A.B. 'Banjo' Paterson

UQP AUSTRALIAN AUTHORS

This is a series of carefully edited selections which represent the full range of an individual author's achievement or which present special themes in anthology form.

General Editor: L.T. Hergenhan,
Reader in Australian Literature,
University of Queensland

Also in this series:

Barbara Baynton edited by Sally Krimmer and Alan Lawson
Rolf Boldrewood edited by Alan Brissenden
Christopher Brennan edited by Terry Sturm
Marcus Clarke edited by Michael Wilding
Robert D. FitzGerald edited by Julian Croft
Joseph Furphy edited by John Barnes
Henry Kingsley edited by J.S.D. Mellick
Henry Lawson edited by Brian Kiernan
James McAuley edited by Leonie Kramer
David Malouf edited by James Tulip
John Shaw Neilson edited by Cliff Hanna
Nettie Palmer edited by Vivian Smith
Hal Porter edited by Mary Lord
Kenneth Slessor edited by Dennis Haskell
Catherine Helen Spence edited by Helen Thomson
Randolph Stow edited by Anthony J. Hassall

The Jindyworobaks edited by Brian Elliott
Writing of the Eighteen Nineties edited by Leon Cantrell
The Australian Short Story edited by Laurie Hergenhan
Eight Voices of the Eighties edited by Gillian Whitlock
Australian Science Fiction edited by Van Ikin
Colonial Voices edited by Elizabeth Webby
New Guinea Images in Australian Literature edited by Nigel Krauth
Five Plays for Stage, Radio and Television edited by Alrene Sykes

In preparation:

Xavier Herbert edited by Frances de Groen and Peter Pierce
Henry Kendall edited by Michael Ackland
Barnard Eldershaw edited by Maryanne Dever
Christina Stead edited by R.G. Geering and Anita Segerberg
Eleanor Dark edited by Barbara Brooks and Judith Clark

A.B. 'Banjo' Paterson

Bush ballads, poems, stories and journalism

Edited by Clement Semmler

University of Queensland Press

First published 1992 by University of Queensland Press
Box 42, St Lucia, Queensland 4067 Australia

Typeset by University of Queensland Press
Printed in Australia by The Book Printer, Victoria

Distributed in the USA and Canada by
International Specialized Book Services, Inc.,
5602 N.E. Hassalo Street, Portland, Oregon 97213-3640

Cataloguing in Publication Data
National Library of Australia

Paterson, A.B. (Andrew Barton), 1864-1941.
  Bush ballads, poems, stories and journalism.

  I. Semmler, Clement, 1914-   . II. Title.
  (Series: UQP Australian authors).

A821.2

ISBN 0 7022 2307 7

For my grandchildren, Heidi, Liam and Ivan,
who have grown up on the Western Plains
that Paterson loved

Contents

Acknowledgments

I am grateful to Dr Laurie Hergenhan of the University of Queensland for his most helpful and valuable advice in my preparation of this anthology, and to my son, Peter, and Maria Lowenstein for their material assistance in its copying and assembling.

Introduction

In 1893 Francis Adams, a young Englishman who had spent five years in Australia from 1884 to 1889, returned to London and wrote of the country:

> The gulf between colony and colony is small and traversable compared to that great fixture that lies between the people of the Slope and of the Interior. Where the marine rainfall flags out and is lost, a new climate, and in a certain sense, a new race begin to unfold themselves.
>
> It is not one hundred, but three and four hundred miles that you must go back from the sea if you would find yourself face to face with the one powerful and unique national type yet produced in the new land. Frankly I find not only all that is genuinely characteristic in Australia and the Australian springing from the heart of the land but also all that is noblest, kindliest and best . . .[1]

As far as literature is concerned, Adams is an almost unknown voice. But in a flash of extraordinary insight, he had glimpsed and fixed for posterity an Australian idea, a spirit, as Henry Lawson had written, "that is roused beyond the Range",[2] a stimulus for popular and literary imagination which, years later, Dr C.E.W. Bean memorably reaffirmed:

> The Australian, one hundred or two hundred years hence, will still live with the consciousness that, if he only goes far enough back over the hills and across the plains he comes in the end to the mysterious half desert country where men have to live the lives of strong men. And the life of that mysterious country will affect the Australian imagination as the life of the sea has affected that of the English . . .[3]

No one saw this more clearly than Andrew Barton Paterson. The words of Adams and Bean are near enough to a statement of his creed, for Paterson was the chronicler and poet of these out-back people, of the Western Plains, of the seemingly illimitable spaces of the interior. Norman Lindsay, reminiscing about Paterson, recalled that "he believed isolation in the Bush made individuals of men".[4] And Paterson's verse and prose abound with these individuals, named or anonymous, through whose agency the legend of the Australian plainsman, the overlander, the mountain rider (even the "Digger" is an offshoot from this legend) has been perpetuated — the Man from Snowy River, Clancy, Saltbush Bill, Old Kiley.

This collection of Paterson's work is therefore intended first of all to introduce the reader to those ballads and prose writings, especially the former, that have endeared him to so many Australians over the last two generations; and second, to illustrate other facets of Paterson's versatility as a writer — as journalist, war correspondent and chronicler of the race track.

Paterson was born on 17 February 1864 at Narambla, near Orange in New South Wales, the eldest of the seven children of Andrew Paterson, a station owner and manager. Young Paterson had the typical bush boyhood of his class, which was best enjoyed from the age of five after his father moved the family to a station called Illalong in the Yass district. Twelve years older than his only brother, he was by his own admission a lonely child who turned for his pleasures and pastimes to the sights and sounds around him. The Yass district, apart from its scenic environment, offered highly romantic possibilities for a young boy. Illalong station was on the main route between Sydney and Melbourne, along which came the exciting traffic of horsemen, bullock teams, drovers and especially coaches, since the famous Cobb and Company coaching system was by 1870 at the peak of its popularity.

It was even more stirring to a young imagination that the gold diggings of Lambing Flat (now called Young) were only a day's ride away, and the gold escort came past twice a week with an armed trooper riding shotgun up front and another in the box with the coachman. The word "bushranger", with its overtones of terror and fascination, was always in the air. From these boyhood experiences, too, came the young Paterson's introduction to the great "characters" of the bush: the bullockies with whom he made friends, who yarned with him and who gave him demonstrations of their terrifying skill with their great whips; the weather-beaten drovers with their dusty herds and myriad dogs; the bush horsemen who loped by, ever ready to pass the time of day even with a small boy and to enquire where tucker could be had.

The other important factor in Paterson's development as a

writer was that he was sent to Sydney to live with his grandmother, Emily Barton, while he completed his secondary education. Mrs Barton was a cultured and well-read woman who not only introduced her grandson to the writings of Carlyle, Ruskin, Swinburne and others of her favourite authors, but also told him many stories of her pioneering days in the bush in the 1840s and 1850s, thus kindling in him ideas of writing about the outback and its people.

Gradually Paterson changed from a shy and awkward bush boy into a young man and lawyer-to-be whose good looks, elegance of dress and manner and his prowess as a sportsman, accomplished horseman and polo player, in particular, earned him a prominent place in the Sydney social scene of the day. By the 1880s, the city had become a thriving and exciting metropolis whose suburbs were expanding rapidly as a result of a land boom. But more than this, it was part of a young nation — though still a group of colonies — that was developing its voice, its writers. Henry Kendall had sung of its beauties as he saw them and Adam Lindsay Gordon, in particular, had pointed the way to a form of literary bush ballad that united both country and city in a kind of self-conscious nationalism which looked particularly to horsemanship and bushcraft among the traditions of outback life. Paterson, barely out of his teens, decided that the time had come when he too could write verse of this kind.

A medium for the effective awakening of Australia to the fact that there was a national literature, although it was at first largely a literature of the bush, was already in existence. In 1880 the *Bulletin* had been founded under the vigorous editorship of J.F. Archibald, who constantly and persistently looked for and encouraged Australian writers. By the mid-1880s it had the widest readership of any journal in Australia, publishing the writings of Henry Lawson, Barcroft Boake, Louis Becke and others. Paterson submitted his first verses in 1885, one of which, "El Mahdi to the Australian Troops" (about a contingent of Australian troops sent to the Sudan), was published anonymously in February of that year. It was in the following year however that his first signed ballad appeared under the pen-name of "The Banjo" (the name of a racehorse, Paterson later admitted, that his family had owned at Illalong). On the manuscript of this and several others that

Paterson had published in that year Archibald wrote comments such as "Doggerel", "Fun in the idea," "Might be re-modelled", "Rough but humorous".[5]

Eventually Archibald summoned Paterson to a meeting. As Paterson recalled:

> In an interview of ten minutes he said he would like me to try some more verse. Did I know anything about the bush? I told him I had been reared there. "All right," he said, "have a go at the bush. Have a go at anything that strikes you. Don't write anything like other people if you can help it. Let's see what you can do."[6]

It was good advice. A cultural upheaval was taking place and it was as if the nation was thirsting for its own literature. Everything Australian had suddenly become worth writing about: the outback, the diggings, the selections, the stock routes, the wheat fields, the outriders. It was against this background that Paterson, obviously heeding Archibald's advice, wrote his first acclaimed ballad, "Old Pardon the Son of Reprieve", published in the *Bulletin* in December 1888.

Paterson went from strength to strength as a balladist. Along with such celebrated and popular writers as Henry Lawson, Roderic Quinn, E.J. Brady, Edward Dyson, Victor Daley and others, his verses were eagerly awaited in the *Bulletin*. By the mid-1890s he had already written some of his most famous ballads — "Clancy of the Overflow", 1890; "The Man from Ironbark", "A Bushman's Song", 1891; "The Geebung Polo Club", 1893; "Shearing at Castlereagh", "The Travelling Post Office", "Saltbush Bill", 1894 — and his reputation was assured.

It was not until 1895 when the established Australian publishing firm of Angus & Robertson produced Paterson's first collection of poems (*The Man from Snowy River and Other Verses*) that "The Banjo's" identity was revealed. Paterson became a celebrity overnight: it was the talk of the town that this young solicitor, so well known in Sydney's sporting and social circles, was the author of these popular verses. His book sold thousands within a few weeks, and its popularity over the years to the present day has been a phenomenon of Australian book publishing.

But the literary significance of Paterson's first collection of verses went far beyond its immediate popularity. It was cardinal in establishing the bushman in the national imagination as a romantic and traditional figure. At the turn of the century, as the historian Russel Ward has written, the bushman "had more influence on the manners and mores of the city-dweller than the latter had on his";[7] and he remains the nearest to the "noble frontiersman" that we shall ever have in our history. Indeed, the Man from Snowy River and Clancy of the Overflow were to become national symbols of the bushman horserider now firmly established in our cultural mythology.

In the last years of the century Paterson's interests began irrevocably turning from the law and city life to journalism and the outback. He made several trips to Northern Australia where he wrote entertainingly of life there and of the opportunities it offered for new experiences and adventure. The outbreak of the Boer War offered him yet another chance to extend his writing talents. In October 1899, as the officially accredited war correspondent for the *Sydney Morning Herald* and the Melbourne *Age*, he sailed for South Africa with the New South Wales Lancers. By January 1900 he was in the thick of all the actions in which the Lancers were involved against the Boers and throughout the year he sent back a series of exciting and vividly written dispatches. He covered General French's relief of Kimberley; the surrender of General Cronje and the capture of Bloemfontein; the fighting round Johannesburg and the taking of Pretoria. These and other war experiences saw him develop into a first-class journalist. The quality of his war reporting attracted the attention of Reuter's news agency and he was appointed as a correspondent for this international organisation.

Yet although he was gaining valuable experience as a newspaperman, Paterson remained a writer who found his best material in personalities and men of action. He recorded memorable pen portraits of the celebrities he met during his Boer War experiences, among them Winston Churchill (a fellow war correspondent in South Africa), Lord Roberts, General French and other military leaders. But perhaps the most affectionate and, from the literary viewpoint, the most useful relationship established by Paterson in South Africa was with Rudyard Kipling whom he met in March 1900 in Bloemfontein. He found they had much in common in their attitudes to writing, particularly in their love of the ballad idiom, and they became firm friends. Later, in his book of autobiographical sketches, *Happy Dispatches* (1934), Paterson paid his highest compliment to Kipling: "You could have dumped Kipling down in a splitters' camp in the backblocks of Australia and he would have been quite at home, and would have gone away leaving the impression that he was a decent sort of bloke who asked a lot of questions . . ."

Back in Australia at the end of 1900, Paterson, now firmly bitten by wanderlust, yearned for more overseas experiences. In mid-1901 he was off again, this time to China and the Boxer Rebellion. He met and admired G.E. "Chinese" Morrison, the famous Australian adventurer (of whom he wrote a couple of memorable pen portraits), but the Boxer War had ended so he went on to London where he renewed his friendship with Kipling and met again a former colleague from his *Bulletin* days, Phil May, the noted cartoonist.

His second book of verse, *Rio Grande's Last Race and Other Verses*, was published in 1902, after he had again returned to Australia. He then embarked on the third phase of his career, being appointed editor of the *Evening News*, the more important of Sydney's two afternoon newspapers, in January 1903. Later that year, in April, he married a Tenterfield woman, Alice Walker. In 1905 he published his collection of early Australian ballads, *Old Bush Songs*, which remains to this day an authoritative source book, followed the next year by *An Outback Marriage*, a conventional enough story but with memorable descriptions of bush life.

By 1908 the call of the bush had become compelling. He sold up in the city, left his editor's desk and with his wife and two children took over a large property called Coodra Vale in the Wee Jasper (NSW) district, surrounded by the rugged bush of his beloved Snowy River country. His few years here were happy ones and he sang of them in such ballads as "The Road to Hogan's Gap" and "The Mountain Squatter":

>   Here in my mountain home
>   On rugged hills and steep

> I sit and watch you come
>> O Riverina sheep . . .

and perhaps with thoughts of "The Man from Snowy River" made particular reference to the expert horsemanship that the terrain demanded:

> These Riverina cracks
>> They do not care to ride
> The half-inch hanging tracks
>> Along the mountain side.
>
> Their horses shake with fear
>> When loosened boulders go
> With leaps like startled deer
>> Down the gulfs below . . .

The outbreak of World War I saw Paterson determined to join up on active service. When his age denied him this he accepted a commission in the 2nd Australian Remount Unit, a job after his heart. Here he commanded squadrons made up of the men he loved: rough riders, jackaroos, horse-breakers, ex-jockeys and buck-jumping riders from country shows. His work included the control and training of army horses in camps in Egypt: he reached the rank of major and his enthusiasm for and efficiency with horses earned him the respect and affection of fighting men throughout the Middle East. In later years he calculated that over sixty thousand horses had passed through his hands.

Paterson returned to Sydney at the end of the war and soon after published a number of his short stories and sketches under the title of *Three Elephant Power and Other Stories* as well as his third volume of ballads, *Saltbush Bill J.P. and Other Verses*. In 1921 he accepted the editorship of the *Sportsman*, which over the next ten years or so gave him the happiest years of his newspaper life. He loved thoroughbred racing and sporting journalism — he had won races at Randwick racecourse in his earlier days as an amateur rider — and in addition to his editing duties he enjoyed reporting the Sydney races each week for the newspaper, *Truth*.

In 1930, at the age of sixty-five, Paterson retired from newspaper life to use his leisure as a freelance writer. At this time he broadcast frequently for the infant ABC about his life and adventures. He also produced in 1933 a charming collection of poems for children entitled *The Animals Noah Forgot*, illustrated by his friend and admirer, Norman Lindsay. He lectured, wrote and lived the life of a respected Sydney clubman during the 1930s, during which time he also published his second novel, *The Shearer's Colt* (1936), one of the best racing novels in our literature, but, perhaps because of its subject matter, almost totally neglected. In January 1939 he was awarded the CBE for his services to Australian literature along with similar honours for Professor Walter Murdoch and Mrs Aeneas Gunn. "The Commonwealth does well," wrote the *Sydney Morning Herald* in its leader of the day, "to recommend royal recognition of the writers who interpret the life and spirit of this land."

Two years later Paterson died after a short illness, on 5 February 1941.

In any assessment of his prose, Paterson the journalist looms large: it is safe to say that he was one of the best of his day and that his journalism was always immensely readable and colloquially literate. He showed quite early in his writing career the capacity to salt description with details of human interest. Reporting, after all, as A.J. Liebling once said,[8] is being interested in everyone you meet: the most casual meetings can turn up fascinating material, offbeat events can create curiosity about people. As early as 1892 Paterson had described for the *Bulletin* a tug-of-war held at Darlinghurst Hall, Sydney:

> Then came what was supposed to be the tug of the evening, Australia v. Ireland. As the teams took their places you could feel the electricity rising in the atmosphere. The Irish were a splendid team, a stone heavier than their opponents all round, but the latter looked, if anything, harder and closer knit. As they took their places the warning yells rang out all over the building: "Now, boys, sunny NSW for it!", "Go it, Australia!" And from the Irish side came a babel of broad, soft, buttery brogue: "Git some chark on yer hands, Dinny!", "Mick, if yez don't win, never come to the wharf no more!", "For the love of God and my fiver, bhoys, pull together!" It was a national Irish team right through — regular Donegal and Tipperary bhoys. They were genuine: every other man answered to the name of Mick. They wore orange and green colours, to give the Pope and Protestants equal show. They spat

on their enormous hands, planted their brogues against the battens, and at the sound of the pistol, while every Australian heart beat high with hope, the Mickies simply gave one enormous drayhorse drag and fetched our countrymen clean away . . .[9]

Any sporting journalist, past or present, would be proud to sign his name to that: it is actuality reporting at its best, rich in atmosphere and with rare touches of style, as in "babel of broad, soft, buttery brogue" and "one enormous drayhorse drag".

This reporting instinct never left him. Thirteen years later with much more status as a journalist Paterson covered for the *Evening News* the first motor reliability trial from Sydney to Melbourne. He still had the reporter's unerring eye for detail to catch the reader's attention immediately:

The road from Goulburn to Yass is in splendid order. We got away badly and ran over a calf. The animal was either purposely left there or wished to commit suicide . . . Friedman in trouble near Gunning: Harry Skinner who is in a Darracq, hit a gully and bent an axle like a hoop. He starts later today. We expect to reach Jugiong safely unless we meet more calves . . .[10]

Undoubtedly his adventures on this trial prompted his motoring short story, "Three Elephant Power", as delightful and ironically amusing a piece as any he wrote.

Many parts of *Happy Dispatches* illustrate Paterson's literary journalism at its best. In his modest foreword he describes himself as a looker-on seeing most of the game, a "not very proficient writer" able to say something about the players. Yet his descriptions, at first hand, are superb — whether of the pony races at Chefoo, the rough-riders at work in Egypt, or his account of a motor ride with Kipling through the Sussex Downs in the latter's new car. But it is in his war dispatches particularly that Paterson shines in translating keen observation and felt experience into graphic prose. I have read the war dispatches of C.E.W. Bean, John Hetherington, Chester Wilmot, Kenneth Slessor, Ronald Monson and other notable war correspondents and I believe that Paterson, in his accounts of actual warfare, stands up to any of them. He was in the thick of the fighting when his unit joined up at the Modder River with General French's forces on the march to Kimberley:

This is something like sport, this shooting at human game with cannon over three thousand yards of country. "Hooray! Give 'em another!" The second gun fires and the shell whizzes away and the same dead silence reigns, when suddenly another note is struck — a discordant note this time. From the rocky tree-covered hill in the direct front only half a mile off, comes a clear tock-tock-tock-tock — a couple of clear double reports, and something seems to whistle by the gunners, making a noise like a heavy wind blowing through a very small crack in the door. Pee-u-uw! It is the thinnest, shrillest sound, this whistle of a bullet at short range. Most of the men duck instinctively as the first bullet goes over. Pee-u-u-uw! Pee-u-u-uw! They come by thick enough now, and each man's heart sinks as he sees what the column is let in for. Here we have marched all the guns and horses without cover, to within half-a-mile of a hill and the Boers have seized it while we were shooting at their mounted men! Pee-u-u-uw! Pee-u-u-uw! That fellow was close! . . .

Paterson's bushman's eye for the tell-tale detail gave particular sharpness to his thumbnail sketches of many great men whom he met, as he put it, "stripped of their official panoply, and sitting, as one might say, in their pyjamas". Certainly, his portraits have stood the test of over sixty years and, by present-day journalistic standards, when the cult of the personality has been so zealously, even ruthlessly exploited, they read entertainingly and vividly in their own right. Churchill, Kipling, "Chinese" Morrison, Haig, French, Phil May — these are vignettes, their etching all the more remarkable since they were by an easy-going and unassuming colonial who had, as he so modestly put it, "started on his travels unencumbered by any knowledge of the world other than what could be gleaned from life in the Australian bush and in a solicitor's office in Sydney".[11] Yet in these pieces there are flashes of unusual insight and epigrammatic assessments that convey more than long passages of descriptive prose — as in his observation of Lord Derby: "a man who stood four-square in a world peopled largely by weathercocks"; of a local Sussex magnate whom he met in his ramblings with Kipling: "as stodgy as a bale of hay"; and of Captain Towse VC as one of those men who "in a regiment, a ship or a shearing shed . . . unobtrusively exerts the same sort of influence that lubricating oil exerts in a motor car".

The abiding characteristic of most of Paterson's prose, as it is of many of his ballads, is his humour: laconic, tinged with the sardonic. As Brian Elliott has perceptively noted, "every nation has its own characteristic humour, maybe this [Paterson's] is ours".[12] For the essence of Paterson's humour lies not in contrived situations, nor in any form of wit, but purely in the everyday manifestations and occurrences of the environment he frequented. For instance, he had studied animals as closely as he had human beings, and his "animal" sketches, such as "The Merino Sheep" and "The Bullock", are masterpieces of quirky humour. In the latter Paterson wrote of the idiosyncrasies of individual bullocks: "the one-eyed bullock that always pokes away to the outside of the mob, the inquisitive bullock that is always walking over to the drover as if he were going to speak to him, the agitator bullock who is always trying to get up a stampede and prodding the others with his horns".

Paterson should long ago have invited more comparison with Henry Lawson as a writer of the bush sketch since this was part of the means by which both men directed the attitudes and values of the nomadic bushworkers towards the framing of a national ethos. Of course, in output there is no comparison: Paterson's is minimal against Lawson's. But there is a quality in much of Paterson's work likely to be just as enduring as Lawson's even though the vogue of the latter has adversely affected the appreciation of the former — just as, by an ironical tit-for-tat, Lawson's verse has been unfairly eclipsed by the public enthusiasm for Paterson's. Admittedly, Paterson wrote nothing that as a short story could be compared with the bush pathos of "The Drover's Wife" or the intense characterisation of the Spicers in "Water Them Geraniums"; but then he did not, like Lawson, see life as quite such a mixture of humour and tragedy: the contradictions of bush humour and misfortune were more clearly dissociated. But where the bush sketch of Paterson seems to me to ring truer than that of Lawson is in the cheerful and uninhibited approach to the scenes and people concerned — what H.M. Green called Paterson's "lyrical glimpses".[13] Lawson, despite what some have said to the contrary, knew the bush, but his knowledge of it was restricted to certain parts of New South Wales. Paterson's familiarity with it was much more wide-ranging, from Darwin and the

Gulf Country to the Snowy Mountains — indeed it went as far as most men had then pushed out — giving his descriptions a greater authenticity. Lawson loved the bush in his fashion — a love-hate relationship at best — as in "His Country — After All" where one sees a nostalgic patriotism. But in Paterson's affection for his country there are no reservations at all — a sardonic appraisal, yes, but that has always been the Australian's privilege.

As for humour, one can take little away from Lawson because throughout his stories humour is woven into their substance, no matter what the theme; even in sadness there is a tinge of it. But Paterson's dry, quiet humour, as in "His Masterpiece", is often like Lawson's, even though it is more prone to veer towards the sardonic. When Paterson chooses, however, to be deliberately comic, as in "Hughey's Dog" and certainly in the uproarious "The Cast-Iron Canvasser", the result is a broader, more open humour, verging on the farcical and just as successful and memorable as Lawson's "The Loaded Dog" and "Bill, the Ventriloquial Rooster". Certainly, because geographically he ranged far more widely than Lawson, Paterson is pre-eminent in such satirically humorous sketches of the Australian scene as "The Cycloon, Paddy Cahill and the G.R." and "Thirsty Island". And when it comes to the bush spielers and conmen, Paterson's "The Downfall of Mulligan" and "Bill and Jim Nearly Get Taken Down" invite comparison with Lawson's "Steelman" stories, and the same is true of Paterson's "The Oracle" sketches where we have the typical Australian "urger" and know-all in full flight.

Undoubtedly Paterson's wide reading as a youth and young man gave poise and gloss to his prose style. In a stimulating study of Paterson's verse, H.P. Heseltine referred to Paterson's Latinisms as they occur in his ballads as "more than humorously remembered scraps from an inert bump of learning he had brushed against in pursuit of the pound, rather they were the relics of that rich cultural matrix which might have given his work a more ample life".[14] I would suggest that this matrix did just that in the case of Paterson's prose, where literary allusions fall sweetly into place and give, sometimes because of their very unexpectedness in the context of his subject, a freshness to his writing. "Virtue herself 'scapes not calumnious strokes'', he quoted in his racing manuscript when writing of the racehorse owner whose horses, sent out as favourites, were beaten; and he used a line from *Hamlet*, ''I speak by the card'', as the heading for his chapter on bookmakers. A punter, like the witness in Dickens, he wrote, had to be ''prepared in a general way for anythink''; often his lot, in the end, is like that of ''Marius sitting in the ruins of Carthage''. In his general writing he drew often on Byron and Swinburne; ''had Kipling been a spectacular person like Gabriel d'Annunzio'' he wrote in *Happy Dispatches*, ''he might have led a great Imperialist movement'' and he compared Kipling, in another passage, to Goethe's hero who ''toiled without haste and without rest''. He referred to Carlyle's *Sartor Resartus* for the word ''hinterschlag'' in describing his schooldays and made it clear that his reading had ranged from Horace to Conan Doyle. Yet there is never a suspicion of conscious literariness in his work; on the contrary, his idiom was invariably that of the bushworkers and battlers he wrote about.

Of those who have written on Paterson, only Brian Elliott[15] has effectively made the point of the wider aspects of Paterson's talents shown in his prose and that here, ''out of his singing robes, he appears in strength'', most himself, as it were, and ''best of all in short passages of digressive reflection''. This, combined with his humour, made him, as Elliott describes him, ''tantalisingly Australian'', because, no matter how or what he wrote, his style was always what has come to be seen as Australian, made up of a sort of indolent cynicism and above all of his intimate knowledge of his country and his people and of the moods of which they were blended. This ''happy intimacy with all sorts of queer people'', as Elliott notes too, gave him an unrivalled capacity to translate Australian dialogue, especially the bush demotic, to the printed word. Indeed I think this is the strongest and likely to be the most enduring quality of Paterson's prose. I can think of no better example than this passage from his novel, *An Outback Marriage*:

> Just as the coach was about to start a drover came out of the bar of the hotel, wiping his lips with the back of his hand. He stared vacantly about him, first up the street and then down, looked hard at a post in front of the hotel, then stared up and down the street again. At last he

walked over, and, addressing the passengers in a body, said, "Did any o' yous see e'er a horse anywheres? I left my prad 'ere and 'es gorn."

A bystander, languidly cutting up a pipeful of tobacco, jerked his elbow down the road.

"That old bloke took 'im," he said. "Old bloke that come in the coach. While yous was all talkin' in the pub, he sneaks out here an' nabs that 'orse, an' away like a rabbit. See that dust on the plain? That's 'im!"

The drover looked helplessly out over the stretch of plain. He seemed quite incapable of grappling with the problem.

"Took my 'orse did he? Well I'm blowed! By Cripes!"

He had another good stare over the plain, and back at the party.

"My oath!" he added.

Then the natural stoicism of the bushman came to his aid and he said, in a resigned tone,

"Oh, well, anyways, I s'pose — s'pose he must 'a been in a hurry to go somewheres. I s'pose 'e'll fetch 'im back some time or other."

As for Paterson the balladist, it has always seemed to me unfair that he should be recorded merely as a stringer together of popular verses, the assumption being that ballads and poetry do not mix. Probably his predilection for the horse (translated more often than not into "the Turf") has been partly responsible for this since literary criticism and horseracing are uneasy bedfellows. It is customary therefore to discuss Paterson merely as a balladist, and thus be spared the necessity of justifying him as a poet. But the poet, I think, stems from the balladist. And as a balladist, Paterson at his best ranks with the best of his time anywhere. After all the London *Times* in reviewing *The Man from Snowy River and Other Verses* compared them favourably with *Barrack Room Ballads,* and Kipling himself (as did Andrew Lang) wrote a congratulatory letter to Angus & Robertson on the book's publication. A.T. Quiller-Couch, in the Introduction to his *The Oxford Book of Ballads*, remarked that the way to define a ballad was to quote lines that had the ring of balladry. Paterson qualifies with distinction: he rings truest in his lines that tell of action and adventure; they are indeed in Douglas Stewart's felicitous phrase, "a minstrelsy of action",[16] encapsulating forever that particular Australia of Paterson's time — the vigorous, sprawling, challenging Australia of the outback.

This landscape of action and the action itself combined, as never before, most tellingly in "The Man from Snowy River":

> Then fast the horseman followed, where the gorges deep and black
>   Resounded to the thunder of their tread,
> And the stockwhips woke the echoes, and they fiercely answered back
>   From cliffs and crags that beetled overhead.
> And upward, ever upward, the wild horses held their way,
>   Where mountain ash and kurrajong grew wide;
> And the old man muttered fiercely, "We may bid the mob good day.
> "*No* man can hold them down the other side."

Often the action seems effortless, like a fine motor car, tuned to perfection, silently and swiftly eating up the distances of a smoothly surfaced highway, so magnificently geared is rhythm to context in such lines as these from "Conroy's Gap":

> He left the camp by the sundown light,
>   And the settlers out on the Marthaguy
> Awoke and heard, in the dead of night,
>   A single horseman hurrying by.
> He crossed the Bogan at Dandaloo,
>   And many a mile of the silent plain
> That lonely rider behind him threw
>   Before they settled to sleep again.
>
> He rode all night and he steered his course
>   By the shining stars with a bushman's skill,
> And every time that he pressed his horse
>   The Swagman answered him gamely still.

But it is not always the action of the saddle, though Paterson has left us in little doubt that this is the finest evocation possible of the adventure and challenge of the outback. There is, too, the everyday excitement of station life — the dust and swirl and confusion of mustering and yarding or the exhilaration of the shearing shed:

> The youngsters picking up the fleece enjoy the merry din,
> They throw the classer up the fleece, he throws it to the bin;
> The pressers standing by the rack are waiting for the wool,
> There's room for just a couple more, the press is nearly full;
> Now jump upon the lever, lads, and heave and heave away,
> Another bale of golden fleece is branded Castlereagh.

and the urgency of "The Flying Gang", the pioneer railwaymen patrolling the country tracks:

> By the uplands bright and the homesteads white
>> With the rush of a western gale —
> And the pilot swayed with the pace we made
>> As she rocked on the ringing rail . . .

This facility to translate experience and imagination into action — with a still-tingling pulse, as A.G. Stephens put it, to sit down and convey the tingle to the pulse of his readers — never deserted Paterson, whether he was retracing in his mind's eye the chase of the bushrangers as they "wheeled their tracks with a wild beast's skill" or setting down on the spot his account of General French's drive to Kimberley, although with an idiom less natural to him:

> The gunners plied their guns amain; the hail of shrapnel flew;
> With rifle fire and lancer charge their squadrons back we threw;
> And through the pass between the hills we swept in furious fray,
> And French was through to Kimberley to drive the Boers away.

Next to their expression of action, the most abiding feature of Paterson's ballads is their humour. His understanding of the humour of daily bush life radiates from his ballads since, after all, as Chaucer has shown from the beginning (and he was a minstrel too) the life and manners of an age can be no less effectively set down in the romps and jokes of its people. In the Australian bush, too, humour could be extracted (as Lawson, Steele Rudd, Edward Dyson and others have shown) from the stoically endured disasters of drought, dust, heat and flood which were part of the scheme of things that Paterson laconically contemplated. But since his was a homely, hearty humour, open as daylight, he looked more often than not for its kindlier manifestations in the outback, as in the explanation of the elements by the Aborigine, "Frying Pan":

> Him drive 'im bullock dray
>> Then thunder go;
> Him shake 'im flour bag —
>> Tumble down snow!

or in the genial Saltbush Bill's Christmas Day version, to his "little rouseabouts", of the story of Isaac and Jacob:

But when the stock were strong and fat with grass and lots of rain,
Then Jacob felt the call to take the homeward track again.
It's strange in every creed and clime, no matter where you roam,
There comes a day when every man would like to make for home.

So off he set with sheep and goats, a mighty moving band,
To battle down the dusty road along the Overland —
It's droving mixed-up mobs like that that makes men cut their throats,
I've travelled rams, which Lord forget, but never travelled goats.

Saltbush Bill, of course, was probably Paterson's best humorous creation in a ballad genre that Douglas Stewart once defined as a new variety, the Australian Comic.[17] In the outback Saltbush Bill was in his kingdom — on the great tracts of land that he claimed were for all, irrespective of boundaries, surveyors and the like.

Then there was the rudimentary humour of the unsophisticated bushman that Paterson sometimes exploited, as in perhaps his best known comic ballad where the former was permitted to have the last laugh on the city slicker, the barber "small and flash", who pretended to cut the throat of the Man from Ironbark, and was upended for his pains:

And now while round the shearing-floor the list'ning shearers gape,
He tells the story o'er and o'er, and brags of his escape.
"Them barber chaps what keeps a tote, By George, I've had enough,
"One tried to cut my bloomin' throat, but thank the Lord it's tough."
And whether he's believed or no, there's one thing to remark,
That flowing beards are all the go way up in Ironbark.

Here, of course, Paterson was tending towards the humour of the larger than life which was the stock-in-trade of the bush humorist — the outback Ananias telling his far-fetched yarns to gaping and gullible audiences in bush pubs and shearers' camps. These were the same listeners and *Bulletin* readers who, Norman Lindsay recalled, stood drinks for many a bogus Lawson and Paterson. And it was a short step from the larger than life to what Paterson wrote into bush legend — Mulga Bill's epic bicycle ride, Saltbush Bill's immortal deed of producing an Australian emu to fight an English gamecock, and William Johnson, down on Snakebite River, seeking his snakebite antidote with the single-mindedness and dedication of a medieval alchemist in search of the philosopher's stone.

Yet in all this Paterson had the instinct of the folk-singer and folk-poet to make sure of the material at hand, to shape it in more telling fashion and give it a national vogue. In words that soon seemed as natural as breathing he made a balladry of the scattered lives of back-country Australians who thought nobody noticed them and who, until then, had scarcely noticed one another. He discovered the simple tunes of their lives: tunes that mostly had the easy, obvious rhythm of a lively barndance. (And indeed, "Waltzing Matilda" is the best of barndances, with everyone joining in and roaring the famous, pseudo-melancholy choruses.)

It was a varied, interesting and above all, lovable country that he revealed to the people of his day and left as a legacy to his readers in future generations: a country where nature was not merely a bitch-goddess, as some soured immigrants had painted it, but had its own beauty and even moments of gentleness. And though we recognise the action and adventure, the humour and the myth-making as essential parts of his balladry, it is in those inspired moments when he takes up the lyre instead of the banjo, when he opens those "occasional windows into the heart of the bush's own music" that Paterson becomes the poet of the Western Plains, the Australian plainsman of our literature. Geographically this area might be thought of as the great hinterland lying between the upper reaches of the Lachlan River to the north and the Eumerella to the south: alternatively, we might think of it, as Paterson probably did, as the whole of the illimitable outback of the Australia he knew and loved from his own travels: western New South Wales, the Snowy country, the Queensland downs (where he wrote "Waltzing Matilda") and the Northern Territory. Or then again, it might well be bounded by the familiar signposts recurring in his ballads: "the land of lots o' time" along the loitering Castlereagh, stretching up to Kiley's Hill and Conroy's Gap, dropping away to Dandaloo and "the black soil flats across by Waddiwong".

At all events this is Paterson's country, where "the plains are all awave with grass, the skies are deepest blue", but where too there is "the fiery dust-storm drifting and the mocking mirage shifting", where there is "waving grass and forest trees on sunlit plains as wide as seas'', but where there is the "drought fiend" too, and the cattle are left lying "with the crows to watch them dying/Grim sextons of the Overland that fasten on their prey''; where there is "the dry sweet scent on the salt bush plain'', but where too "fierce hot winds have set the pine and myall bows asweep" — so vast a country indeed that the lonely rider is seen as "a speck upon the waste of plain''.

In this setting Paterson opened his heart and his talent to the outback he loved. There was the smell of it in "The Wind's Message'':

> It brought a breath of mountain air from off the hills of pine,
> A scent of eucalyptus trees in honey-laden bloom;
> And drifting, drifting far away along the southern line
> It caught from leaf and grass and fern a subtle strange perfume . . .

and its music:

> The waving of grasses,
> The song of the river
> That sings as it passes
> For ever and ever,
> The hobble-chain's rattle,
> The calling of birds,
> The lowing of cattle
> Must blend with the words . . .

and, as well, its magic which often seems to have been absorbed into his very verse:

> By the winding Wollondilly where the weeping willows weep,
> And the shepherd with his billy, half-awake and half-asleep . . .

And especially, there were its characteristic sights evoking lines of true landscape poetry, as in "Brumby's Run'':

> The traveller by the mountain-track
>   May bear their hoof-beats pass,
> And catch a glimpse of brown and black
>   Dim shadows on the grass

and in "White Cockatoos'':

> Over the mountain peaks outlying
> Clear, against the blue

Comes a scout in silence flying
One white cockatoo . . .

As Douglas Stewart has remarked[18] (and he seems to me to have
read Paterson's verse with more affection and understanding than
most critics), only a man who was truly a poet at heart could have
soared into such stanzas as these from "Black Swans":

O! ye wild black swans, 'twere a world of wonder
For a while to join in your westward flight,
With the stars above and the dim earth under,
Through the cooling air of the glorious night.
As we swept along on our pinions winging,
We could catch a chime of a church-bell ringing,
Or the distant note of a torrent singing,
Or the far-off flash of a station light.

As frequently and felicitously as any poet in our literature who
has written of our great hinterland Paterson has caught its light
and colour, hinted at its mystery and magic:

Land of plenty or land of want, where the grey Companions dance,
Feast or famine, or hope or fear, and in all things land of chance,
Where Nature pampers or Nature slaps, in her ruthless, red romance,
And we catch a sound of a fairy's song, as the wind goes whipping by,
Or a scent like incense drifts along from the herbage ripe and dry
— Or the dust-storms dance on their ball-room floor, where the bones
of the cattle lie.

In these lines from "Sunrise on the Coast":

Like mariners calling the roll of their number
   The sea-fowl put out to the infinite deep.
And far overhead — singing softly to slumber —
   Worn out by their watching the stars fall asleep . . .

Paterson sometimes can claim to have justified H.M. Green's observation that "the quality that in the end he stands by is after all
a poetic quality"[19] and John Manifold's contention that "Paterson is a far richer, more subtle and more versatile poet than people
appear to believe today".[20]

NOTES

1. Francis Adams in *The Australians: A Social Sketch* (London, 1893).
2. Henry Lawson, "The Natives of the Range", in *Henry Lawson: Collected Works,* ed. L. Cronin (Sydney: Lansdowne, 1984).
3. C.E.W. Bean, *The Dreadnought of the Darling* (Sydney: Angus & Robertson, 1956).
4. Norman Lindsay, ABC radio documentary broadcast, 17 April 1964.
5. Manuscripts held Mitchell Library, Sydney.
6. A.B. Paterson, reminiscences, *Sydney Morning Herald*, February/March 1939.
7. Russel Ward, *The Australian Legend* (Melbourne: Oxford University Press, 1978), p. 22.
8. *The Most of A.J. Liebling*, ed. William Cole (New York: Simon & Schuster, 1963).
9. *Bulletin*, 20 February 1892.
10. *Evening News*, 22 February 1905.
11. A.B. Paterson, *Happy Dispatches* (Sydney: Angus & Robertson, 1934), Preface.
12. Brian Elliott, "Australian Paterson", *Singing to the Cattle* (Melbourne: Georgian House, 1947), pp. 142-54.
13. H.M. Green, *A History of Australian Literature* (Sydney: Angus & Robertson, 1961), Vol. 1.
14. H.P. Heseltine, "Banjo Paterson, a Poet Nearly Anonymous", *Meanjin* 4 (1964): 400.
15. Elliott, "Australian Paterson".
16. Douglas Stewart, "Banjo, the Minstrel", *Bulletin*: Red Page (date unknown).
17. Stewart, "Banjo, the Minstrel".
18. Stewart, "Banjo, the Minstrel".
19. Green, *History of Australian Literature*, p. 365.
20. John Manifold, *Who Wrote the Ballads* (Sydney: Australian Book Society, 1964), p. 115.

Textual Note

The categories into which I have placed Paterson's work are designed to enable the reader to appreciate better his versatility as a writer, especially in his prose works, even though for most he will remain pre-eminent as a balladist. In reprinting Paterson's work, I have used the following sources: *The Man from Snowy River and Other Verses* (Sydney: Angus & Robertson, 1895) [MSR]; *Rio Grande's Last Race and Other Verses* (Sydney: Angus & Robertson, 1902) [RGLR]; *Collected Verse* (Sydney: Angus & Robertson, 1921) [CV]; *The Animals Noah Forgot* (Sydney: Endeavour Press, 1933) [ANF]; *Happy Dispatches* (Sydney: Angus & Robertson, 1934) [HD]. Material not included in these collections has been taken from original sources, for example newspapers and journals. I have indicated the date and place of first publication of each item, followed where appropriate by the abbreviated title in square brackets of the source from which I have taken the version used, and in each section a chronological order is followed. Of course, many of the ballads and prose pieces have been reprinted frequently down the years in various anthologies and collections and recently in two volumes, *Singer of the Bush* and *Song of the Pen* (Sydney: Lansdowne, 1983), compiled by Paterson's grandchildren, Rosamund Campbell and Philippa Harvie, and represented as his *Complete Works 1885-1941*.

The only changes made here to original versions are the use of double quotation marks, where single may have been used originally, and their placement either inside or outside punctuation, in accordance with house style.

1
Bush Ballads

EDITOR'S NOTE

Between 1885 and 1889 Banjo Paterson published twenty-one ballads and poems, all in the Sydney *Bulletin* (except for two which appeared in the *Sydney Mail*). In December of 1889 "Clancy of the Overflow", the first ballad included in this section, appeared in the *Bulletin*. Most of his earlier efforts, which are not included in this collection, are amateurish by Paterson's later standards with the exception of three: "Old Pardon the Son of Reprieve", "Mulligan's Mare", and "An Idyll of Dandaloo", ballads of horseracing where Paterson, in this early period, was on surer ground. These are accordingly included in the later section, Racehorses and Racing.

It is worthy of comment that in only one of his ballads or verses, as far as I can ascertain, did Paterson intrude his personal emotions. This was "The Road to Gundagai", in which he described his meeting with "a maiden fair of face" on the bush track between Tumut and Gundagai, where they kissed and parted — she to Sydney and as for him:

> I turned and travelled with a sigh
> The lonely road to Gundagai.

In her biography, *Miles Franklin in America: Her Unknown Brilliant Career* (1981), Verna Coleman reveals that early in 1902 Paterson and Miles (Stella) had had what in those days was called a "romance" and that he had proposed marriage to her. However, according to Coleman, the episode was over by the end of the year. In a paper on Paterson, read by Richard Walsh at the Warana Writers' Week in Brisbane in 1987, he put forward the suggestion that "The Road to Gundagai" was written by Paterson to his lost love. Certainly, there is enough evidence in the poem to support this view: the woman he encounters was "bred among the mountain snows" and Miles Franklin, of course, was born and spent her childhood in the Snowy Mountains country. It is significant that Paterson, perhaps regarding this as a "private" poem, did not submit it to the *Bulletin* or any other journal, but included it in his second collection, *Rio Grande's Last Race and Other Verses*, published at the end of 1902.

"Waltzing Matilda", which Paterson wrote at Dagworth Station near Winton in Queensland's central west where he was holidaying in 1895, was not printed until it appeared in sheet music form, published by Allans Ltd in 1903. Thereafter it was included in the many reprints of Paterson's *Collected Verse* (1921) that have appeared over the years. Undoubtedly there are hundreds of thousands of Australians and many people overseas who have sung the song without ever having seen it in the printed form. For this reason, perhaps, there are variations in the words both in the oral and printed versions, but the text used here is the version in the *Collected Verse*.

Bush Ballads

CLANCY OF THE OVERFLOW

I had written him a letter which I had, for want of better
    Knowledge, sent to where I met him down the Lachlan, years
        ago,
He was shearing when I knew him, so I sent the letter to him,
    Just "on spec", addressed as follows, "Clancy, of The
        Overflow".

And an answer came directed in a writing unexpected,
    (And I think the same was written with a thumb-nail dipped in
        tar)
'Twas his shearing mate who wrote it, and *verbatim* I will quote
    it:
    "Clancy's gone to Queensland droving, and we don't know
       where he are.

* * * * *

In my wild erratic fancy visions come to me of Clancy
    Gone a-droving "down the Cooper" where the Western
       drovers go;
As the stock are slowly stringing, Clancy rides behind them
       singing,
    For the drover's life has pleasures that the townsfolk never
       know.

And the bush hath friends to meet him, and their kindly voices
       greet him
    In the murmur of the breezes and the river on its bars,
And he sees the vision splendid of the sunlit plains extended,
    And at night the wond'rous glory of the everlasting stars.

* * * * *

I am sitting in my dingy little office, where a stingy
    Ray of sunlight struggles feebly down between the houses tall,
And the foetid air and gritty of the dusty, dirty city
    Through the open window floating spreads its foulness over all

And in place of lowing cattle, I can hear the fiendish rattle
   Of the tramways and the 'buses making hurry down the street,
And the language uninviting of the gutter children fighting,
   Comes fitfully and faintly through the ceaseless tramp of feet.

And the hurrying people daunt me, and their pallid faces haunt
      me
   As they shoulder one another in their rush and nervous haste,
With their eager eyes and greedy, and their stunted forms and
      weedy,
   For townsfolk have no time to grow, they have no time to
      waste.

And I somehow rather fancy that I'd like to change with Clancy,
   Like to take a turn at droving where the seasons come and go,
While he faced the round eternal of the cash-book and the
      journal —
   But I doubt he'd suit the office, Clancy, of "The Overflow".

                                             Bulletin, 21 December 1889 [MSR]

THE MAN FROM SNOWY RIVER

There was movement at the station, for the word had passed
      around
   That the colt from old Regret had got away,
And had joined the wild bush horses — he was worth a thousand
      pound,
   So all the cracks had gathered to the fray.
All the tried and noted riders from the stations near and far
   Had mustered at the homestead overnight,
For the bushmen love hard riding where the wild bush horses are,
   And the stock-horse snuffs the battle with delight.

There was Harrison, who made his pile when Pardon won the
      cup,
   The old man with his hair as white as now;
But few could ride beside him when his blood was fairly up —
   He would go wherever horse and man could go.
And Clancy of the Overflow came down to lend a hand,

No better horseman ever held the reins;
For never horse could throw him while the saddle-girths would
         stand,
      He learnt to ride while droving on the plains.

And one was there, a stripling on a small and weedy beast,
      He was something like a racehorse undersized,
With a touch of Timor pony — three parts thoroughbred
         at least —
      And such as are by mountain horsemen prized.
He was hard and tough and wiry — just the sort that won't say
         die —
      There was courage in his quick impatient tread;
And he bore the badge of gameness in his bright and fiery eye,
      And the proud and lofty carriage of his head.

But still so slight and weedy, one would doubt his power to stay,
      And the old man said, "That horse will never do
For a long and tiring gallop — lad, you'd better stop away,
      "Those hills are far too rough for such as you."
So he waited sad and wistful — only Clancy stood his friend —
      "I think we ought to let him come," he said;
"I warrant he'll be with us when he's wanted at the end,
      "For both his horse and he are mountain bred.

"He hails from Snowy River, up by Kosciusko's side,
      "Where the hills are twice as steep and twice as rough,
"Where a horse's hoofs strike firelight from the flint stones
         every stride,
      "The man that holds his own is good enough.
"And the Snowy River riders on the mountains make their home,
      "Where the river runs those giant hills between;
"I have seen full many horsemen since I first commenced to
         roam,
      "But nowhere yet such horsemen have I seen."

So he went — they found the horses by the big mimosa clump —
      They raced away towards the mountain's brow,
And the old man gave his orders, "Boys, go at them from the
         jump,
      "No use to try for fancy riding now.

And, Clancy, you must wheel them, try and wheel them to the
    right.
  "Ride boldly, lad, and never fear the spills,
"For never yet was rider that could keep the mob in sight,
  "If once they gain the shelter of those hills."

So Clancy rode to wheel them — he was racing on the wing
  Where the best and boldest riders take their place,
And he raced his stock-horse past them, and he made the ranges
    ring
  With the stockwhip, as he met them face to face.
Then they halted for a moment, while he swung the dreaded lash,
  But they saw their well-loved mountain full in view,
And they charged beneath the stockwhip with a sharp and
    sudden dash,
  And off into the mountain scrub they flew.

Then fast the horsemen followed, where the gorges deep and
    black
  Resounded to the thunder of their tread,
And the stockwhips woke the echoes, and they fiercely answered
    back
  From cliffs and crags that beetled overhead.
And upward, ever upward, the wild horses held their way,
  Where mountain ash and kurrajong grew wide;
And the old man muttered fiercely, "We may bid the mob good
    day.
  "*No* man could hold them down the other side."

When they reached the mountain's summit, even Clancy took a
    pull,
  It well might make the boldest hold their breath,
The wild hop scrub grew thickly, and the hidden ground was full
  Of wombat holes, and any slip was death.
But the man from Snowy River let the pony have his head,
  And he swung his stockwhip round and gave a cheer,
And he raced him down the mountain like a torrent down its bed,
  While the others stood and watched in very fear.

He sent the flint stones flying, but the pony kept his feet,
  He cleared the fallen timber in his stride,

And the man from Snowy River never shifted in his seat —
    It was grand to see that mountain horseman ride.
Through the stringy barks and saplings, on the rough and
        broken ground,
    Down the hillside at a racing pace he went;
And he never drew the bridle till he landed safe and sound,
    At the bottom of that terrible descent.

He was right among the horses as they climbed the further hill,
    And the watchers on the mountain standing mute,
Saw him ply the stockwhip fiercely, he was right among them
        still,
    As he raced across the clearing in pursuit.
Then they lost him for a moment, where two mountain gullies
        met
    In the ranges, but a final glimpse reveals
On a dim and distant hillside the wild horses racing yet,
    With the man from Snowy River at their heels.

And he ran them single-handed till their sides were white with
        foam.
    He followed like a bloodhound on their track,
Till they halted cowed and beaten, then he turned their heads for
        home,
    And alone and unassisted brought them back.
But his hardy mountain pony he could scarcely raise a trot,
    He was blood from hip to shoulder from the spur;
But his pluck was still undaunted, and his courage fiery hot,
    For never yet was mountain horse a cur.

And down by Kosciusko, where the pine-clad ridges raise
    Their torn and rugged battlements on high,
Where the air is clear as crystal, and the white stars fairly blaze
    At midnight in the cold and frosty sky,
And where around the Overflow the reedbeds sweep and away
    To the breezes, and the rolling plains are wide,
The man from Snowy River is a household word to-day,
    And the stockmen tell the story of his ride.

Bulletin, 26 April 1890 [MSR]

THOSE NAMES

The shearers sat in the firelight, hearty and hale and strong,
After the hard day's shearing, passing the joke along:
The "ringer" that shore a hundred, as they never were shorn
    before,
And the novice who, toiling bravely, had tommy-hawked half a
    score,
The tarboy, the cook, and the slushy, the sweeper that swept the
    board,
The picker-up, and the penner, with the rest of the shearing
    horde.
There were men from the inland stations where the skies like a
    furnace glow,
And men from the Snowy River, the land of the frozen snow;
There were swarthy Queensland drovers who reckoned all land
    by miles,
And farmers' sons from the Murray, where many a vineyard
    smiles.
They started at telling stories when they wearied of cards and
    games,
And to give these stories a flavour they threw in some local
    names,
And a man from the bleak Monaro, away on the tableland,
He fixed his eyes on the ceiling, and he started to play his hand.

He told them of Adjintoothbong, where the pine-clad mountains
    freeze,
And the weight of the snow in summer breaks branches off the
    trees,
And, as he warmed to the business, he let them have it strong —
Nimitybelle, Conargo, Wheeo, Bongongolong;
He lingered over them fondly, because they recalled to mind
A thought of the old bush homestead, and the girl that he left
    behind.
Then the shearers all sat silent till a man in the corner rose;
Said he, "I've travelled a-plenty but never heard names like
    those,

"Out in the western districts, out on the Castlereagh
"Most of the names are easy — short for a man to say.

"You've heard of Mungrybambone and the Gunda-bluey pine,
"Quobbotha, Girilambone, and Terramungamine,
"Quambone, Eunonyhareenyha, Wee Waa, and Buntijo —"
But the rest of the shearers stopped him: "For the sake of your
      jaw, go slow,
"If you reckon those names are short ones out where such names
      prevail,
"Just try and remember some long ones before you begin the
      tale."
And the man from the western district, though never a word he
      said,
Just winked with his dexter eyelid, and then he retired to bed.

Bulletin, 20 September 1890 [MSR]

ON KILEY'S RUN

The roving breezes come and go
      On Kiley's Run,
The sleepy river murmurs low,
And far away one dimly sees
Beyond the stretch of forest trees —
Beyond the foothills dusk and dun —
The ranges sleeping in the sun
      On Kiley's Run.

'Tis many years since first I came
      To Kiley's Run,
More years than I would care to name
Since I, a stripling, used to ride
For miles and miles at Kiley's side,
The while in stirring tones he told
The stories of the days of old
      On Kiley's Run.

I see the old bush homestead now
      On Kiley's Run,
Just nestled down beneath the brow

Of one small ridge above the sweep
Of river-flat, where willows weep
And jasmine flowers and roses bloom,
The air was laden with perfume
     On Kiley's Run.

We lived the good old station life
     On Kiley's Run,
With little thought of care or strife.
Old Kiley seldom used to roam,
He liked to make the Run his home,
The swagman never turned away
With empty hand at close of day
     From Kiley's Run.

We kept a racehorse now and then
     On Kiley's Run,
And neighb'ring stations brought their men
To meetings where the sport was free,
And dainty ladies came to see
Their champions ride; with laugh and song
The old house rang the whole night long
     On Kiley's Run.

The station hands were friends I wot
     On Kiley's Run,
A reckless, merry-hearted lot —
All splendid riders, and they knew
The "boss" was kindness through and through.
Old Kiley always stood their friend,
And so they served him to the end
     On Kiley's Run.

But droughts and losses came apace
     To Kiley's Run,
Till ruin stared him in the face;
He toiled and toiled while lived the light,
He dreamed of overdrafts at night:
At length, because he could not pay,
His bankers took the stock away
     From Kiley's Run.

Old Kiley stood and saw them go
    From Kiley's Run.
The well-bred cattle marching slow;
His stockmen, mates for many a day,
They wrung his hand and went away.
Too old to make another start,
Old Kiley died — of broken heart,
    On Kiley's Run.

* * * * *

The owner lives in England now
    Of Kiley's Run.
He knows a racehorse from a cow;
But that is all he knows of stock:
His chiefest care is how to dock
Expenses, and he sends from town
To cut the shearers' wages down
    On Kiley's Run.

There are no neighbours anywhere
    Near Kiley's Run.
The hospitable homes are bare,
The gardens gone; for no pretence
Must hinder cutting down expense:
The homestead that we held so dear
Contains a half-paid overseer
    On Kiley's Run.

All life and sport and hope have died
    On Kiley's Run.
No longer there the stockmen ride;
For sour-faced boundary riders creep
On mongrel horses after sheep,
Through ranges where, at racing speed,
Old Kiley used to "wheel the lead"
    On Kiley's Run.

There runs a lane for thirty miles
    Through Kiley's Run.
On either side the herbage smiles,
But wretched trav'lling sheep must pass

Without a drink or blade of grass
Thro' that long lane of death and shame:
The weary drovers curse the name
       Of Kiley's Run.

The name itself is changed of late
       Of Kiley's Run.
They call it "Chandos Park Estate."
The lonely swagman through the dark
Must hump his swag past Chandos Park
The name is English, don't you see,
The old name sweeter sounds to me
       Of "Kiley's Run."

I cannot guess what fate will bring
       To Kiley's Run —
For chances come and changes ring —
I scarcely think 'twill always be
Locked up to suit an absentee;
And if he lets it out in farms
His tenants soon will carry arms
       On Kiley's Run.

Bulletin, 20 December 1890 [MSR]

CONROY'S GAP

This was the way of it, don't you know —
    Ryan was "wanted" for stealing sheep,
And never a trooper, high or low,
    Could find him — catch a weasel asleep!
Till Trooper Scott, from the Stockman's Ford —
    A bushman, too, as I've heard them tell —
Chanced to find him drunk as a lord
    Round at the Shadow of Death Hotel.

D'you know the place? It's a wayside inn,
    A low grog-shanty — a bushman trap,
Hiding away in its shame and sin
    Under the shelter of Conroy's Gap —

Under the shade of that frowning range,
    The roughest crowd that ever drew breath —
Thieves and rowdies, uncouth and strange,
    Were mustered round at the Shadow of Death.

The trooper knew that his man would slide
    Like a dingo pup, if he saw the chance;
And with half a start on the mountain side
    Ryan would lead him a merry dance.
Drunk as he was when the trooper came,
    To him that did not matter a rap —
Drunk or sober, he was the same,
    The boldest rider in Conroy's Gap.

''I want you, Ryan,'' the trooper said,
    ''And listen to me, if you dare resist,
''So help me heaven, I'll shoot you dead!''
    He snapped the steel on his prisoner's wrist,
And Ryan, hearing the handcuffs click,
    Recovered his wits as they turned to go,
For fright will sober a man as quick
    As all the drugs that the doctors know.

There was a girl in that rough bar
    Went by the name of Kate Carew
Quiet and shy as the bush girls are,
    But ready-witted and plucky, too.
She loved this Ryan, or so they say,
    And passing by, while her eyes were dim
With tears, she said in a careless way,
    ''The Swagman's round in the stable, Jim.''

Spoken too low for the trooper's ear.
    Why should she care if he heard or not?
Plenty of swagmen far and near,
    And yet to Ryan it meant a lot.
That was the name of the grandest horse
    In all the district from east to west
In every show ring, on every course
    They always counted the Swagman best.

He was a wonder, a raking bay —
  One of the grand old Snowdon strain —
One of the sort that could race and stay
  With his mighty limbs and his length of rein.
Born and bred on the mountain side,
  He could race through scrub like a kangaroo,
The girl herself on his back might ride,
  And the Swagman would carry her safely through.

He would travel gaily from daylight's flush
  Till after the stars hung out their lamps,
There was never his like in the open bush,
  And never his match on the cattle-camps.
For faster horses might well be found
  On racing tracks, or a plain's extent,
But few, if any, on broken ground
  Could see the way that the Swagman went.

When this girl's father, old Jim Carew,
  Was droving out on the Castlereagh
With Conroy's cattle, a wire came through
  To say that his wife couldn't live the day.
And he was a hundred miles from home,
  As flies the crow, with never a track,
Through plains as pathless as ocean's foam,
  He mounted straight on the Swagman's back.

He left the camp by the sundown light,
  And the settlers out on the Marthaguy
Awoke and heard, in the dead of night,
  A single horseman hurrying by.
He crossed the Bogan at Dandaloo,
  And many a mile of the silent plain
That lonely rider behind him threw
  Before they settled to sleep again.

He rode all night and he steered his course
  By the shining stars with a bushman's skill,
And every time that he pressed his horse
  The Swagman answered him gamely still.
He neared his home as the east was bright,

The doctor met him outside the town:
"Carew! How far did you come last night?"
    "A hundred miles since the sun went down."

And his wife got round, and an oath he passed,
    So long as he or one of his breed
Could raise a coin, though it took their last
    The Swagman never should want a feed.
And Kate Carew, when her father died,
    She kept the horse and she kept him well;
The pride of the district far and wide,
    He lived in style at the bush hotel.

Such was the Swagman; and Ryan knew
    Nothing about could pace the crack;
Little he'd care for the man in blue
    If once he got on the Swagman's back.
But how to do it? A word let fall
    Gave him the hint as the girl passed by;
Nothing but "Swagman — stable-wall;
    "Go to the stable and mind your eye."

He caught her meaning, and quickly turned
    To the trooper: "Reckon you'll gain a stripe
"By arresting me, and it's easily earned;
    "Let's go to the stable and get my pipe,
"The Swagman has it." So off they went,
    And soon as ever they turned their backs
The girl slipped down, on some errand bent
    Behind the stable, and seized an axe.

The trooper stood at the stable door
    While Ryan went in quite cool and slow,
And then (the trick had been played before)
    The girl outside gave the wall a blow.
Three slabs fell out of the stable wall —
    'Twas done 'fore ever the trooper knew —
And Ryan, as soon as he saw them fall,
    Mounted the Swagman and rushed him through.

The trooper heard the hoof-beats ring
   In the stableyard, and he slammed the gate,
But the Swagman rose with a mighty spring
   At the fence, and the trooper fired too late,
As they raced away and his shots flew wide
   And Ryan no longer need care a rap,
For never a horse that was lapped in hide
   Could catch the Swagman in Conroy's Gap.

And that's the story. You want to know
   If Ryan came back to his Kate Carew;
Of course he should have, as stories go,
   But the worst of it is, this story's true:
And in real life it's a certain rule,
   Whatever poets and authors say
Of high-toned robbers and all their school,
   These horsethief fellows aren't built that way.

Come back! Don't hope it — the slinking hound,
   He sloped across to the Queensland side,
And sold the Swagman for fifty pound,
   And stole the money, and more beside.
And took to drink, and by some good chance
   Was killed — thrown out of a stolen trap.
And that was the end of this small romance,
   The end of the story of Conroy's Gap.

Bulletin, 20 December 1890 [MSR]

A MOUNTAIN STATION

I bought a run a while ago,
   On country rough and ridgy,
Where wallaroos and wombats grow —
   The Upper Murrumbidgee.
The grass is rather scant, it's true,
   But this a fair exchange is,
The sheep can see a lovely view
   By climbing up the ranges.

And "She-oak Flat"'s the station's name,
    I'm not surprised at that, sirs:
The oaks were there before I came,
    And I supplied the flat, sirs.
A man would wonder how it's done,
    The stock so soon decreases —
They sometimes tumble off the run
    And break themselves to pieces.

I've tried to make expenses meet.
    But wasted all my labours,
The sheep the dingoes didn't eat
    Were stolen by the neighbours.
They stole my pears — my native pears —
    Those thrice-convicted felons,
And ravished from me unawares
    My crop of paddy-melons.

And sometimes under sunny skies,
    Without an explanation,
The Murrumbidgee used to rise
    And overflow the station.
But this was caused (as now I know)
    When summer sunshine glowing
Had melted all Kiandra's snow
    And set the river going.

And in the news, perhaps you read:
    "Stock passings. Puckawidgee,
"Fat cattle: Seven hundred head
    "Swept down the Murrumbidgee;
"Their destination's quite obscure,
    "But, somehow, there's a notion,
"Unless the river falls, they're sure
    "To reach the Southern Ocean."

So after that I'll give it best;
    No more with Fate I'll battle.
I'll let the river take the rest,
    For those were all my cattle.
And with one comprehensive curse
    I close my brief narration,

And advertise it in my verse —
  "For Sale! A Mountain Station."

Bulletin, 19 December 1891 [MSR]

THE MAN FROM IRONBARK

It was the man from Ironbark who struck the Sydney town,
He wandered over street and park, he wandered up and down.
He loitered here, he loitered there, till he was like to drop,
Until at last in sheer despair he sought a barber's shop.
"Ere! shave my beard and whiskers off, I'll be a man of mark,
"I'll go and do the Sydney toff up home in Ironbark."

The barber man was small and flash, as barbers mostly are,
He wore a strike-your-fancy sash, he smoked a huge cigar:
He was a humorist of note and keen at repartee,
He laid the odds and kept a "tote", whatever that may be,
And when he saw our friend arrive, he whispered "Here's a lark!
"Just watch me catch him all alive, this man from Ironbark."

There were some gilded youths that sat along the barber's wall.
Their eyes were dull, their heads were flat, they had no brains at
      all;
To them the barber passed the wink, his dexter eyelid shut,
"I'll make this bloomin' yokel think his bloomin' throat is cut."
And as he soaped and rubbed it in he made a rude remark:
"I s'pose the flats is pretty green up there in Ironbark."

A grunt was all reply he got; he shaved the bushman's chin,
Then made the water boiling hot and dipped the razor in.
He raised his hand, his brow grew black, he paused awhile to
      gloat,
Then slashed the red-hot-razor-back across his victim's throat;
Upon the newly-shaven skin it made a livid mark —
No doubt it fairly took him in — the man from Ironbark.

He fetched a wild up-country yell might wake the dead to hear,
And though his throat, he knew full well, was cut from ear to
      ear,
He struggled gamely to his feet, and faced the murd'rous foe:

"You've done for me! you dog, I'm beat! one hit before I go!
"I only wish I had a knife, you blessed murdering shark!
"But you'll remember all your life, the man from Ironbark."

He lifted up his hairy paw, with one tremendous clout
He landed on the barber's jaw, and knocked the barber out.
He set to work with tooth and nail, he made the place a wreck;
He grabbed the nearest gilded youth, and tried to break his neck.
And all the while his throat he held to save his vital spark,
And "Murder! Bloody Murder!" yelled the man from Ironbark.

A peeler man who heard the din came in to see the show;
He tried to run the bushman in, but he refused to go.
And when at last the barber spoke, and said "Twas all in fun —
"'Twas just a little harmless joke, a trifle overdone."
"A joke!" he cried, "By George, that's fine; a lively sort of lark;
"I'd like to catch that murdering swine some night in Ironbark."

And now while round the shearing floor the list'ning shearers
    gape,
He tells the story o'er and o'er, and brags of his escape.
"Them barber chaps what keeps a tote, By George, I've had
    enough,
"One tried to cut my bloomin' throat, but thank the Lord it's
    tough."
And whether he's believed or no, there's one thing to remark,
That flowing beards are all the go way up in Ironbark.

Bulletin, 17 December 1892 [MSR]

A BUSHMAN'S SONG

I'm travellin' down the Castlereagh, and I'm a station hand,
I'm handy with the ropin' pole, I'm handy with the brand,
And I can ride a rowdy colt, or swing the axe all day,
But there's no demand for a station-hand along the Castlereagh.

So it's shift boys, shift, for there isn't the slightest doubt
That we've got to make a shift to the stations further out,
With the pack-horse runnin' after, for he follows like a dog.
We must strike across the country at the old jig-jog.

This old black horse I'm riding — if you'll notice what's his
    brand,
He wears the crooked R, you see — none better in the land.
He takes a lot of beatin', and the other day we tried,
For a bit of a joke, with a racing bloke, for twenty pounds a side.

It was shift, boys, shift, for there wasn't the slightest doubt
That I had to make him shift, for the money was nearly out;
But he cantered home a winner, with the other one at the flog —
He's a red-hot sort to pick up with his old jig-jog.

I asked a cove for shearin' once along the Marthaguy
"We shear non-union here," says he. "I call it scab, says I.
I looked along the shearin' floor before I turned to go —
There were eight or ten dashed Chinamen a-shearin in a row.

It was shift, boys, shift, for there wasn't the slightest doubt
It was time to make a shift with the leprosy about.
So I saddled up my horses, and I whistled to my dog,
And I left his scabby station at the old jig-jog.

I went to Illawarra, where my brother's got a farm,
He has to ask his landlord's leave before he lifts his arm;
The landlord owns the country side — man, woman, dog and cat,
They haven't the cheek to dare to speak without they touch their
    hat.

It was shift, boys, shift, for there wasn't the slightest doubt
Their little landlord god and I would soon have fallen out;
Was I to touch my hat to him? — was I his bloomin dog?
So I makes for up the country at the old jig-jog.

But it's time that I was movin', I've a mighty way to go
Till I drink artesian water from a thousand feet below;
Till I meet the overlanders with the cattle comin' down,
And I'll work a while till I make a pile, then have a spree in town.

So, it's shift, boys, shift, for there isn't the slightest doubt
We've got to make a shift to the stations further out;
The pack-horse runs behind us, for he follows like a dog,
And we cross a lot of country at the old jig-jog.

Bulletin, 24 December 1892 [MSR]

BLACK SWANS

As I lie at rest on a patch of clover
In the Western Park when the day is done,
I watch as the wild black swans fly over
With their phalanx turned to the sinking sun;
And I hear the clang of their leader crying
To a lagging mate in the rearward flying,
And they fade away in the the darkness dying,
Where the stars are mustering one by one.

Oh! ye wild black swans, 'twere a world of wonder
For a while to join in your westward flight,
With the stars above and the dim earth under,
Through the cooling air of the glorious night.
As we swept along on our pinions winging,
We should catch the chime of a church-bell ringing,
Or the distant note of a torrent singing,
Or the far-off flash of a station light.

From the northern lakes with the reeds and rushes,
Where the hills are clothed with a purple haze,
Where the bell-birds chime and the songs of thrushes
Make music sweet in the jungle maze,
They will hold their course to the westward ever,
Till they reach the banks of the old grey river,
Where the waters wash, and the reed-beds quiver
In the burning heat of the summer days.

Oh! ye strange wild birds, will ye bear a greeting
To the folk that live in that western land?
Then for every sweep of your pinions beating,
Ye shall bear a wish to the sunburnt band,
To the stalwart men who are stoutly fighting
With the heat and drought and the dust-storm smiting,
Yet whose life somehow has a strange inviting,
When once to the work they have put their hand.

Facing it yet! Oh, my friend stout-hearted,
What does it matter for rain or shine,
For the hopes deferred and the gain departed?

Nothing could conquer that heart of thine.
And thy health and strength are beyond confessing
As the only joys that are worth possessing.
May the days to come be as rich in blessing
As the days we spent in the auld lang syne.

I would fain go back to the old grey river,
To the old bush days when our hearts were light,
But, alas! those days they have fled for ever,
They are like the swans that have swept from sight.
And I know full well that the strangers' faces
Would meet us now in our dearest places;
For our day is dead and has left no traces
But the thoughts that live in my mind to-night.

There are folk long dead, and our hearts would sicken —
We would grieve for them with a bitter pain,
If the past could live and the dead could quicken,
We then might turn to that life again.
But on lonely nights we would hear them calling,
We should hear their steps on the pathways falling,
We should loathe the life with a hate appalling
In our lonely rides by the ridge and plain.

* * * * *

In the silent park is a scent of clover,
And the distant roar of the town is dead,
And I hear once more as the swans fly over
Their far-off clamour from overhead.
They are flying west, by their instinct guided,
And for man likewise is his fate decided,
And griefs apportioned and joys divided
By a mighty power with a purpose dread.

Sydney Mail, 22 July 1893 [MSR]

THE GEEBUNG POLO CLUB

It was somewhere up the country, in a land of rock and scrub,
That they formed an institution called the Geebung Polo Club.
They were long and wiry natives from the rugged mountain side,

And the horse was never saddled that the Geebungs couldn't ride;
But their style of playing polo was irregular and rash —
They had mighty little science, but a mighty lot of dash:
And they played on mountain ponies that were muscular and
     strong,
Though their coats were quite unpolished, and their manes and
     tails were long.
And they used to train those ponies wheeling cattle in the scrub:
They were demons, were the members of the Geebung Polo Club

It was somewhere down the country, in a city's smoke and steam,
That a polo club existed, called "The Cuff and Collar Team".
As a social institution 'twas a marvellous success,
For the members were distinguished by exclusiveness and dress.
They had natty little ponies that were nice, and smooth, and
     sleek,
For their cultivated owners only rode 'em once a week.
So they started up the country in pursuit of sport and fame,
For they meant to show the Geebungs how they ought to play
     the game;
And they took their valets with them — just to give their boots a
     rub
Ere they started operations on the Geebung Polo Club.

Now my readers can imagine how the contest ebbed and flowed,
When the Geebung boys got going it was time to clear the road;
And the game was so terrific that ere half the time was gone
A spectator's leg was broken — just from merely looking on.
For they waddied one another till the plain was strewn with dead,
While the score was kept so even that they neither got ahead.
And the Cuff and Collar Captain, when he tumbled off to die,
Was the last surviving player — so the game was called a tie.

Then the Captain of the Geebungs raised him slowly from the
     ground,
Though his wounds were mostly mortal, yet he fiercely gazed
     around;
There was no one to oppose him — all the rest were in a trance,
So he scrambled on his pony for his last expiring chance,

For he meant to make an effort to get victory to his side;
So he struck at goal — and missed it — then he tumbled off and
    died.

*   *   *   *   *

By the old Campaspe River, where the breezes shake the grass,
There's a row of little gravestones that the stockmen never pass,
For they bear a crude inscription saying, "Stranger, drop a tear,
"For the Cuff and Collar players and the Geebung boys lie
    here."
And on misty moonlit evenings, while the dingoes howl around,
You can see their shadows flitting down that phantom polo
    ground;
You can hear the loud collisions as the flying players meet,
And the rattle of the mallets, and the rush of ponies' feet,
Till the terrified spectator rides like blazes to the pub —
He's been haunted by the spectres of the Geebung Polo Club.

Antipodean, December 1893 [MSR]

SHEARING AT CASTLEREAGH

The bell is set a-ringing, and the engine gives a toot,
There's five and thirty shearers here are shearing for the loot,
So stir yourselves, you penners-up, and shove the sheep along,
The musterers are fetching them a hundred thousand strong,
And make your collie dogs speak up — what would the buyers
    say
In London if the wool was late this year from Castlereagh?

The man that "rung" the Tubbo shed is not the ringer here,
That stripling from the Cooma side can teach him how to shear.
They trim away the ragged locks, and rip the cutter goes,
And leaves a track of snowy fleece from brisket to the nose;
It's lovely how they peel it off with never stop nor stay,
They're racing for the ringer's place this year at Castlereagh.

The man that keeps the cutters sharp is growling in his cage,
He's always in a hurry and he's always in a rage —
"You clumsy-fisted mutton-heads, you'd turn a fellow sick,
"You pass yourselves as shearers, you were born to swing a pick.

"Another broken cutter here, that's two you've broke to-day,
"It's awful how such crawlers come to shear at Castlereagh."

The youngsters picking up the fleece enjoy the merry din,
They throw the classer up the fleece, he throws it to the bin;
The pressers standing by the rack are waiting for the wool,
There's room for just a couple more, the press is nearly full;
Now jump upon the lever, lads, and heave and heave away,
Another bale of golden fleece is branded Castlereagh.

Bulletin, 10 February 1894 [MSR]

THE TRAVELLING POST OFFICE

The roving breezes come and go, the reed beds sweep and away,
The sleepy river murmurs low, and loiters on its way,
It is the land of lots o' time along the Castlereagh.

*   *   *   *   *

The old man's son had left the farm, he found it dull and slow,
He drifted to the great North-west where all the rovers go.
"He's gone so long," the old man said, "he's dropped right out
     of mind,
"But if you'd write a line to him I'd take it very kind;
"He's shearing here and fencing there, a kind of waif and stray,
He's droving now with Conroy's sheep along the Castlereagh.

"The sheep are travelling for the grass, and travelling very slow;
"They may be at Mundooran now, or past the Overflow,
"Or tramping down the black soil flats across by Waddiwong,
"But all those little country towns would send the letter wrong,
"The mailman, if he's extra tired, would pass them in his sleep,
"It's safest to address the note to 'Care of Conroy's sheep,'
"For five and twenty thousand head can scarcely go astray,
"You write to 'Care of Conroy's sheep along the Castlereagh'."

*   *   *   *   *

By rock and ridge and riverside the western mail has gone,
Across the great Blue Mountain Range to take that letter on.
A moment on the topmost grade while open fire doors glare,
She pauses like a living thing to breathe the mountain air,
Then launches down the other side across the plains away
To bear that note to "Conroy's sheep along the Castlereagh".

And now by coach and mailman's bag it goes from town to
    town,
And Conroy's Gap and Conroy's Creek have marked it "further
    down".
Beneath a sky of deepest blue where never cloud abides,
A speck upon the waste of plain the lonely mailman rides.
Where fierce hot winds have set the pine and myall boughs
    asweep
He hails the shearers passing by for news of Conroy's sheep.
By big lagoons where wildfowl play and crested pigeons flock,
By camp fires where the drovers ride around their restless stock,
And past the teamster toiling down to fetch the wool away
My letter chases Conroy's sheep along the Castlereagh.

Bulletin, 10 March 1894 [MSR]

HOW GILBERT DIED

There's never a stone at the sleeper's head,
    There's never a fence beside,
And the wandering stock on the grave may tread
    Unnoticed and undenied,
But the smallest child on the Watershed
    Can tell you how Gilbert died.

For he rode at dusk, with his comrade Dunn
    To the hut at the Stockman's Ford,
In the waning light of the sinking sun
    They peered with a fierce accord.
They were outlaws both — and on each man's head
    Was a thousand pounds reward.

They had taken toll of the country round,
    And the troopers came behind
With a black that tracked like a human hound
    In the scrub and the ranges blind:
He could run the trail where a white man's eye
    No sign of a track could find.

He had hunted them out of the One Tree Hill
  And over the Old Man Plain,
But they wheeled their tracks with a wild beast's skill,
  and they made for the range again.
Then away to the hut where their grandsire dwelt,
  They rode with a loosened rein.

And their grandsire gave them a greeting bold:
  "Come in and rest in peace,
"No safer place does the country hold —
  "With the night pursuit must cease,
"And we'll drink success to the roving boys,
  "And to hell with the black police."

But they went to death when they entered there,
  In the hut at the Stockman's Ford,
For their grandsire's words were as false as fair —
  They were doomed to the hangman's cord.
He had sold them both to the black police
  For the sake of the big reward.

In the depth of night there are forms that glide
  As stealthy as serpents creep,
And around the hut where the outlaws hide
  They plant in the shadows deep,
And they wait till the first faint flush of dawn
  Shall waken their prey from sleep.

But Gilbert wakes while the night is dark —
  A restless sleeper, aye,
He has heard the sound of a sheep-dog's bark,
  And his horse's warning neigh,
And he says to his mate, "There are hawks abroad
  "And it's time that we went away."

Their rifles stood at the stretcher head,
  Their bridles lay to hand,
They wakened the oldman out of his bed,
  When they heard the sharp command:
"In the name of the Queen lay down your arms,
  "Now, Dunn and Gilbert, stand!"

Then Gilbert reached for his rifle true
   That close at his hand he kept,
He pointed it straight at the voice and drew,
   But never a flash outleapt,
For the water ran from the rifle breech —
   It was drenched while the outlaws slept.

Then he dropped the piece with a bitter oath,
   And he turned to his comrade Dunn:
"We are sold," he said, "we are dead men both,
   "But there may be a chance for one;
"I'll stop and I'll fight with the pistol here,
   "You take to your heels and run."

So, Dunn crept out on his hands and knees
   In the dim, half-dawning light,
And he made his way to a patch of trees,
   And vanished among the night,
And the trackers hunted his tracks all day,
   But they never could trace his flight.

But Gilbert walked from the open door
   In a confident style and rash;
He heard at his side the rifles roar,
   And he heard the bullets crash.
But he laughed as he lifted his pistol-hand,
   And he fired at the rifle flash.

Then out of the shadows the troopers aimed
   At his voice and the pistol sound,
With the rifle flashes the darkness flamed,
   He staggered and spun around,
And they riddled his body with rifle balls
   As it lay on the blood-soaked ground.

There's never a stone at the sleeper's head,
   There's never a fence beside,
And the wandering stock on the grave may tread
   Unnoticed and undenied,
But the smallest child on the Watershed
   Can tell you how Gilbert died.

Bulletin, 2 June 1894 [MSR]

SALTBUSH BILL

Now this is the law of the Overland that all in the West obey,
A man must cover with travelling sheep a six-mile stage a day;
But this is the law which the drovers make, right easily understood,
They travel their stage where the grass is bad, but they camp
      where the grass is good;
They camp, and they ravage the squatter's grass till never a blade
      remains,
Then they drift away as the white clouds drift on the edge of the
      saltbush plains,
From camp to camp and from run to run they battle it hand to
      hand,
For a blade of grass and the right to pass on the track of the
      Overland.
For this is the law of the Great Stock Routes, 'tis written in white
      and black —
The man that goes with a travelling mob must keep to a
      half-mile track;
And the drovers keep to a half-mile track on the runs where the
      grass is dead.
But they spread their sheep on a well-grassed run till they go with
      a two-mile spread.
So the squatters hurry the drovers on from dawn till the fall of night,
And the squatters' dogs and the drovers' dogs get mixed in a
      deadly fight;
Yet the squatters' men, though they hunt the mob, are willing
      the peace to keep,
For the drovers learn how to use their hands when they got with
      the travelling sheep;
But this is the tale of a Jackaroo that came from a foreign strand,
And the fight that he fought with Saltbush Bill, the King of the
      Overland.

Now Saltbush Bill was a drover tough, as ever the country knew,
He had fought his way on the Great Stock Routes from the sea
      to the big Barcoo;
He could tell when he came to a friendly run that gave him a
      chance to spread,

And he knew where the hungry owners were that hurried his
    sheep ahead;
He was drifting down in the Eighty drought with a mob that
    could scarcely creep,
(When the kangaroos by the thousands starve, it is rough on the
    travelling sheep),
And he camped one night at the crossing-place on the edge of the
    Wilga run,
"We must manage a feed for them here," he said, "or the half
    of the mob are done!"
So he spread them out when they left the camp wherever they
    liked to go,
Till he grew aware of a Jackaroo with a station-hand in tow,
And they set to work on the straggling sheep, and with many a
    stockwhip crack
They forced them in where the grass was dead in the space of the
    half-mile track;
So William prayed that the hand of fate might suddenly strike
    him blue
But he'd get some grass for his starving sheep in the teeth of that
    Jackaroo
So he turned and he cursed the Jackaroo, he cursed him alive or
    dead,
From the soles of his great unwieldy feet to the crown of his ugly
    head,
With an extra curse on the moke he rode and the cur at his heels
    that ran,
Till the Jackaroo from his horse got down and he went for the
    drover-man;
With the station-hand for his picker-up, though the sheep ran
    loose the while,
They battled it out on the saltbush plain in the regular prize-ring
    style.

Now, the new chum fought for his honour's sake and the pride
    of the English race,
But the drover fought for his daily bread with a smile on his
    bearded face;

So he shifted ground and he sparred for wind and he made it a
　　lengthy mill,
And from time to time as his scouts came in they whispered to
　　Saltbush Bill —
"We have spread the sheep with a two-mile spread, and the grass
　　it is something grand,
You must stick to him, Bill, for another round for the pride of
　　the Overland."
The new chum made it a rushing fight, though never a blow got
　　home,
Till the sun rode high in the cloudless sky and glared on the
　　brick-red loam,
Till the sheep drew in to the shelter-trees and settled them down
　　to rest,
Then the drover said he would fight no more and he gave his
　　opponent best.
So the new chum rode to the homestead straight and he told
　　them a story grand
Of the desperate fight that he fought that day with the King of
　　the Overland.
And the tale went home to the Public Schools of the pluck of the
　　English swell,
How the drover fought for his very life, but blood in the end
　　must tell.
But the travelling sheep and the Wilga sheep were boxed on the
　　Old Man Plain.
'Twas a full week's work ere they drafted out and hunted them
　　off again,
With a week's good grass in their wretched hides with a curse
　　and a stockwhip crack,
They hunted them off on the road once more to starve on the
　　half-mile track.
And Saltbush Bill, on the Overland, will many a time recite
How the best day's work that ever he did was the day that he lost
　　the fight.

Bulletin, 15 December 1894 [MSR]

HAY AND HELL AND BOOLIGAL

"You come and see me, boys," he said;
"You'll find a welcome and a bed
    "And whisky any time you call;
"Although our township hasn't got
"The name of quite a lively spot —
    "You see, I live in Booligal.

"And people have an awful down
"Upon the district and the town —
    "Which worse than hell itself they call;
"In fact, the saying far and wide
"Along the Riverina side
    "Is 'Hay and Hell and Booligal'.

"No doubt it suits 'em very well
"To say it's worse than Hay or Hell,
    'But don't you heed their talk at all;
"Of course, there's heat — no one denies —
"And sand and dust and stacks of flies,
    "And rabbits, too, at Booligal.

"But such a pleasant, quiet place,
"You never see a stranger's face —
    "They hardly ever care to call;
"The drovers mostly pass it by;
"They reckon that they'd rather die
    "Than spend a night in Booligal.

"The big mosquitoes frighten some —
"You'll lie awake to hear 'em hum —
    "And snakes about the township crawl;
"But shearers, when they get their cheque,
"They never come along and wreck
    "The blessed town of Booligal.

"But down in Hay the shearers come
"And fill themselves with fighting-rum,
    "And chase blue devils up the wall,
"And fight the snaggers every day,

"Until there is the deuce to pay —
　"There's some of that in Booligal.

"Of course, there isn't much to see —
"The billiard-table used to be
　"The great attraction for us all,
"Until some careless, drunken curs
"Got sleeping on it in their spurs,
　"And ruined it, in Booligal.

"Just now there is a howling drought
"That pretty near has starved us out —
　"It never seems to rain at all;
"But, if there *should* come any rain,
"You couldn't cross the black-soil plain —
　"You'd have to stop in Booligal."

* * * * *

"We'd have to stop!" With bated breath
We prayed that both in life and death
　Our fate in other lines might fall:
"Oh, send us to our just reward
"In Hay or Hell, but, gracious Lord,
　"Deliver us from Booligal!"

Bulletin, 25 April 1896 [MSR]

MULGA BILL'S BICYCLE

'Twas Mulga Bill, from Eaglehawk, that caught the cycling
　　craze;
He turned away the good old horse that served him many days;
He dressed himself in cycling clothes, resplendent to be seen;
He hurried off to town and bought a shining new machine;
And as he wheeled it through the door, with air of lordly pride,
The grinning shop assistant said, "Excuse me, can you ride?"

"See, here, young man," said Mulga Bill, "from Walgett to the
　　sea,
"From Conroy's Gap to Castlereagh, there's none can ride like
　　me.

"I'm good all round at everything, as everybody knows,
"Although I'm not the one to talk — I *hate* a man that blows.
"But riding is my special gift, my chiefest, sole delight;
"Just ask a wild duck can it swim, a wild cat can it fight.
"There's nothing clothed in hair or hide, or built of flesh or steel,
"There's nothing walks or jumps, or runs, on axle, hoof, or
      wheel,
"But what I'll sit, while hide will hold and girths and straps are
      tight:
"I'll ride this here two-wheeled concern right straight away at
      sight."

'Twas Mulga Bill, from Eaglehawk, that sought his own abode,
That perched above the Dead Man's Creek, beside the mountain
      road.
He turned the cycle down the hill and mounted for the fray,
But ere he'd gone a dozen yards it bolted clean away.
It left the track, and through the trees, just like a silver streak,
It whistled down the awful slope, towards the Dead Man's
      Creek.

It shaved a stump by half an inch, it dodged a big white-box:
The very wallaroos in fright went scrambling up the rocks,
The wombats hiding in their caves dug deeper underground,
As Mulga Bill, as white as chalk, sat tight to every bound.
It struck a stone and gave a spring that cleared a fallen tree,
It raced beside a precipice as close as close could be;
And then as Mulga Bill let out one last despairing shriek
It made a leap of twenty feet into the Dead Man's Creek.

'Twas Mulga Bill, from Eaglehawk, that slowly swam ashore:
He said, "I've had some narrer shaves and lively rides before;
"I've rode a wild bull round a yard to win a five pound bet,
"But this was the most awful ride that I've encountered yet.
"I'll give that two-wheeled outlaw best; it's shaken all my nerve
"To feel it whistle through the air and plunge and buck and
      serve.
"It's safe at rest in Dead Man's Creek, we'll leave it lying still;
"A horse's back is good enough henceforth for Mulga Bill."

Sydney Mail, 25 July 1896 [RGLR]

SONG OF THE ARTESIAN WATER

Now the stock have started dying, for the Lord has sent a
    drought;
But we're sick of prayers and Providence — we're going to do
    without;
With the derricks up above us and the solid earth below,
We are waiting at the lever for the word to let her go.
      Sinking down, deeper down,
      Oh, we'll sink it deeper down:
As the drill is plugging downward at a thousand feet of level,
If the Lord won't send us water, oh, we'll get it from the devil;
Yes, we'll get it from the devil deeper down.

Now, our engine's built in Glasgow by a very canny Scot,
And he marked it twenty horse-power, but he don't know what
    is what:
When Canadian Bill is firing with the sun-dried gidgee logs,
She can equal thirty horses and a score or so of dogs.
      Sinking down, deeper down,
      Oh, we're going deeper down:
If we fail to get the water then it's ruin to the squatter,
For the drought is on the station and the weather's growing
    hotter,
But we're bound to get the water deeper down.

But the shaft has started caving and the sinking's very slow,
And the yellow rods are bending in the water down below,
And the tubes are always jamming and they can't be made to
    shift
Till we nearly burst the engine with a forty horse-power lift.
      Sinking down, deeper down,
      Oh, we're going deeper down
Though the shaft is always caving, and the tubes are always
    jamming,
Yet we'll fight our way to water while the stubborn drill is
    ramming —
While the stubborn drill is ramming deeper down.

But there's no artesian water, though we've passed three
    thousand feet,
And the contract price is growing and the boss is nearly beat.
But it must be down beneath us, and it's down we've got to go,
Though she's bumping on the solid rock four thousand feet
    below.
    Sinking down, deeper down,
    Oh, we're going deeper down:
And it's time they heard us knocking on the roof of Satan's
    dwellin';
But we'll get artesian water if we cave the roof of hell in —
Oh! we'll get artesian water deeper down.

But it's hark! the whistle's blowing with a wild, exultant blast,
And the boys are madly cheering, for they've struck the flow at
    last,
And it's rushing up the tubing from four thousand feet below
Till it spouts above the casing in a million-gallon flow.
    And it's down, deeper down —
    Oh, it comes from deeper down;
It is flowing, ever flowing, in a free, unstinted measure
From the silent hidden places where the old earth hides her
    treasure —
Where the old earth hides her treasure deeper down.

And it's clear away the timber, and it's let the water run:
How it glimmers in the shadow, how it flashes in the sun!
By the silent belts of timber, by the miles of blazing plain
It is bringing hope and comfort to the thirsty land again.
    Flowing down, further down;
    It is flowing further down
To the tortured thirsty cattle, bringing gladness in its going;
Through the droughty days of summer it is flowing, ever
    flowing —
It is flowing, ever flowing, further down.

Bulletin, 12 December 1896 [RGLR]

THE ROAD TO GUNDAGAI

The mountain road goes up and down,
From Gundagai to Tumut Town.
And branching off there runs a track,
Across the foothills grim and black,

Across the plains and grey
To Sydney city far away.

       *   *   *   *   *   *

It came by chance one day that I
From Tumut rode to Gundagai.

And reached about the evening tide
The crossing where the roads divide;

And, waiting at the crossing place,
I saw a maiden fair of face,

With eyes of deepest violet blue,
And cheeks to match the rose in hue —

The fairest maids Australia knows
Are bred among the mountain snows.

Then, fearing I might go astray,
I asked if she could show the way.

Her voice might well a man bewitch —
Its tones so supple, deep, and rich.

"The tracks are clear," she made reply,
"And this goes down to Sydney town,
"And that one goes to Gundagai."

Then slowly, looking coyly back,
She went along the Sydney track.

And I for one was well content
To go the road the lady went;

But round the turn a swain she met —
The kiss she gave him haunts me yet!

       *   *   *   *   *

I turned and travelled with a sigh
The lonely road to Gundagai.

Rio Grande's Last Race, 1902

SALTBUSH BILL ON THE PATRIARCHS

Come all you little rouseabouts and climb upon my knee;
Today, you see, is Christmas Day, and so it's up to me
To give you some instruction like — a kind of Christmas tale —
So name your yarn, and off she goes. What, "Jonah and the
      Whale?"

Well, whales is sheep I've never shore; I've never been to sea,
So all them great Leviathans is mysteries to me;
But there's a tale the Bible tells I fully understand,
About the time the Patriarchs were settling on the land.

Those Patriarchs of olden time, when all is said and done,
They lived the same as far-out men on many a Queensland run —
A lot of roving, droving men who drifted to and fro,
The same we did out Queensland way a score of years ago.

Now Isaac was a squatter man, and Jacob was his son,
And when the boy grew up, you see, he wearied of the run.
You know the way that boys grow up — there's some that stick
      at home;
But any boy that's worth his salt will roll his swag and roam.

So Jacob caught the roving fit and took the drovers' track
To where his uncle had a run, beyond the outer back;
You see they made for out-back runs for room to stretch and
      grow,
The same we did out Queensland way a score of years ago.

Now, Jacob knew the ways of stock — that's most uncommon
      clear —
For, when he got to Laban's Run, they made him overseer;
He didn't ask a pound a week, but bargained for his pay
To take the roan and strawberry calves — the same we'd take
      today.

The duns and blacks and "Goulburn roans" (that's brindles),
      coarse and hard,
He branded them with Laban's brand, in Old Man Laban's yard;
So, when he'd done the station work for close on seven year,
Why, all the choicest stock belonged to Laban's overseer.

It's often so with overseers — I've seen the same thing done
By many a Queensland overseer on many a Queensland run.
But when the mustering time came on old Laban acted straight,
And gave him country of his own outside the boundary gate.

He gave him stock, and offered him his daughter's hand in troth;
And Jacob first he married one, and then he married both;
You see, they weren't particular about a wife or so —
No more were we up Queensland way a score of years ago.

But when the stock were strong and fat with grass and lots of
        rain,
Then Jacob felt the call to take the homeward track again.
It's strange in every creed and clime, no matter where you roam,
There comes a day when every man would like to make for
        home.

So off he set with sheep and goats, a mighty moving band,
To battle down the dusty road along the Overland —
It's droving mixed-up mobs like that that makes men cut their
        throats,
I've travelled rams, which Lord forget, but never travelled goats.

But Jacob knew the ways of stock, for (so the story goes)
When battling through the Philistines — selectors, I suppose —
And down the road from run to run, his hand 'gainst every hand,
He moved that mighty mob of stock across the Overland.

The thing is made so clear and plain, so solid in and out,
There isn't any room at all for any kind of doubt.
It's just a plain straightforward tale — a tale that lets you know
The way they lived in Palestine three thousand years ago.

It's strange to read it all today, the shifting of the stock;
You'd think you see the caravans that loaf behind the flock,
The little donkeys and the mules, the sheep that slowly spread,
And maybe Dan or Naphthali a-ridin' on ahead.

The long, dry, dusty summer days, the smouldering fires at night;
The stir and bustle of the camp at break of morning light;
The little kids that skipped about, the camels' dead-slow
        tramp —
I wish I'd done a week or two in Old Man Jacob's camp!

But if I keep the narrer path some day, perhaps, I'll know
How Jacob bred them strawberry calves three thousand years
    ago.

Evening News, 19 December 1903 [CV]

WALTZING MATILDA
(Carrying a Swag.)

Oh! there once was a swagman camped in a Billabong,
    Under the shade of a Coolabah tree;
And he sang as he looked at his old billy boiling,
    "Who'll come a-waltzing Matilda with me?"

    Who'll come a-waltzing Matilda, my darling,
      Who'll come a-waltzing Matilda with me?
    Waltzing Matilda and leading a water-bag —
      Who'll come a-waltzing Matilda with me?

Down came a jumbuck to drink at the water-hole,
    Up jumped the swagman and grabbed him in glee;
And he sang as he stowed him away in his tucker-bag,
    You'll come a-waltzing Matilda with me."

Down came the Squatter a-riding his thoroughbred;
    Down came Policemen — one, two and three.
      "Whose is the jumbuck you've got in the tucker-bag?
    You'll come a-waltzing Matilda with me."

But the swagman, he up and he jumped in the water-hole,
    Drowning himself by the Coolabah tree;
And his ghost may be heard as it sings in the Billabong
    "Who'll come a-waltzing Matilda with me?"

Sheet music, 1903 (written 1895) [CV]

THE MAN FROM GOONDIWINDI, Q.

I

This is the sunburnt bushman who
Came down from Goodiwindi, Q.

II

This is the Push from Waterloo
That spotted the sunburnt bushman who
Came down from Goondiwindi, Q.

III

These are the wealthy uncles — two,
Part of the Push from the Waterloo
That spotted the sunburnt bushman who
Came down from Goondiwindi, Q.

IV

This is the game, by no means new,
Played by the wealthy uncles — two,
Part of the Push from Waterloo
That spotted the sunburnt bushman who
Came down from Goondiwindi, Q.

V

This is the trooper dressed in blue
Who busted the game by no means new
Played by the wealthy uncles — two,
Part of the Push from Waterloo
That spotted the sunburnt bushman who
Came down from Goondiwindi, Q.

VI

This is the magistrate who knew
Not only the trooper dressed in blue,
But also the game by no means new,
And likewise the wealthy uncles — two,
And ditto the Push from Waterloo
That spotted the sunburnt bushman who
Came down from Goondiwindi, Q.

VII

This is the tale that has oft gone through
On Western plains where the skies are blue,
Till the native bear and the kangaroo
Have heard of the magistrate who knew
Not only the trooper dressed in blue,

But also the game by no means new,
And likewise the wealthy uncles — two,
And ditto the Push from Waterloo
That spotted the sunburnt bushman who
Came down from Goondiwindi, Q.

Evening News, 17 December 1904

SALTBUSH BILL, J.P.

Beyond the land where Leichhardt went,
    Beyond Sturt's Western track,
The rolling tide of change has sent
    Some strange J.P.'s out back.

And Saltbush Bill, grown old and grey,
    And worn for want of sleep,
Received the news in camp one day
    Behind the travelling sheep.

That Edward Rex, confiding in
    His known integrity,
By hand and seal on parchment skin
    Had made him a J.P.

He read the news with eager face
    But found no word of pay.
"I'd like to see my sister's place
    And kids on Christmas Day.

"I'd like to see green grass again,
    And watch clear water run,
Away from this unholy plain,
    And flies, and dust, and sun."

At last one little clause he found
    That might some hope inspire,
"A magistrate may charge a pound
    For inquest on a fire."

A big blacks' camp was built close by,
    And Saltbush Bill, says he,

"I think that camp might well supply
   A job for a J.P."

That night, by strange coincidence,
   A most disastrous fire
Destroyed the country residence
   Of Jacky Jack, Esquire.

'Twas mostly leaves, and bark, and dirt;
   The party most concerned
Appeared to think it wouldn't hurt
   If forty such were burned.

Quite otherwise thought Saltbush Bill,
   Who watched the leaping flame.
"The home is small," said he, "but still
   The principle's the same.

"Midst palaces though you should roam,
   Or follow pleasure's tracks,
You'll find," he said, "no place like home —
   At least like Jacky Jack's.

"Tell every man in camp, 'Come quick,'
   Tell every black Maria
I give tobacco, half a stick —
   Hold inquest long-a fire."

Each juryman received a name
   Well suited to a Court.
"Long Jack" and "Stumpy Bill" became
   "John Long" and "William Short".

While such as "Tarpot", "Bullock Dray",
   And "Tommy Wait-a-While",
Became, for ever and a day,
   "Scott", "Dickens", and "Carlyle".

And twelve good sable men and true
   Were soon engaged upon
The conflagration that o'erthrew
   The home of John A. John.

Their verdict, "Burnt by act of Fate",
   They scarcely had returned
When, just behind the magistrate,
   Another humpy burned!

The jury sat again and drew
   Another stick of plug.
Said Saltbush Bill, "It's up to you
   Put some one long-a Jug."

"I'll camp the sheep," he said, "and sift
   The evidence about."
For quite a week he couldn't shift,
   The way the fires broke out.

The jury thought the whole concern
   As good as any play.
They used to "take him oath" and earn
   Three sticks of plug a day.

At last the tribe lay down to sleep
   Homeless, beneath a tree;
And onward with his travelling sheep
   Went Saltbush Bill, J.P.

The sheep delivered, safe and sound,
   His horse to town he turned,
And drew some five-and-twenty pound
   For fees that he had earned.

And where Monaro's ranges hide
   Their little farms away —
His sister's children by his side —
   He spent his Christmas Day.

The next J.P. that went out back
   Was shocked, or pained, or both,
At hearing every pagan black
   Repeat the juror's oath.

No matter though he turned and fled
   They followed faster still;
"You make it inkwich, boss," they said,
   "All same like Saltbush Bill."

They even said that they'd let him see
   The fires originate.
When he refused they said that he
   Was "No good magistrate".

And out beyond Sturt's Western track,
   And Leichhardt's farthest tree,
They wait till fate shall send them back
   Their Saltbush Bill, J.P.

Evening News, 16 December 1905 [CV]

THE ROAD TO HOGAN'S GAP

Now look, you see, it's this way like —
   You cross the broken bridge
And run the crick down, till you strike
   The second right-hand ridge.

The track is hard to see in parts,
   But still it's pretty clear;
There's been two Injun hawkers' carts
   Along that road this year.

Well, run that right-hand ridge along —
   It ain't, to say, too steep —
There's two fresh tracks might put you wrong
   Where blokes went out with sheep.

But keep the crick upon your right,
   And follow pretty straight
Along the spur, until you sight
   A wire and sapling gate.

Well, that's where Hogan's old grey mare
   Fell off and broke her back;
You'll see her carcass lyin' there,
   Jist down below the track.

And then you drop two mile, or three,
   It's pretty steep and blind;

You want to go and fall a tree
   And tie it on behind.

And then you pass a broken cart
   Below a granite bluff;
And that is where you strike the part
   They reckon pretty rough.

But by the time you've got that far
   It's either cure or kill,
So turn your horses round the spur
   And face 'em up the hill.

For look, if you should miss the slope
   And get below the track,
You haven't got the slightest hope
   Of ever gettin' back.

An' half way up you'll see the hide
   Of Hogan's brindled bull;
Well, mind and keep the right-hand side.
   The left's too steep to pull.

And both the banks is full of cracks;
   An' just about at dark
You'll see the last year's bullock tracks
   Where Hogan drew the bark.

The marks is old and pretty faint —
   O'ergrown with scrub and such;
Of course the track to Hogan's ain't
   A road that's travelled much.

But turn and run the tracks along
   For half a mile or more,
And then, of course, you can't go wrong —
   You're right at Hogan's door.

When first you come to Hogan's gate
   He mightn't show perhaps;
He's pretty sure to plant, and wait
   To see it ain't the traps.

I wouldn't call it good enough
   To let your horses out;

There's some that's pretty extra rough
  Is livin' round about.

It's likely, if your horses did
  Get feedin' near the track,
It's going to cost at least a quid
  Or more to get them back.

So, if you find they're off the place,
  It's up to you to go
And flash a quid in Hogan's face —
  He'll know the blokes that know.

But listen — if you're feelin' dry,
  Just see there's no one near,
And go and wink the other eye
  And ask for ginger beer.

The blokes come in from near and far
  To sample Hogan's pop;
They reckon once they breast the bar
  They stay there till they drop.

On Sundays you can see them spread
  Like flies around the tap.
It's like that song "The Livin' Dead"
  Up there at Hogan's Gap.

They like to make it pretty strong
  Whenever there's a chance;
So when a stranger comes along
  They always hold a dance.

There's recitations, songs, and fights —
  A willin' lot you'll meet.
There's one long bloke up there recites;
  I tell you he's a treat.

They're lively blokes all right up there,
  It's never dull a day.
I'd go myself if I could spare
  The time to get away.

* * * * *

The stranger turned his horses quick.
    He didn't cross the bridge;
He didn't go along the crick
    To strike the second ridge;

He didn't make the trip, because
    He wasn't feeling fit.
His business up at Hogan's was
    To serve him with a writ.

He reckoned, if he faced the pull
    And climbed the rocky stair,
The next to come might find his hide
A landmark on the mountain side,
Along with Hogan's brindled bull
    And Hogan's old grey mare!

Lone Hand, 1 July 1914 [CV]

SONG OF THE WHEAT

We have sung the song of the droving days,
    Of the march of the travelling sheep —
How by silent stages and lonely ways
    Thin, white battalions creep.
But the man who now by the land would thrive
    Must his spurs to a ploughshare beat;
And the bush bard, changing his tune, may strive
    To sing the song of the Wheat!

It's west by south of the Great Divide
    The grim grey plains run out,
Where the old flock-masters lived and died
    In a ceaseless fight with drought.
Weary with waiting and hope deferred
    They were ready to own defeat,
Till at last they heard the master-word —
    And the master-word was Wheat.

Yarran and Myall and Box and Pine —
    'Twas axe and fire for all;

They scarce could tarry to blaze the line
    Or wait for the trees to fall
Ere the team was yoked, and the gates flung wide,
    And the dust of the horses' feet
Rose up like a pillar of smoke to guide
    The wonderful march of Wheat.

Furrow by furrow, and fold by fold,
    The soil is turned on the plain;
Better than silver and better than gold
    Is the surface-mine of the grain.
Better than cattle and better than sheep
    In the fight with drought and heat;
For a streak of stubbornness, wide and deep,
    Lies hid in a grain of Wheat.

When the stock is swept by the hand of fate,
    Deep down on his bed of clay
The brave brown Wheat will die and wait
    For the resurrection day —
Lie hid while the whole world thinks him dead;
    But the Spring-rain, soft and sweet,
Will over the steaming paddocks spread
    The first green flush of the Wheat.

Green and amber and gold it grows
    When the sun sinks late in the West;
And the breeze sweeps over the rippling rows
    Where the quail and the skylark nest.
Mountain or river or shining star,
    There's never a sight can beat —
Away to the sky-line stretching far —
    A sea of the ripening Wheat.

When the burning harvest sun sinks low,
    And shadows stretch on the plain,
The roaring strippers come and go
    Like ships on a sea of grain.
Till the lurching, groaning waggons bear
    Their tale of the load complete.

Of the world's great work he has done his share
　　Who has garnered a crop of wheat.

Princes, Potentates, Kings and Czars,
　　They travel in regal state,
But old King Wheat has a thousand cars
　　For his trip to the water-gate;
And his thousand steamships breast the tide
　　And plough through the wind and sleet
To the lands where the teeming millions bide
　　That say: "Thank God for Wheat!"

Lone Hand, 2 November 1914 [CV]

THE MOUNTAIN SQUATTER

Here in my mountain home,
　　On rugged hills and steep,
I sit and watch you come,
　　O Riverina Sheep!

You come from fertile plains
　　Where saltbush (sometimes) grows,
And flats that (when it rains)
　　Will blossom like the rose.

But when the summer sun
　　Gleams down like burnished brass,
You have to leave your run
　　And hustle off for grass.

'Tis then that — forced to roam —
　　You come to where I keep,
Here in my mountain home,
　　A boarding-house for sheep.

Around me where I sit
　　The wary wombat goes —
A beast of little wit,
　　But what he knows, he *knows*.

The very same remark
　　Applies to me also;

I don't give out a spark,
  But what I know, I *know*.

My brain perhaps would show
  No convolutions deep,
But anyhow I know
  The way to handle sheep.

These Riverina cracks,
  They do not care to ride
The half-inch hanging tracks
  Along the mountain side.

Their horses shake with fear
  When loosened boulders go
With leaps, like startled deer,
  Down to the gulfs below.

Their very dogs will shirk,
  And drop their tails in fright
When asked to go and work
  A mob that's out of sight.

My little collie pup
  Works silently and wide;
You'll see her climbing up
  Along the mountain side.

As silent as a fox
  You'll see her come and go,
A shadow through the rocks
  Where ash and messmate grow.

Then, lost to sight and sound
  Behind some rugged steep,
She works her way around
  And gathers up the sheep;

And, working wide and shy,
  She holds them rounded up.
The cash ain't coined to buy
  That little collie pup.

And so I draw a screw
   For self and dog and keep
To boundary-ride for you,
   O Riverina Sheep!

And, when the autumn rain
   Has made the herbage grow,
You travel off again,
   And glad — no doubt — to go.

But some are left behind
   Around the mountain's spread,
For those we cannot find
   We put them down as dead.

So, when we say adieu
   And close the boarding job,
I always find a few
   Fresh ear-marks in my mob.

And, with with those I sell,
   And what with those I keep,
You pay me pretty well,
   O Riverina Sheep!

It's up to me to shout
   Before we say good-bye —
"Here's to a howlin' drought
   All west of Gundagai!"

Lone Hand, July 1915 [CV]

THE GUNDAROO BULLOCK

Oh, there's some that breeds the Devon that's as solid as a stone,
And there's some that breeds the brindle which they call the
    "Goulburn Roan";
But amongst the breeds of cattle there are very, very few
Like the hairy-whiskered bullock that they bred at Gundaroo.

Far away by Grabben Gullen, where the Murrumbidgee flows,
There's a block of broken country-side where no one ever goes;

For the banks have gripped the squatters, and the free selectors
    too,
And their stock are always stolen by the men of Gundaroo.

There came a low informer to the Grabben Gullen side,
And he said to Smith the squatter, "You must saddle up and
    ride,
For your bullock's in the harness-cask of Morgan Donahoo —
He's the greatest cattle-stealer in the whole of Gundaroo."
"Oh, ho!" said Smith, the owner of the Grabben Gullen run,
"I'll go and get the troopers by the sinking of the sun,
And down into his homestead tonight we'll take a ride,
With warrants to identify the carcass and the hide."

That night rode down the troopers, the squatter at their head,
They rode into the homestead, and pulled Morgan out of bed.
"Now, show to us the carcass of the bullock that you slew —
The hairy-whiskered bullock that you killed in Gundaroo."

They peered into the harness-cask, and found it wasn't full,
But down among the brine they saw some flesh and bits of wool.
"What's this?" exclaimed the trooper; "an infant, I declare;"
Said Morgan. "'Tis the carcass of an old man native bear.
I heard that ye were coming, so an old man bear I slew,
Just to give you kindly welcome to my home in Gundaroo.

"The times are something awful, as you can plainly see,
The banks have broke the squatters, and they've broke the likes
    of me;
We can't afford a bullock — such expense would never do —
So an old man bear for breakfast is a treat in Gundaroo."
And along by Grabben Gullen, where the rushing river flows,
In the block of broken country where there's no one ever goes,
On the Upper Murrumbidgee, they're a hospitable crew —
But you mustn't ask for "bullock" when you go to Gundaroo.

Saltbush Bill and Other Verses, 1917 [CV]

2
Bush Sketches, Short Stories and Other Prose

EDITOR'S NOTE

Paterson began writing his bush sketches and stories at the time when he was contributing his early verses to the *Bulletin*, and "Hughey's Dog" was his first prose piece published in that journal, in November 1889. It was not, however, Paterson's first published prose effort. At the end of 1888, when he was managing clerk of a law firm that handled the business of several banks, he became appalled at the plight of many small property-holders and the treatment meted out to them by the banks in harassing and foreclosing on them. Accordingly he wrote a pamphlet, *Australia for the Australians*, published by Gordon & Gotch early in 1889, in which, in unusually passionate terms, he bitterly attacked the system of granting away land in fee simple. The pamphlet also deplored the incidence of unemployment in the colony, the absurdity of country people flocking to the towns, the overcrowding of the professions, and especially the evils of absentee landlordism. Paterson later regretted writing *Australia for the Australians* and blamed it on his youthful infatuation with the teachings of Henry George. Nevertheless both he and his father had suffered as a result of the system he attacked and some of his bitterness about it emerges in his poem "On Kiley's Run". Moreover many others who had seen the evils of the land grant system, including some of the poets and writers of the day (especially Barcroft Boake, Henry Lawson, "Breaker" Morant and Will Ogilvie), would have agreed with him.

The pieces I have selected are, I believe, most representative of Paterson's best prose. He is shown to much better advantage in his sketches and short stories than in his two novels, *An Outback Marriage* and *The Shearer's Colt*. The shorter sketch came as naturally to him as the writing of his ballads but he had not studied the form and structure of the novel sufficiently to master it effectively, nor did he have the patience to develop his characterisation. Nevertheless it must be said that those parts of his novels where he was on familiar ground — the mountain country and the plains of the outback — remain in the memory and the people he writes about are eminently recognisable as bush types.

From *Australia for the Australians*

It may be said, "We have plenty of land; there is no need to make an outcry about it being granted away — you can get acres and acres out back at the selection price." "Out back" you can; but every day the words "out back" mean further and further out. At present the far back land has little value except what the owners add to it; but every day there is less and less available land worth taking up. It is all very well to point to dry waterless plains and say, "There is land — plenty of it — what are you complaining about the land system for? If you want land, go and take up some of this." But there is an almighty difference between such land as this, and the rich lands on the coast rivers, down about Illawarra, and on the banks of the Hunter and Macleay. The injustice, the stupidity, of the arrangement, consists in the fact that our immediate predecessors granted away for ever and ever, in fee simple, free of rent, the best lands we had, and left the present generation the wilderness. They should never have allowed any absolute ownership free of rent to be acquired in land. As the land gets more and more scarce, those who enjoy the advantage of using the picked lands of the colony should also enjoy the privilege of paying something to the community for it.

It is evident that once all the available land gets into the hands of owners, they have the rest of us at their mercy. Writers who deal with the subject as it presents itself in older countries are very fond of denouncing the tyranny of the landlord over the tenant. This phase of the matter has not yet forced itself upon our community to any extent. The country is too new for landlord and tenant disputes to have sprung up; but we will have them, sure enough. We are creating the largest landed proprietors yet known — men who count their freehold acres by the hundred thousand. As soon as we leave our cities with their pitiful little subdivisions and crowded buildings, we can run in the train through miles and miles of freehold estates all belonging to individual owners. These will all be cut up into farms some day and leased out, and then the fun will begin. We will have all the things which make life in Ireland so enjoyable — plenty of good landlord shooting then. We all know the bitter hatred between the tenants and their landlords, not only in Ireland, but in Scotland, England and Wales. That sort of thing will come here some day — the poverty and all, unless we mend our system.

As to the question of discouraging improvements, many people are under the impression that our present system, of what is practically absolute ownership, is the only one that encourages improvements. "If you make the tenure of land subject to a rent," say they, "or to any restrictions, there will be no money spent on the land, no improvements made, and great deterioration will set in. We will have wooden houses instead of stones, paling fences instead of walls." But a very little thought will show them that this is erroneous. It is only when the owner realises that he can only add to the value of his land by making improvements that improvements will be made in real earnest. Under the present system it generally pays better not to improve; improvements cost money. Any man who has tried his hand at building and laying out a garden knows that in nine cases out of ten it would have paid him better to let the land be idle, and wait for an increase in value. It is only when we get rid of this increase in value through no good deed of the owner, that we will get proper increase in value by way of improvements.

As to the locking-up of land; it is astonishing how far this locking-up system prevails. Nearly every country town in New South Wale is cursed by the proximity of some large estate which can neither be bought nor leased. Think of the loss to the community caused by this. Every day's work done on bad land while better land is lying idle is done at so much loss. Every unfortunate selector who is driven out on to the Macquarie and the Bogan to take up the dry plain, while land is lying idle on the rich river flats all over the colony, is working at a dead loss to himself and the community. It is on the success of such men as these that city men live. Our present system is direct encouragement to the owners to hold land idle and wait for a rise. The thing has taken a great hold in this colony, and the cleverest man is not the man who can use a bit of land and make something out of it, but the man who can make a rise out of a railway being made to his property.

For city properties the evil is intensified. When we hear of George Street property fetching a thousand pounds per foot, we say, "How prosperous the country must be! What wonderful advances we are making! A few years ago it could have been bought for a hundred pounds an acre!" What we ought to say is, "What a dreadful handicap on the colony it is, that men should be able to get such a lot of the colony's products for land which was increased in value by the State. What fools we are to allow it to go on!" That is what we ought to say. To anyone who understands the matter, it is a cruel thing to see the settlers in the interior of our colony, striving day after day on their little properties, with no comforts, no leisure, no hopes nor aspirations beyond making a decent living, and to think that it is owing to the labour of these men and such as these that the owners of Sydney are living luxuriously, travelling between this colony and England, drawing large rentals, or spending the large values which they never did a hand's turn to earn or deserve.

There is one stock argument which seems to go down with a lot of people. It is said that the people who buy land when it is worth little, and hold on to it till it rises in value, are risking their money, and that if the land falls in value they lose, so that they surely ought to be allowed to profit if it rises. The answer to this is that we should never have to go into the risk at all. It is too great a certainty that land will rise in any fertile unsettled country. The man who buys runs a very small risk, and has the chance of a huge profit. The community on the other hand make a very small profit if the land falls in value after it is sold, and they make a huge loss if it rises.

Land which was bought for a pound an acre has often risen in value to twenty thousand pounds per acre by the exertions of the community, and the owner has reaped the benefit. Land buying in the early stage of a settlement is a kind of lottery, in which the inventor is pretty certain to win; and where the fortunate men profit at the expense of their fellow men, not for once but for all time, and not merely for themselves but for their descendants. We have prohibited all other lotteries, and yet none of them ever did one-millionth part of the harm which this has done. There is no sense in abusing the men who have taken advantage of this state of affairs. The way was open to them, and they adopted it. I expect most of my readers only wish that their forefathers had secured a few acres about Sydney at the time when they could be bought for a keg of rum. Their descendants need do very little work now; other people would have to work for them.

There is another argument sometimes advanced, which looks well on paper but carries little weight. It is argued that if a man pays money for land and lets the land lie idle, he is entitled to profit by any advance in its value, because he has lost interest on his money. This is a rotten argument. If a man likes to lock up his capital in unproductive, unused land, it is his own fault. The land is handed over to him to use, not to look at. If he uses the land he can get a return for it, which will pay his interest. If a man bought a mare for a hundred pounds and never rode her or bred from her, by the time she was twenty years of age he would, if he calculated up the interest on her price, expect to get for her several thousands of pounds, whereas he would really get nothing for so old an animal, nor would he expect it. He would ride her and breed from her, and so get a return for his money year by year. In the same way let the owners use the land if they want interest.

This is where we want to make a reform. Our land system is bad: it drives the men into the cities; it causes good land to be locked up; it enables some men to live at the expense of others; it enables a man to say by his will that for twenty-one years after his death no one shall use his land. Fancy that; a dead man's will that can override the needs of the living. We have created a land-grabbing mania — an earth hunger. Five hundred and fifty-two persons in a population of over a million own upwards of seventeen million acres of freehold; they possess in fee simple over one-half the alienated lands of New South Wales. Squatters have been forced to buy where they would rather have taken a good lease on secure tenure. To buy the land they have had to borrow largely from England capital, and our lands are mortgaged up to the hilt; the purchase money has been spent in wasteful extravagance in public buildings, in useless courthouses, etc., in one-horse country towns. Where we ought to have spent money in irrigation we have spent it in building tramways and bridges, and such like city works, which add nothing to the productive power of the country. This is the thing which cries aloud for a reform . . .

Hughey's Dog

Hughey was butcher on the station, and his soul yearned for a dog. Dogs there were about in plenty, but he wanted something special, and as the super was going to Sydney, Hughey commissioned him to buy him a dog. "Buy a dog," he said, "as can fight. I don't put no value on pedigree — I don't want no pedigree, I want a dog, get a dog as can fight, and he'll fill the bill." Wherefore, there appeared shortly in a Sydney paper, in the somewhat inaccurate grammar of the super:

Wanted, at once, a dog as can fight. Apply Bushman's Hotel.

Next morning the men with dogs commenced to roll up. The dogs were of all sorts and colours, having only one thing in common — they each and all looked as if they would tear a man's leg off on the slightest pretext. When the super went down and admitted them into the bar-parlour, he and the landlord had to get up on the table to obtain anything like an unprejudiced view of the competitors. They soon weeded them down to two, one a villainous-looking half-breed devil, and the other a pure-bred bulldog of undeniable quality, a truculent ruffian with milk-white skin and bloodshot eyes, by whose noble proportions the soul of the landlord was much gratified. The other dog, however, was evidently the better in the fight, because the gentleman in charge of him said he thought the best way to decide was 'to let the two dawgs 'ave a go in, to see which is the best dawg''. The one-eyed nobleman who represented the bulldog, saw that his dog would have no chance in a fight, but being himself of the pugilistic persuasion, he tied his dog to the leg of a table and advanced on the other man with his fists up. "Suppose me an' you has a go in," he said, "to see which is the best dawg?"

This proposal would have been promptly acceded to but for the arrival of another man with a dog — a big brown dog with a coarse, heavy-jawed head, big round the ribs, fairly long and light in the legs, evidently as active as a cat and hard as nails. But the previous dog-owners knew him and apparently recognized that they and their canines were in the presence of a master. "'Ere's 'Arrison's dawg," they said, "an in corse if you want a dawg to fight —." So the super explained that that was just what he did want, and he became the purchaser of the brown animal, which duly arrived among us and was installed as Hughey's dog. As he had no tail, Hughey, of course, christened him "Stumpy".

And he could fight. He "counted out" every dog in the place the first two days he was there. His great activity, combined with his powerful jaws, made him a Czar among tykes. After the first two days not a dog dared heave in sight while Hughey's dog was taking a walk. He chased the kangaroo dogs away up the paddock; he fought two rounds with the bullock-driver's dog, and would have killed him only for the arrival of the bullocky with the whip; and as he was intercepted in hot pursuit of the boss's favourite collie, Hughie thought it was best to tie him up. This made him worse, and whenever he managed to slip his collar or break the chain there would be a procession of dogs making full speed for the river, with Stumpy after them kicking the dust up in hot pursuit. Once they got to the river they were safe, as he was an indifferent swimmer and would not take to the water. Whenever any traveller or teamster came along with a dog that he fancied could fight, Hughey's dog was always trotted out to maintain the honour of the station, which he invariably did with a vengeance.

Soon his fame spread far and wide. Long, gawky, cornstalk youths used to ride miles to see him, and a kind of exhibition used to be given on a Sunday for the benefit of visitors. Stumpy was chained up by a fairly long chain, and the entertainment consisted of taking a dog, one that knew Stumpy's prowess for choice, and then getting Stumpy out to the full length of his chain and giving him a fair hold of the visiting dog's tail. A most exciting struggle would ensure. The hospitable Stumpy would drag with might and main to get his guest within the reach of his chain, and the frenzied excitement in his face as he felt the other dog's tail slipping out of his teeth was awful to witness. The other dog meanwhile industriously scratched gravel to get away. Sometimes he turned and confronted Stumpy, but no dog ever did that more than once; once was more than enough, and on any second appearance they would devote all their energies to pulling away, and praying that their tails would break. Sometimes the tail was bitten through by Stumpy, and on these occasions the dog was, if possible, recaptured and the affair was started fresh, fair and square. If Stumpy pulled the dog into his reach he used to drag him back into the centre of the circle covered by his chain, shorten his hold on the tail in a workmanlike manner until he got him right up close to him, when he would suddenly release the tail and make a spring for the dog's neck. This was a most exciting moment, because if Stumpy missed his spring the other dog would probably dash away out of reach, and it was with breathless interest the assembled crowd would watch Stumpy nerving himself for this critical rush. If Stumpy got a fair hold the game was stopped and the dog released.

One night some dingoes came howling round the homestead, scaring the sheep in the yard, frightening the cows and calves and small dogs, making the fowls cackle and the cocks crow, and stirring up the deuce generally. It was bright moonlight, and the big, grey expanse of the plain lay open and clear almost as day when the men slipped down to the back and let Stumpy go. They reckoned this dingo business would be right into his hand, and when they got down there he was straining at the collar so hard that he nearly choked. They let him go, and he dashed madly off into the moonlight in the direction of the howling dingoes, breathing murder and dogs-meat and the men followed at a run, one of them carrying an old carbine. "Lord help the dingo as Stumpy gets hold on!" gasped out Hughey as they ran along. They soon lost sight of Stumpy in the dim distance, and the howling had abruptly ceased. They ran on until out of breath, when they pulled up and listened: a dead silence reigned, there was no sound of dog or dingo, and nothing in sight on the plain but the clumps of saltbush. "I expect he's follerin' them away into the scrub," said Hughey. "I reckon they'd better take to the river if they want to keep their hides outside their gizzards," said another. They waited a while and whistled and called, but nothing came, so they tramped off home. As they drew near the sheepyard it became evidence something was wrong; the sheep were "ringing" wildly, rushing in all direction to escape some foe.

"By Jove, there's a dingo in the yard," said Hughey, and they rushed up at the double. The carbine was handed to one of the blackfellows, a noted shot, and as the party ran up he got a clear view of the marauder in the yard worrying a struggling ewe. The blackfellow put the carbine to his shoulder and was just going to let drive, when Hughey knocked up the muzzle of the weapon. "Don't fire," he said, "it's Stumpy."

And so it was. That amiable animal, finding that he could not catch the dingoes, had come back to give the sheep a turn. After this he was tied up at night and only occasionally let loose in the day time, and on one of these excursions an event happened which sealed his fate.

Hughey used to kill the sheep for eating, and, of course, Stumpy came in for the lion's share of the waste meat. The men's cook was a big Dutchman, a half-witted chap who occasionally went religion-mad, and between him and Stumpy there was a vendetta. Stumpy, you see, had killed his dog, and he had poured boiling water on Stumpy on the only occasion when the latter visited the kitchen; so it was not to be wondered at that when the cook walked rather carelessly, and perhaps swaggeringly, past Stumpy, who was devouring some sheep's liver, Stumpy went after him and bit him severely. The cook went to Hughey, who was putting the ornamental touches on the ribs of the dead sheep by cutting patterns with his knife.

"Hughey," he said, "your tam tog was pite me!"

"What do I care!" responded Hughey. "I suppose it won't poison him — did he swaller the piece?"

The Dutch cook looked at Hughey in a curious way and walked on. Late that night when the episode was forgotten, the cook announced his intention of going out to shoot some possums. "Don't shoot yourself!" was the only advice he got, but he again smiled that curious smile as he replied, "I vill shoot a bossum — a big one."

Then he set forth into the night with all the dogs in the place accompanying him. A couple of shots were heard down by the river, and soon the Dutchman came back and put the gun away, and went off to the house. He asked for the boss, and much to the boss's astonishment said he meant to leave next morning.

"You can't leave," said the boss — "you are under agreement to give a certain amount of notice — you can't leave all at once."

"Vell," responded the Dutchman slowly, "it is all in de agreement but I must go. De stars is gettin' very close togedder, and I haf a heap of preachin' to do — as soon as dem stars get togedder de vorld vill be purnt up and I must go and preach to the beeples.''

"Off his nanny again," thought the boss, "the sooner he goes the better." So the cook returned to the hut, and the men heard him packing and rolling things at all hours of the night; then he went out again and quiet reigned.

Next morning he was gone. The men had to cook their own breakfast, which annoyed them greatly, and then they went down to the house to see if the boss knew anything of the cook's disappearance, and learnt that he had given notice.

"He seems to have taken my dog," groaned Hughey. "I can't see him anywhere."

Then Hughey went off to the meat-house to get the sheep he had killed on the previous day. There it hung, wrapped round by a white cover just as he had left it. As he took it down he noticed that it felt strangely light but he carried it to the kitchen, laid it on the chopping block and took off the cover. Then he found out why it was so light. In the place of the sheep there lay, skinned, dressed and ornamented in true butcher fashion, the corpse of Stumpy. The Dutchman had shot him and butchered him the previous night, and had gone forth to do his "preaching to the peoples" for fear of the consequences.

Hughey swore an oath of vengeance, but he never came across the cook again. The latter got into a lunatic asylum and spends his days in asserting that the Prince of Wales meanly cut him out of the affection of Alexandra, to whom he (the mad butcher) was engaged to be married, and in the contemplation of that romantic matter he has forgotten all about Hughey's dog.

Bulletin, 2 November 1889

His Masterpiece

Greenhide Billy was a stockman on a Clarence River cattle-station, and admittedly the biggest liar in the district. He had been for many years pioneering in the Northern Territory, the other side of the sundown — a regular "furthest-out man" — and this assured his reputation among station-hands who award rank according to amount of experience.

Young men who have always hung around the home districts, doing a job of shearing here or a turn at horse-breaking there, look with reverence on Riverine or Macquarie River shearers who came in with tales of runs where they have 300,000 acres of free-hold land and shear 250,000 sheep; these again pale their ineffectual fires before the glory of the Northern Territory man who has all-comers on toast, because no one can contradict him or check his figures. When two of them meet, however, they are not fools enough to cut down quotations and spoil the market; they lie in support of each other, and make all other bushmen feel mean and pitiful and inexperienced.

Sometimes a youngster will timidly ask Greenhide Billy about the *terra incognita*: "What sort of a place is it, Billy — how big are the properties? How many acres had you in the place you were on?"

"Acres be d—d!" Billy would scornfully reply; "hear him talking about acres! D'ye think we were blanked cockatoo selectors! Out there we reckon country by the hundred miles. You orter say, 'How many thousand miles of country?' and then I'd understand you."

Furthermore, according to Billy, they reckoned the rainfall in the Territory by yards, not inches. He had seen blackfellows who could jump at least three inches higher than anyone else had ever seen a blackfellow jump, and every bushman had seen or personally known a blackfellow who could jump over six feet. Billy had seen higher droughts, better country, fatter cattle, faster horses, and cleverer dogs, than any other man on the Clarence River. But one night when the rain was on the roof, and the river was rising with a moaning sound, and the men were gathered round the fire in the hut smoking and staring at the coals, Billy turned himself loose and gave us his masterpiece.

"I was drovin' with cattle from Mungrybanbone to old Corlett's station on the Buckadowntown River" (Billy always started his stories with some paralysing bush names). "We had a thousand head of store-cattle, wild, mountain-bred wretches that'd charge you on sight; they were that handy with their horns they could skewer a mosquito. There was one or two one-eyed cattle among 'em — and you know how a one-eyed beast always keeps movin' away from the mob, pokin' away out to the edge of them so as they won't git on his blind side, so that by stirrin' about he keeps the others restless.

"They had been scared once or twice, and stampeded and gave us all we could do to keep them together; and it was wet and dark and thundering, and it looked like a real bad night for us. It was my watch. I was on one side of the cattle, like it might be here, with a small bit of a fire; and my mate, Barcoo Jim, he was right opposite on the other side of the cattle, and had gone to sleep under a log. The rest of the men were in the camp fast asleep. Every now and again I'd get on my horse and prowl round the cattle quiet like, and they seemed to be settled down all right, and I was sitting by my fire holding my horse and drowsing, when all of a sudden a blessed possum ran out from some saplings and scratched up a tree right alongside me. I was half-asleep, I suppose, and was startled; anyhow, never thinking what I was doing, I picked up a firestick out of the fire and flung it at the possum.

"Whoop! Before you could say Jack Robertson, that thousand head of cattle were on their feet, and made one wild, headlong, mad rush right over the place where poor old Barcoo Jim was sleeping. There was no time to hunt up materials for the inquest; I had to keep those cattle together, so I sprang into the saddle, dashed the spurs into the old horse, dropped my head on his mane, and sent him as hard as he could leg it through the scrub to get to the lead of the cattle and steady them. It was brigalow, and you know what that is.

"You know how the brigalow grows," continued Bill; "saplings about as thick as a man's arm, and that close together a dog can't open his mouth to bark in 'em. Well, those cattle swept through that scrub, levelling it like as if it had been cleared for a railway line. They cleared a track a quarter of a mile wide, and smashed every stick, stump, and sapling on it. You could hear them roaring and their hoofs thundering and the scrub smashing three or four miles off.

"And where was I? I was racing parallel with the cattle, with my head down on the horse's neck, letting him pick his way through the scrub in the pitchy darkness. This went on for about four miles. Then the cattle began to get winded, and I dug into the old stock-horse with the spurs, and got in front, and began to crack the whip and sing out, so as to steady them a little; after a while they dropped slower and slower, and I kept the whip going. I got them all together in a patch of open country, and there I rode round and round 'em all night till daylight.

"And how I wasn't killed in the scrub, goodness only knows; for a man couldn't ride in the daylight where I did in the dark. The cattle were all knocked about — horns smashed, legs broken, ribs torn; but they were all there, every solitary head of 'em; and as soon as the daylight broke I took 'em back to the camp — that is, all that could travel, because I had to leave a few broken-legged ones."

Billy paused in his narrative. He knew that some suggestions would be made, by way of compromise, to tone down the awful strength of the yarn, and he prepared himself accordingly. His motto was "No surrender"; he never abated one jot of his statements; if anyone chose to remark on them, he made them warmer and stronger, and absolutely flattened out the intruder.

"That was a wonderful bit of ridin' you done, Billy," said one of the men at last, admiringly. "It's a wonder you wasn't killed. I suppose your clothes was pretty well tore off your back with the scrub?"

"Never touched a twig," said Billy.

"Ah!" faltered the inquirer, "then no doubt you had a real ringin' good stock-horse that could take you through a scrub like that full-split in the dark, and not hit you against anything."

"No, he wasn't a good 'un," said Billy decisively, "he was the worst horse in the camp. Terrible awkward in the scrub he was, al-

ways fallin' down on his knees; and his neck was so short you
could sit far back on him and pull his ears."

Here that interrogator retired hurt; he gave Billy best. After a
pause another took up the running.

"How did you mate get on, Billy? I s'pose he was trampled to a
mummy!"

"No," said Billy, "he wasn't hurt a bit. I told you he was sleeping under the shelter of a log. Well, when those cattle rushed they
swept over that log a thousand strong; and every beast of that herd
took the log in his stride and just missed landing on Barcoo Jimmy
by about four inches."

The men waited a while and smoked, to let this statement soak
well into their systems; at last one rallied and had a final try.

"It's a wonder then, Billy," he said, "that your mate didn't
come after you and give you a hand to steady the cattle."

"Well, perhaps it was," said Billy, "only that there was a bigger
wonder than that at the back of it."

"What was that?"

"My mate never woke up all through it."

Then the men knocked the ashes out of their pipes and went to
bed.

Bulletin, 4 April 1891

The History of a Jackaroo

IN FIVE LETTERS

1. *Letter from Jocelyn de Greene, of Wiltshire, England, to college friend.*

DEAR GUS — The Governor has fixed things up for me at last. I am not go to India, but to Australia. It seems the Governor met some old Australian swell named Moneygrub at a dinner in the City. He has thousands of acres of land and herds of sheep, and I am to go out and learn the business of sheep-raising. Of course it is not quite the same as going to India; but some really decent people do go out to Australia sometimes, I am told, and I expect it won't be so bad. In India one generally goes into the Civil Service, nothing to do and lots of niggers to wait on you, but the Australian Civil Service no fellow can well go into — it is awful low business, I hear. I have been going in for gun and revolver practice so as to be able to hold my own against the savages and serpents in the woods of Australia. Mr Moneygrub says there isn't much fighting with the savages nowadays; but, he says, the Union shearers will give me all the fight I want. What is a Union shearer, I wonder? My mother has ordered an extra-artist's umbrella for me to take with me for fear of sunstroke, and I can hold it over me while watching the flocks. She didn't half like my going until Mr Moneygrub said that they always dressed for dinner at the head station, and that a Church of England clergyman visits there twice a month. I am only to pay a premium of £500 for the experience, and Mr Moneygrub says I'll be able to make that out of scalps in my spare time. He says there is a Government reward for scalps. I don't mind a brush with the savages, but if he thinks I'm going to scalp my enemies he is mistaken. Anyhow, I sail next week, so no more from yours, outward bound, JOCELYN DE GREENE.

2. *Letter from Moneygrub and Co., London, to the manager of the company's "Drybone" Station, Paroo River, Australia.*

DEAR SIR — We beg to advise you of having made arrangements to take a young gentleman named Greene as colonial-experiencer, and he will be consigned to you by the next boat. His premium is £500, and you will please deal with him in the usual way. Let us know when you have vacancies for any more colonial-experiencers, as several are now asking about it, and the premiums are forthcoming. You are on no account to employ Union shearers this year; and you must cut expenses as low as you can. Would it not be feasible to work the station with the colonial-experience men and Chinese labour? &c., &c., &c.

3. *Letter from Mr Robert Saltbush, of Fryingpan Station, to a friend.*

DEAR BILLY — Those fellows over at Drybone Station have been at it again. You know it joins us, and old Moneygrub, who lives in London, sends out an English bloke every now and again to be a jackaroo. He gets £500 premium for each one, and the manager puts the jackaroo to boundary-ride a tremendous great paddock at the back of the run, and he gives him a week's rations and tells him never to go through a gate, because so long as he only gets lost in the paddock he can always be found somehow, but if he gets out of the paddock, Lord knows whether he'd ever be seen again. And there these poor English devils are, riding round the fences and getting lost and not seeing a soul until they go near mad from loneliness; and then they run away at last, and old Macgregor, the manager, he makes a great fuss and goes after them with a whip, but he takes care to have a stockman pick their tracks up and take them to the nearest township, and then they go on the spree and never come back, and old Moneygrub collars the £500 and sends out another jackaroo. It's a great game. The last one they had was a fellow called Greene. They had him at the head station for a while, letting him get pitched off the station horses. He said, "They're awfully beastly horses in this country, by Jove; they're not content with throwing you off, but they'd kick you afterwards if you don't be careful." When they got full up of him at the head station they sent him out to the big paddock to an old hut full of fleas, and left him there with his tucker and two old screws of horses. The horses, of course, gave him the slip, and he got lost for two days looking for them, and his meat was gone bad when he got home. He killed a sheep for tucker, and how do you think he killed it? He *shot* it! It was a ram, too, one of Moneygrub's best rams, and there will be the deuce to pay when they find out. About the fourth day a swagman turned up, and he gave the swaggy a gold watch-chain to show him the way to the nearest town, and he is there now — on the spree, I believe. He had a fine throat for whisky, anyhow, and the hot climate has started him in earnest. Before he left the hut and the fleas, he got a piece of raddle and wrote on the door:

HELL
S.R.O.

whatever that means. I think it must be some sort of joke. The brown colt I got from Ginger is a clinker, a terror to kick, but real fast. He takes a lot of rubbing out for half a mile, &c., &c., &c.

4. *Letter from Sandy Macgregor, manager of Drybone Station, to Messrs Moneygrub & Co., London.*

DEAR SIR; — I regret to have to inform you that the young gentleman, Mr Greene, whom you sent out, has seen fit to leave his employment and go away to the township. No doubt he found the work somewhat rougher than he had been used to, but if young gentlemen are sent out here to get experience they must expect to rough it like other bushmen. I hope you will notify his friends of the fact: and if you have applications for any more colonial-experiencers we now have a vacancy for one. There is great trouble this year over the shearing and a lot of grass will be burnt unless some settlement is arrived at, &c., &c., &c.

5. *Extract from evidence of Senior-Constable Rafferty, taken at an inquest before Lushington, P.M. for the North-east by South Paroo district, and a jury.*

I AM a senior-constable, stationed at Walloopna beyant. On the 5th instant, I received information that a man was in the horrors at Flanagan's hotel. I went down and saw the man, whom I recognized as the deceased. He was in the horrors: he was very bad. He had taken all his clothes off, and was hiding in a fowlhouse to get away from the devils which were after him. I went to arrest him, but he avoided me, and escaped over a paling-fence on to the Queensland side of the border, where I had no power to arrest him. He was foaming at the mouth and acting like a madman. He had been on the spree for several days. From inquiries made, I believe his name to be Greene, and that he had lately left the employment of Mr Macgregor, at Drybone. He was found dead on the roadside by the carriers coming into Walloopna. He had evidently wandered away from the township, and died from the effects of the sun and the drink.

VERDICT OF JURY: "That deceased came to his death by sunstroke and exposure during a fit of *delirium tremens*, caused by excessive drinking. No blame attached to anybody." Curator of intestate advertises for next of kin to J. Greene, and nobody comes forward. Curtain!

Bulletin, 5 September 1891

The Cast-Iron Canvasser

The firm of Sloper and Dodge, publishers and printers, was in great distress. These two enterprising individuals had worked up an enormous business in time-payment books, which they sold all over Australia by means of canvassers. They had put all the money they had into the business; and now, just when everything was in thorough working order, the public had revolted against them.

Their canvassers were molested by the country folk in divers strange bush ways. One was made drunk, and then a two-horse harrow was run over him; another was decoyed into the ranges on pretence of being shown a gold-mine, and his guide galloped away and left him to freeze all night in the bush. In mining localities the inhabitants were called together by beating a camp-oven lid with a pick, and the canvasser was given ten minutes in which to get out of the town alive. If he disregarded the hint he would, as likely as not, fall accidentally down a disused shaft.

The people of one district applied to their M.P. to have canvassers brought under the "Noxious Animals Act", and demanded that a reward should be offered for their scalps. Reports appeared in the country press about strange, gigantic birds that appeared at remote selections and frightened the inhabitants to death — these were Sloper and Dodge's sober and reliable agents, wearing neat, close-fitting suits of tar and feathers.

In fact, it was altogether too hot for the canvassers, and they came in from North and West and South, crippled and disheartened, to tender their resignations. To make matters worse, Sloper and Dodge had just got out a large *Atlas of Australia*, and if they couldn't sell it, ruin stared them in the face; and how could they sell it without canvassers?

The members of the firm sat in their private office. Sloper was a long, sanctimonious individual, very religious and very bald. Dodge was a little fat American, with bristly, black hair and beard, and quick, beady eyes. He was eternally smoking a reeking black pipe, and puffing the smoke through his nose in great whiffs, like a locomotive on a steep grade. Anybody walking into one of those whiffs was liable to get paralysis.

Just as things were at their very blackest, something had turned up that promised to relieve all their difficulties. An inventor had offered to supply them with a patent cast-iron canvasser — a figure which (he said) when wound up would walk, talk, collect orders, and stand any amount of ill-usage and wear and tear. If this could indeed be done, they were saved. They had made an appointment with the Genius; but he was half an hour late, and the partners were steeped in gloom.

They had begun to despair of his appearing at all, when a cab rattled up to the door. Sloper and Dodge rushed unanimously to the window. A young man, very badly dressed, stepped out of the cab, holding over his shoulder what looked like the upper half of a man's body. In his disengaged hand he held a pair of human legs with boots and trousers on. Thus burdened he turned to ask his fare, but the cabman gave a yell of terror, whipped up his horse, and disappeared at a hand-gallop; and a woman who happened to be going by, ran down the street, howling that Jack the Ripper had come to town. The man bolted in at the door, and toiled up the dark stairs tramping heavily, the legs and feet, which he dragged after him, making an unearthly clatter. He came in and put his burden down on the sofa.

"There you are, gents," he said; "there's your canvasser."

Sloper and Dodge recoiled in horror. The upper part of the man had a waxy face, dull, fishy eyes, and dark hair; he lounged on the sofa like a corpse at ease, while his legs and feet stood by, leaning stiffly against the wall. The partners gazed at him for a while in silence.

"Fix him together, for God's sake," said Dodge. "He looks awful."

The Genius grinned, and fixed the legs on.

"Now he looks better," said Dodge, poking about the figure — "looks as much like life as most — ah, would you, you brute!" he exclaimed, springing back in alarm, for the figure had made a violent La Blanche swing at him.

"That's all right," said the Inventor. "It's no good having his face knocked about, you know — lot of trouble to make that face.

His head and body are full of springs, and if anybody hits him in the face, or in the pit of the stomach — favourite place to hit canvassers, the pit of the stomach — it sets a strong spring in motion, and he fetches his right hand round with a swipe that'll knock them into the middle of next week. It's an awful hit. Griffo couldn't dodge it, and Slavin couldn't stand up against it. No fear of any man hitting *him* twice.

"And he's dog-proof, too. His legs are padded with tar and oakum, and if a dog bites a bit out of him, it will take that dog weeks to pick his teeth clean. Never bite anybody again, that dog won't. And he'll talk, talk, talk, like a suffragist gone mad; his phonograph can be charged for a hundred thousand words, and all you've got to do is to speak into it what you want him to say, and he'll say it. He'll go on saying it till he talks his man silly, or gets an order. He has an order-form in his hand, and as soon as anyone signs it and gives it back to him, that sets another spring in motion, and he puts the order in his pocket, turns round, and walks away. Grand idea, isn't he? Lor' bless you, I fairly love him."

He beamed affectionately on his monster.

"What about stairs?" said Dodge.

"No stairs in the bush," said the Inventor, blowing a speck of dust off his apparition; "all ground-floor houses. Anyhow, if there were stairs we could carry him up and let him fall down afterwards, or get flung down like any other canvasser."

"Ha! Let's see him walk," said Dodge.

The figure walked all right, stiff and erect.

"Now let's hear him yabber."

The Genius touched a spring, and instantly, in a queer, tin-whistly voice, he began to sing, "Little Annie Rooney".

"Good!" said Dodge; "he'll do. We'll give you your price. Leave him here to-night, and come in tomorrow. We'll send you off to the back country with him. Ninemile would be a good place to start in. Have a cigar?"

Mr Dodge, much elated, sucked at his pipe, and blew through his nose a cloud of nearly solid smoke, through which the Genius sidled out. They could hear him sneezing and choking all the way down stairs.

Ninemile is a quite little place, sleepy beyond description. When the mosquitoes in that town settle on anyone, they usually go to sleep, and forget to bite him. The climate is so hot that the very grasshoppers crawl into the hotel parlours out of the sun, climb up the window curtains, and then go to sleep. The Riot Act has never had to be read in Ninemile. The only thing that can arouse the inhabitants out of their lethargy is the prospect of a drink at somebody else's expense.

For these reasons it had been decided to start the Cast-iron Canvasser there, and then move him on to more populous and active localities if he proved a success. They sent up the Genius, and one of their men who knew the district well. The Genius was to manage the automation, and the other was to lay out the campaign, choose the victims, and collect the money, geniuses being notoriously unreliable and loose in their cash. They got through a good deal of whisky on the way up, and when they arrived at Ninemile were in a cheerful mood, and disposed to take risks.

"Who'll we begin on?" said the Genius.

"Oh, hang it all," said the other, "let's make a start with Macpherson."

Macpherson was a Land Agent, and the big bug of the place. He was a gigantic Scotchman, six feet four in his socks, and freckled all over with freckles as big as half-crowns. His eyebrows would have made decent-sized moustaches for a cavalryman, and his moustaches looked like horns. He was a fighter from the ground up, and had a desperate "down" on canvassers generally, and on Sloper and Dodge's canvassers in particular.

Sloper and Dodge had published a book called *Remarkable Colonials*, and Macpherson had written out his own biography for it. He was intensely proud of his pedigree and his relations, and in his narrative made out that he was descended from the original Fhairshon who swam round Noah's Ark with his title-deeds in his teeth. He showed how his people had fought under Alexander the Great and Timour, and had come over to Scotland some centuries before William the Conqueror landed in England. He proved that he was related in a general way to one emperor, fifteen kings, twenty-five dukes, and earls and lords and viscounts innumerable. And then, after all, the editor of *Remarkable Colonials* managed to mix him up with some other fellow, some low-bred Irish McPherson, born in Dublin of poor but honest parents.

It was a terrible outrage. Macpherson became president of the Western District Branch of the *Remarkable Colonials* Defence League, a fierce and homicidal association got up to resist, legally and otherwise, paying for the book. He had further sworn by all he held sacred that every canvasser who came to harry him in future should die, and had put up a notice on his office door, "Canvassers come in at their own risk."

He had a dog of what he called the Hold 'em breed, who could tell a canvasser by his walk, and would go for him on sight. The reader will understand, therefore, that when the Genius and his mate proposed to start on Macpherson, they were laying out a capacious contract for the Cast-iron Canvasser, and could only have been inspired by a morbid craving for excitement, aided by the influence of backblock whisky.

The Inventor wound the figure up in the back parlour of the pub. There were a frightful lot of screws to tighten before the thing would work, but at last he said it was ready, and they shambled off down the street, the figure marching stiffly between them. It had a book tucked under its arm and an order-form in its hand. When they arrived opposite Macpherson's office, the Genius started the phonograph working, pointed the figure straight at Macpherson's door, and set it going. Then the two conspirators waited, like Guy Fawkes in his cellar.

The automaton marched across the road and in at the open door, talking to itself loudly in a hoarse, unnatural voice.

Macpherson was writing at his table, and looked up.

The figure walked bang through a small collection of flowerpots, sent a chair flying, tramped heavily in the spittoon, and then brought up against the table with a loud crash and stood still. It was talking all the time.

"I have here," it said, "a most valuable work, an *Atlas of Australia*, which I desire to submit to your notice. The large and increasing demand of bush residents for time-payment works has induced the publishers of this —"

"My God!" said Macpherson, "it's a canvasser. Here, Tom Sayers, Tom Sayers!" and he whistled and called for his dog.

"Now," he said, "will you go out of this office quietly, or will you be thrown out? It's for yourself to decide, but you've only got while a duck wags his tail to decide in. Which'll it be?"

" — works of modern ages," said the canvasser. "Every person subscribing to this invaluable work will receive, in addition, a flat-iron, a railway pass for a year, and a pocket-compass. If you will please sign this order —"

Just then Tom Sayers came tearing through the office, and without waiting for orders hitched straight on to the canvasser's calf. To Macpherson's amazement the piece came clear away, and Tom Sayers rolled about on the floor with his mouth full of sticky substance which seemed to surprise him badly.

The long Scotchman paused awhile before this mystery, but at last he fancied he had got the solution. "Got a cork leg, have you?" said he — "Well, let's see if your ribs are cork too," and he struck the canvasser an awful blow on the fifth button of the waistcoat.

Quicker than lightning came that terrific right-hand cross-counter. Macpherson never even knew what happened to him. The canvasser's right hand, which had been adjusted by his inventor for a high blow, had landed on the butt of Macpherson's ear and dropped him like a fowl. The gasping, terrified bull-dog fled the scene, and the canvasser stood over his fallen foe, still intoning the virtues of his publication. He had come there merely as a friend, he said, to give the inhabitants of Ninemile a chance to buy a book which had recently earned the approval of King O'Malley and His Excellency the Governor-General.

The Genius and his mate watched this extraordinary drama through the window. The stimulant habitually consumed by the Ninemilers had induced in them a state of superlative Dutch courage, and they looked upon the whole affair as a wildly hilarious joke.

"By Gad! he's done him," said the Genius, as Macpherson went down, "done him in one hit. If he don't pay as a canvasser I'll take him to town and back him to fight Les Darcy. Look out for yourself; don't you handle him!" he continued as the other approached the figure. "Leave him to me. As like as not, if you get fooling about him, he'll give you a clout that'll paralyse you."

So saying, he guided the automaton out of the office and into the street, and walked straight into a policeman.

By a common impulse the Genius and his mate ran rapidly away in different directions, leaving the figure alone with the officer.

He was a fully-ordained sergeant — by name Aloysius O'Grady; a squat, little Irishman. He hated violent arrests and all that sort of thing, and had a faculty of persuading drunks and disorderlies and other fractious persons to "go quietly along wid him", that was little short of marvellous. Excited revellers, who were being carried by their mates, struggling violently, would break away to prance gaily along to the lock-up with the sergeant. Obstinate drunks who had done nothing but lie on the ground and kick their feet in the air, would get up like birds, serpent-charmed, go to with him to durance vile.

As soon as he saw the canvasser, and noted his fixed, unearthly stare, and listened to his hoarse, unnatural voice, the sergeant knew what was the matter; it was a man in the horrors, a common enough spectacle at Ninemile. He resolved to decoy him into the lock-up, and accosted him in a friendly, free-and-easy way.

"Good day t'ye," he said.

" — most magnificent volume ever published, jewelled in fourteen holes, working on a ruby roller, and in a glass case," said the book-canvasser. "The likeness of the historical personages are so natural that the book must not be left open on the tble, or the mosquitoes will ruin it by stinging the portraits."

It then dawned on the sergeant that this was no mere case of the horrors — he was dealing with a book-canvasser.

"Ah, sure," he said, "fwat's the use uv tryin' to sell books at all, at all; folks does be peltin' them out into the street, and the nanny-goats lives on them these times. Oi send the childer out to pick 'em up, and we have 'em at me place in barrow-loads. Come along wid me now, and Oi'll make you nice and comfortable for the night," and he laid his hand on the outstretched palm of the figure.

It was a fatal mistake. He had set in motion the machinery which operated the figure's left arm, and it moved that limb in towards its body, and hugged the sergeant to its breast with a vice-like grip. Then it started in a faltering and uneven, but dogged, way to walk towards the river.

"Immortal Saints!" gasped the sergeant, "he's squeezin' the livin' breath out uv me. Lave go now loike a dacent sowl, lave go. And oh, for the love uv God, don't be shpakin' into me ear that way"; for the figure's mouth was pressed tight against the sergeant's ear, and its awful voice went through and through the little man's head, as it held forth about the volume. The sergeant struggled violently, and by so doing set some more springs in motion, and the figure's right arm made terrific swipes in the air. A following of boys and loafers had collected by this time. "Blimey, how does he lash out!" was the remark they made. But they didn't interfere, notwithstanding the sergeant's frantic appeals, and things were going hard with him when his subordinate, Constable Dooley, appeared on the scene.

Dooley, better known as The Wombat because of his sleepy disposition, was a man of great strength. He had originally been quartered at Sydney, and had fought many bitter battles with the notorious "pushes" of Bondi, Surry Hills, and The Rocks. After that, duty at Ninemile was child's play, and he never ran in fewer than two drunks at a time; it was beneath his dignity to be seen capturing a solitary inebriate. If they wouldn't come any other way, he would take them by the ankles and drag them after him. When The Wombat saw the sergeant in the grasp of an inebriate he bore down on the fray full of fight.

"I'll soon make him lave go, sergeant," he said, and he caught hold of the figure's right arm, to put on the "police twist". Unfortunately, at that exact moment the sergeant touched one of the springs in the creature's breast. With the suddenness and severity of a horse-kick, it lashed out with its right hand, catching the redoubtable Dooley a thud on the jaw, and sending him to grass as if he had been shot.

For a few minutes he "lay as only dead men lie". Then he got up bit by bit, wandered off home to the police barracks, and mentioned casually to his wife that John L. Sullivan had come to town, and had taken the sergeant away to drown him. After which, having given orders that anybody who called was to be told that he had gone fifteen miles out of town to serve a summons on a man for not registering a dog, he locked himself up in a cell for the rest of the day.

Meanwhile, the Cast-iron Canvasser, still holding the sergeant tightly clutched to its breast, was marching straight towards the river. Something had disorganised its vocal arrangements, and it was now positively shrieking in the sergeant's ear, and, as it yelled, the little man yelled still louder.

"Oi don't want yer accursed book. Lave go uv me, Oi say!" He beat with his fists on its face, and kicked its shins without avail. A short, staggering rush, a wild shriek from the officer, and they both toppled over the steep bank and went souse into the depths of Ninemile Creek.

That was the end of the matter. The Genius and his mate returned to town hurriedly, and lay low, expecting to be indicted for murder. Constable Dooley drew up a report for the Chief of Police which contained so many strange statements that the Police Department concluded the sergeant must have got drunk and drowned himself, and that Dooley saw him do it, but was too drunk to pull him out.

Anyone unacquainted with Ninemile might expect that a report of the occurrence would have reached the Sydney papers. As a matter of fact the storekeeper did think of writing one, but decided that it was too much trouble. There was some idea of asking the Government to fish the two bodies out of the river; but about that time an agitation was started in Ninemile to have the Federal Capital located there, and nothing else mattered.

The Genius discovered a pub in Sydney that kept the Ninemile brand of whisky, and drank himself to death; the Wombat became a Sub-Inspector of Police; Sloper entered the Christian ministry; Dodge was elected to the Federal Parliament; and a vague tradition about "a bloke who came up here in the horrors, and drowned poor old O'Grady", is the only memory that remains of that wonderful creation, the Cast-iron Canvasser.

Bulletin, 19 December 1891

White-When-He's-Wanted

Buckalong was a big freehold of some 80,000 acres, belonging to an absentee syndicate and therefore run in most niggardly style. There was a manager on £200 a year, Sandy M'Gregor to wit — a hard-headed old Scotchman known as "four-eyed M'Gregor", because he wore spectacles. For assistants, he had half a dozen of us — jackaroos and colonial experiencers — who got nothing a year, and earned it.

We had, in most instances, paid premiums to learn the noble art of squatting — which now appears to me hardly worth studying, for so much depends on luck that a man with a head as long as a horse's has little better chance than the fool just imported. Besides the manager and the jackaroos, there were a few boundary riders to prowl round the fences of the vast paddocks. This constituted the whole station staff.

Buckalong was on one of the main routes by which stock were taken to market, or from the plains to the tablelands, and *vice versa*. Great mobs of travelling sheep constantly passed through the run, eating up the grass and vexing the soul of the manager. By law, sheep must travel six miles per day, and they must be kept to within half a mile of the road. Of course we kept all the grass near the road eaten bare, to discourage travellers from coming that way.

Such hapless wretches as did venture through Buckalong used to try hard to stray from the road and pick up a feed, but old Sandy was always ready for them, and would have them dogged right through the run. This bred feuds, and bad language, and personal combats between us and the drovers, whom we looked upon as natural enemies.

The men who came through with mobs of cattle used to pull down the paddock fences at night, and slip the cattle in for refreshments, but old Sandy often turned out at 2 or 3 a.m. to catch a mob of bullocks in the horse-paddock, and then off they went to Buckalong pound. The drovers, as in duty bound, attributed the trespass to accident — broken rails, and so on — and sometimes they tried to rescue the cattle, which again bred strife and police-court summonses.

Besides having a particular aversion to drovers, old M'Gregor had a general "down" on the young Australians whom he comprehensively described a "feckless, horrse-dealin', horrse-stealin', crawlin' lot o' wretches". According to him, a native-born would sooner work a horse to death than work for a living any day. He hated any man who wanted to sell him a horse.

"As aw walk the street," he used to say, "the fouk disna stawp me to buy claes nor shoon, an' wheerfore should they stawp me to buy horses? It's 'Mister M'Gregor, will ye purchase a horrse?' Let them wait till I ask them to come wi' their horrses."

Such being his views on horseflesh and drovers, we felt no little excitement when one Sunday, at dinner, the cook came in to say there was "a drover-chap outside wanted the boss to come and have a look at a horse." M'Gregor simmered a while, and muttered something about the "Sawbath day"; but at last he went out, and we filed after him to see the fun.

The drover stood by the side of his horse, beneath the acacia-trees in the yard. He had a big scar on his face, apparently the result of a collision with a fence; he looked thin and sickly and seemed poverty-stricken enough to disarm hostility. Obviously, he was down on his luck. Had it not been for that indefinable self-reliant look which drovers — the Ishmaels of the bush — always acquire, one might have taken him for a swagman. His horse was in much the same plight. It was a ragged, unkempt pony, pitifully poor and very footsore, at first sight, an absolute "moke"; but a second glance showed colossal round ribs, square hips, and a great length of rein, the rest hidden beneath a wealth of loose hair. He looked like "a good journey horse", possibly something better.

We gathered round while M'Gregor questioned the drover. The man was monosyllabic to a degree, as the real bushmen generally are. It is only the rowdy and the town-bushy that are fluent of speech.

"Guid mornin'," said M'Gregor.

"Mornin', boss," said the drover, shortly.

"Is this the horrse ye hae for sale?"

"Yes."

"Ay," and M'Gregor looked at the pony with a business-like don't-think-much-of-him air, ran his hand lightly over the hard legs, and opened the passive creature's mouth. "H'm," he said. Then he turned to the drover. "Ye seem a bit oot o'luck. Ye're thin like. What's been the matter?"

"Been sick with fever — Queensland fever. Just come through from the North. Been out on the Diamantina last."

"Ay. I was there mysel'," said M'Gregor. "Hae ye the fever on ye still?"

"Yes — goin' home to get rid of it."

A man can only get Queensland fever in a malarial district, but he can carry it with him wherever he goes. If he stays, it will sap his strength and pull him to pieces; if he moves to a better climate, the malady moves with him, leaving him by degrees, and coming back at regular intervals to rack, shake, burn, and sweat its victim. Gradually it wears itself out, often wearing its patient out at the same time. M'Gregor had been through the experience, and there was a slight change in his voice as he went on with his palaver.

"Whaur are ye makin' for the noo?"

"Monaro — my people live in Monaro."

"Hoo will yet get to Monaro gin ye sell the horrse?"

"Coach and rail. Too sick to care about ridin'," said the drover, while a wan smile flitted over his yellow-grey features. "I've rode him far enough. I've rode that horse a thousand miles. I wouldn't sell him, only I'm a bit hard up. Sellin' him now to get the money to go home."

"How auld is he?"

"Seven."

"Is he a guid horse on a camp?" asked M'Gregor.

"No better camp-horse in Queensland," said the drover. "You can chuck the reins on his neck, an' he'll cut out a beast by himself."

M'Gregor's action in this matter puzzled us. We spent our time crawling after sheep, and a camp-horse would be about as much use to us as side-pockets to a pig. We had expected Sandy to rush the fellow off the place at once, and we couldn't understand how it was that he took so much interest in him. Perhaps the fever-racked drover and the old camp-horse appealed to him in a way incomprehensible to us. We had never been on the Queensland cattle-camps, nor shaken and shivered with the fever, nor lived the roving life of the overlanders. M'Gregor had done all this, and his heart (I can see it all now) went out to the man who brought the old days back to him.

"Ah, weel," he said, "we hae'na muckle use for a camp-horrse here, ye ken; wi'oot some of these lads wad like to try theer han' cuttin' oot the milkers' cawves frae their mithers." And the old man laughted contemptuously, while we felt humbled in the sight of the man from far back. "An' what'll ye be wantin' for him?" asked M'Gregor.

"Reckon he's worth fifteen notes," said the drover.

This fairly staggered us. Our estimates had varied between thirty shillings and a fiver. We thought the negotiations would close abruptly; but M'Gregor, after a little more examination, agreed to give the price, provided the saddle and bridle, both grand specimens of ancient art, were given in. This was agreed to, and the drover was sent off to get his meals in the hut before leaving by the coach.

"The mon is verra harrd up, an' it's a sair thing that Queensland fever," was the only remark M'Gregor made. But we knew now that there was a soft spot in his heart somewhere.

Next morning the drover got a crisp-looking cheque. He said no word while the cheque was being written, but, as he was going away, the horse happened to be in the yard, and he went over to the old comrade that had carried him so many miles, and laid a hand on his neck.

"He ain't much to look at," said the drover, speaking slowly and awkwardly, "but he's white when he's wanted." And just before the coach rattled off, the man of few words leant down from the box and nodded impressively, and repeated, "Yes, he's white when he's wanted."

We didn't trouble to give the new horse a name. Station horses are generally called after the man from whom they are bought. "Tom Devine", "The Regan Mare", "Black M'Carthy", and "Bay M'Carthy" were among the appellations of our horses at that time. As we didn't know the drover's name, we simply called the animal "The new horse" until a still newer horse was one day acquired. Then, one of the hands being told to take the new horse, said, "D'yer mean the *new* horse or the *old* new horse?"

"Naw," said the boss, "not the new horrse — that bay horrse we bought frae the drover. The one he said was white when he's wanted."

And so, by degrees, the animal came to be referred to as the horse that's white when he's wanted, and at last settled down to the definite name of "White-when-he's-wanted".

White-when-he's-wanted didn't seem much of an acquisition. He was sent out to do slavery for Greenhide Billy, a boundary-rider who plumed himself on having once been a cattleman. After a week's experience of "White", Billy came into the homestead disgusted. The pony was so lazy that he had to build a fire under him to get him to move, and so rough that it made a man's nose bleed to ride him more than a mile. "The boss must have been off his head to give fifteen notes for such a cow."

M'Gregor heard this complaint. "Verra weel, Mr Billy," said he, hotly, "ye can just tak' ane of the young horrses in yon paddock, an' if he bucks wi' ye an' kills ye, it's yer ain fault. Ye're a cattleman — so ye say — dommed if ah believe it. Ah believe ye're a dairy-farmin' body frae Illawarra. Ye ken neither horrse nor cattle. Mony's the time ye never rode buckjumpers, Mr Billy" — and with this parting-shot the old man turned into the house, and White-when-he's-wanted came back to the head station.

For a while he was a sort of pariah. He used to yard the horses, fetch up the cows, and hunt travelling sheep through the run. He really was lazy and rough, and we all decided that Billy's opinion of him was correct, until the day came to make one of our periodical raids on the wild horses in the hills at the back of the run.

Every now and again we formed parties to run in some of these animals, and, after nearly galloping to death half a dozen good horses, we would capture three or four brumbies, and bring them in triumph to the homestead to be broken in. By the time they had thrown half the crack riders on the station, broken all the bridles, rolled on all the saddles, and kicked all the dogs, they would be marketable (and no great bargains) at about thirty shillings a head.

Yet there is no sport in the world to be mentioned in the same volume as "running horses", and we were very keen on it. All the crack nags were got as fit as possible, and fed up beforehand; and on this particular occasion White-when-he's-wanted, being in good trim, was given a week's hard feed and lent to a harum-scarum fellow from the Upper Murray, who happened to be working in a survey camp on the run. How he did open our eyes!

He ran the mob from hill to hill, from range to range, across open country and back again to the hills, over flats and gullies, through hop-scrub and stringybark ridges; and all the time White-when-he's-wanted was on the wing of the mob, pulling double. The mares and foals dropped out, the colts and young stock pulled up dead beat, and only the seasoned veterans were left. Most of our horses caved in altogether; one or two were kept in the hunt by judicious nursing and shirking the work. But White-when-he's-wanted was with the quarry from end to end of the run, doing double his share; and at the finish, when a chance offered to wheel them into the trapyard, he simply smothered them for pace, and slewed them into the wings before they knew where they were. Such a capture had not fallen to our lot for many a day, and the fame of White-when-he's-wanted was speedily noised abroad.

He was always fit for work, always hungry, always ready to lie down and roll, and always lazy. But when he heard the rush of the brumbies' feet in the scrub he became frantic with excitement. He could race over the roughest ground without misplacing a hoof or altering his stride, and he could sail over fallen timber and across gullies like a kangaroo. Nearly every Sunday we were after the brumbies, until they got as lean as greyhounds and as cunning as policemen. We were always ready to back White-when-he's-wanted to run-down, single-handed, any animal in the bush that we liked to put him after — wild horses, wild cattle, kangaroos, emus, dingoes, kangaroo-rats — we barred nothing, for, if he couldn't beat them for pace, he would outlast them.

And then one day he disappeared from the paddock, and we never saw him again. We knew there were plenty of men in the district who would steal him; but, as we knew also of many more who would ''inform'' for a pound or two, we were sure that it could not have been local ''talent'' that had taken him. We offered good rewards and set some of the right sort to work, but heard nothing of him for about a year.

Then the surveyor's assistant turned up again, after a trip to the interior. He told us the usual string of backblock lies, and wound up by saying that out on the very fringe of settlement he had met an old acquaintance.

"Who was that?"

"Why, that little bay horse that I rode after the brumbies that time. The one you called White-when-he's-wanted."

"The deuce you did! Are you sure? Who had him?"

"Sure! I'd swear to him anywhere. A little drover fellow had him. A little fellow, with a big scar across his forehead. Came from Monaro way somewhere. He said he bought the horse from you for fifteen notes."

The King's warrant doesn't run much out west of Boulia, and it is not likely that any of us will ever see the drover again, or will ever again cross the back of "White-when-he's-wanted".

Bulletin, 12 December 1896

Sitting in Judgment

The show ring was a circular enclosure of about four acres, with a spiked batten fence round it, and a listless crowd of back-country settlers propped along the fence. Behind them were the sheds for produce, and the machinery sections where steam threshers and earth scoops hummed and buzzed and thundered unnoticed. Crowds of sightseers wandered past the cattle stalls to gape at the fat bullocks; sideshows flourished, a blasé goose drew marbles out of a tin canister, and a boxing showman displayed his muscles outside his tent, while his partner urged the youth of the district to come in and be thumped for the edification of the spectators.

Suddenly a gate opened at the end of the show ring, and horses, cattle, dogs, vehicles, motor-cars, and bicyclists crowded into the arena. This was the general parade, but it would have been better described as a general chaos. Trotting horses and ponies, in harness, went whirling round the ring, every horse and every driver fully certain that every eye was fixed on them; the horses — the vainest creatures in the world — arching their necks and lifting their feet, whizzed past in bewildering succession, till the onlookers grew giddy. Inside the whirling circle blood stallions stood on their hind legs, screaming defiance to the world at large; great shaggy-fronted bulls, with dull vindictive eyes, paced along, looking as though they were trying to remember who it was that struck them last. A showground bull always seems to be nursing a grievance.

Mixed up with the stallions and bulls were dogs and donkeys. The dogs were led by attendants, apparently selected on the principle of the larger the dog the smaller the custodian; while the donkeys were the only creatures unmoved by their surroundings, for they slept peaceably through the procession, occasionally waking up to bray their sense of boredom.

In the centre of the ring a few lady-riders, stern-featured women for the most part, were being "judged" by a trembling official, who feared to look them in the face, but hurriedly and apologetically examined horses and saddles, whispered his award to the stewards, and fled at top speed to the official stand — his sanctuary from the fury of spurned beauty. The defeated ladies immediately began to "perform" — that is, to ask the universe at large whether anyone ever heard the like of that. But the stewards strategically slipped away, and the injured innocents had no resource left but to ride haughtily round the ring, glaring defiance at the spectators.

All this time stewards and committee-men were wandering among the competitors, trying to find the animals for judgment. The clerk of the ring — a huge man on a small cob — galloped around, roaring like a bull: "This way for the fourteen stone 'acks! Come on, you twelve 'and ponies!" and by degrees various classes got judged, and dispersed grumbling. Then the bulls filed out with their grievances still unsettled, the lady riders were persuaded to withdrew, and the clerk of the ring sent a sonorous bellow across the ground: "Where's the jumpin' judges?"

From the official stand came a brisk, dark-faced, wiry little man. He had been a steeplechase rider and a trainer in his time. Long experience of that tricky animal, the horse, had made him reserved and slow to express an opinion. He mounted the table, and produced a notebook. From the bar of the booth came a large, hairy, red-faced man, whose face showed fatuous self-complacency. He was a noted show-judge because he refused, on principle, to listen to others' opinions; or in those rare cases when he did, only to eject a scornful contradiction. The third judge was a local squatter, who was overwhelmed with a sense of his own importance.

They seated themselves on a raised platform in the centre of the ring, and held consultation. The small dark man produced his notebook.

"I always keep a scale of points," he said. "Give 'em so many points for each fence. Then give 'em so many for make, shape, and quality, and so many for the way they jump."

The fat man looked infinite contempt. "I never want any scale of points," he said. "One look at the 'orses is enough for me. A man that judges by points ain't a judge at all, I reckon. What do you think?" he went on, turning to the squatter. "Do you go by points?"

"Never," said the squatter, firmly; which, as he had never judged before in his life, was strictly true.

"Well, we'll each go our own way," said the little man. "I'll keep points. Send 'em in."

"Number One, Conductor!" roared the ring steward in a voice like thunder, and a long-legged grey horse came trotting into the ring and sidled about uneasily. His rider pointed him for the first jump, and went at it at a terrific pace. Nearing the fence the horse made a wild spring, and cleared it by feet, while the crowd yelled applause. At the second jump he raced right under the obstacle, propped dead, and rose in the air with a leap like a goat, while the crowd yelled their delight again, and said, "My oath! ain't he clever?" As he neared the third fence he shifted about uneasily, and finally took it at an angle, clearing a wholly unnecessary thirty feet. Again the hurricane of cheers broke out. "Don't he fly 'em," said one man, waving his hat. At the last fence he made his spring yards too soon; his forelegs got over all right, but his hind legs dropped on the rail with a sounding rap, and he left a little tuft of hair sticking on it.

"I like to see 'em feel their fences," said the fat man. "I had a boy 'orse once, and he felt every fence he ever jumped; shows their confidence."

"I think he'll feel that one for a while," said the little dark man. "What's this now?"

"Number Two, Homeward Bound!" An old, solid chestnut horse came out and cantered up to each jump, clearing them cooly and methodically. The crowd was not struck by the performance, and the fat man said: "No pace!" but surreptitiously made two strokes (to indicate Number Two) on the cuff of his shirt.

"Number Eleven, Spite!" This was a leggy, weedy chestnut, half-race-horse, half-nondescript, ridden by a terrified amateur, who went at the fence with a white, set face. The horse raced up to the fence, and stopped dead, amid the jeers of the crowd. The rider let daylight into him with his spurs, and rushed him at it again. This time he got over.

Round he went, clouting some fences with his front legs, others with his hind legs. The crowd jeered, but the fat man, from a sheer spirit of opposition, said, "that would be a good horse if he was rode better.'' And the squatter remarked, ''Yes, he belongs to a young feller just near me. I've seen him jump splendidly out in the bush, over brush fences.''

The little dark man said nothing, but made a note in his book.

''Number Twelve, Gaslight!''

''Now you'll see a horse,'' said the fat man. ''I've judged this 'orse in twenty different shows, and gave him first prize every time!''

Gaslight turned out to be a fiddle-headed, heavy-shouldered brute, whose long experience of jumping in shows where they give points for pace — as if the affair was a steeplechase — had taught him to get the business over as quickly as he could. He went thundering round the ring, pulling double, and standing off his fences in a style that would infallibly bring him to grief if following hounds across roads or through broken timber.

''Now,'' said the fat man, ''that's a 'unter, that is. What I say is, when you come to judge at a show, pick out the 'orse you'd soonest be on if Ned Kelly was after you, and there you have the best 'unter.''

The little man did not reply, but made the usual scrawl in his book, while the squatter hastened to agree with the fat man. ''I like to see a bit of pace myself,'' he ventured.

The fat man sat on him heavily. ''You don't call that pace, do you?'' he said. ''He was going dead slow.''

Various other competitors did their turn round the ring, some propping and bucking over the jumps, others rushing and tearing at their fences; not one jumped as a hunter should. Some got themselves into difficulties by changing feet or misjudging the distance, and were loudly applauded by the crowd for ''cleverness'' in getting themselves out of the difficulties they had themselves created.

A couple of rounds narrowed the competitors down to a few, and the task of deciding was entered on.

''I have kept a record,'' said the little man, ''of how they jumped each fence, and I give them points for style of jumping, and for their make and shape and hunting qualities. The way I bring it out is that Homeward Bound is the best, with Gaslight second.''

"Homeward Bound!" said the fat man. "Why, the pace he went wouldn't head a duck. He didn't go as fast as a Chinaman could trot with two baskets of stones. I want to have three of 'em in to have another look at 'em." Here he looked surreptitiously at his cuff, saw a note "No. II", mistook it for "Number Eleven", and said, "I want Number Eleven to go another round."

The leggy, weedy chestnut, with the terrified amateur up, came sidling and snorting out into the ring. The fat man looked at him with scorn.

"What is that fiddle-headed brute doing in the ring?" he said.

"Why," said the ring steward, "you said you wanted him."

"Well," said the fat man, "if I said I wanted him I do want him. Let him go the round."

The terrified amateur went at his fences with the rashness of despair, and narrowly escaped being clouted off on two occasions. This put the fat man in a quandary. He had kept no record, and all the horses were jumbled up in his head; but he had one fixed idea, to give the first prize to Gaslight; as to the second he was open to argument. From sheer contrariness he said that Number Eleven would be "all right if he were rode better", and the squatter agreed. The little man was overruled, and the prizes went — Gaslight, first; Spite, second; Homeward Bound, third.

The crowd hooted loudly as Spite's rider came round with the second ribbon, and small boys suggested to the fat judge in shrill tones that he ought to boil his head. The fat man stalked majestically into the steward's stand, and on being asked how he came to give Spite the second prize, remarked oracularly, "I judge the 'orse. I don't judge the rider." This silenced criticism, and everyone adjourned to have a drink.

Over the flowing bowl the fat man said, "You see, I don't believe in this nonsense about points, I can judge 'em without that."

Twenty dissatisfied competitors vowed they would never bring another horse there in their lives. Gaslight's owner said, "Blimey, I knew it would be all right with old Billy judging. 'E knows this 'orse."

Three Elephant Power

"Them things," said Alfred the chauffeur, tapping the speed indicator with his fingers, "them things are all right for the police. But, Lord, you can fix 'em up if you want to. Did you ever hear about Henery, that used to drive for old John Bull — about Henery and the elephant?"

Alfred was chauffeur to a friend of mine who owned a very powerful car. Alfred was part of that car. Weirdly intelligent, of poor physique, he might have been any age from fifteen to eighty. His education had been somewhat hurried, but there was no doubt as to his mechanical ability. He took to a car like a young duck to water. He talked motor, thought motor, and would have accepted — I won't say with enthusiasm, for Alfred's motto was *Nil admirari* — but without hesitation, an offer to drive in the greatest race in the world. He could drive really well, too; as for belief in himself, after six months' apprenticeship in a garage he was prepared to vivisect a six-cylinder engine with the confidence of a diploma'd bachelor of engineering.

Barring a tendency to flash driving, and a delight in persecuting slow cars by driving just in front of them and letting them come up and enjoy his dust, and then shooting away again, he was a respectable member of society. When his boss was in the car he cloaked the natural ferocity of his instincts; but this day, with only myself on board, and a clear run of a hundred and twenty miles up to the station before him, he let her loose, confident that if any trouble occurred I would be held morally responsible.

As we flew past a somnolent bush pub, Alfred, whistling softly, leant forward and turned on a little more oil.

"You never heard about Henery and the elephant?" he said. "It was dead funny. Henery was a bushwhacker, who went clean mad on motorin'. He was wood and water joey at some squatter's place until he seen a motor-car go past one day, the first that ever they had in the district.

" 'That's my game,' says Henery; 'no more wood and water joey for me.'

"So he comes to town and gets a job off Miles that had that garage at the back of Allison's. An old cove that they called John Bull — I don't know his right name, he was a fat old cove — he used to come there to hire cars, and Henery used to drive him. And this old John Bull he had lots of stuff, so at last he reckons he's going to get a car for himself, and he promises Henery a job to drive it. A queer cove this Henery was — half mad, I think, but the best hand with a car ever I see.''

While he had been talking, we topped a hill, and opened up a new stretch of blue-grey granite-like road. Down at the foot of the hill was a teamster's wagon in camp; the horses in their harness munching at their nose-bags, while the teamster and a mate were boiling a billy a little off to the side of the road. There was a turn in the road just below the wagon which looked a bit sharp, so of course Alfred bore down on it like a whirlwind. The big stupid team-horses huddled together and pushed each other awkwardly as we passed. A dog that had been sleeping in the shade of the wagon sprang out right in front of the car, and was exterminated without ever knowing what struck him.

There was just room to clear the tail of the wagon and negotiate the turn. Alfred, with the calm decision of a Napoleon, swung round the bend to find that the teamster's hack, fast asleep, was tied to the tail of the wagon. Nothing but a lightning-like twist of the steering-wheel prevented our scooping the old animal up, and taking him on board as a passenger. As it was, we carried off most of his tail as a trophy on the brass of the lamp. The old steed, thus rudely awakened, lashed out good and hard, but by that time we were gone, and he missed the car by a quarter of a mile.

During this strenuous episode Alfred never relaxed his professional stolidity, and, when we were clear, went on with his story in the tone of a man who found life wanting in animation.

''Well, at fust, the old man would only buy one of these little eight-horse rubby-dubbys that go strugglin' up 'ills with a death-rattle in its throat, and all the people in buggies passin' it. O' course that didn't suit Henery. He used to get that spiked when a car passed him, he'd nearly go mad. And one day he nearly got the sack for dodgin' about up a steel 'ill in front of one o' them big twenty-four Darracqs, full of 'owlin' toffs, and not lettin' 'em get a chance to go past till they got to the top. But at last he persuaded

old John Bull to let him go to England and buy a car for him. He
was to do a year in the shops, and pick up all the wrinkles, and get
a car for the old man. Bit better than wood and water joeying,
wasn't it?''

Our progress here was barred by our rounding a corner right on
to a flock of sheep, that at once packed together into a solid mass
in front of us, blocking the whole road from fence to fence.

"Silly cows o' things, ain't they?" said Alfred, putting on his
emergency brake, and skidding up till the car came softly to rest
against the cushion-like mass — a much quicker stop that any
horse-drawn vehicle could have made. A few sheep were crushed
somewhat, but it is well known that a sheep is practically inde-
structible by violence. Whatever Alfred's faults were, he certainly
could drive.

"Well," he went on, lighting a cigarette, unheeding the growls
of the drovers, who were trying to get the sheep to pass the car,
"well, as I was sayin', Henery went to England, and he got a car.
Do you know wot he got?''

"No, I don't."

"'E got a ninety," said Alfred slowly, giving time for the words
to soak in.

"A ninety! What do you mean?"

"'E got a ninety — a ninety horse-power racin' engine wot was
made for some American millionaire and wasn't as fast as wot
some other millionaire had, so he sold it for the price of the iron,
and Henery got it, and had a body built for it, and he comes out
here and tells us all it's a twenty mongrel — you know, one of
them cars that's made part in one place and part in another, the
body here and the engine there, and the radiator another place.
There's lots of cheap cars made like that.

"So Henery he says that this is a twenty mongrel — only a four-
cylinder engine; and nobody drops to what she is till Henery goes
out one Sunday and waits for the big Napier that Scotty used to
drive — it belonged to the same bloke wot owned that big racehorse wot won all the races. So Henery and Scotty they have a fair
go round the park while their bosses is at church, and Henery beat
him out o' sight — fair lost him — and so Henery was reckoned
the boss of the road. No one would take him on after that.''

A nasty creek-crossing here required Alfred's attention. A little girl, carrying a billy-can of water, stood by the stepping stones, and smiled shyly as we passed. Alfred waved her a salute quite as though he were an ordinary human being. I felt comforted. He had his moments of relaxation evidently, and his affections like other people.

"What happened to Henry and the ninety-horse machine?" I asked. "And where does the elephant come in?"

Alfred smiled pityingly.

"Ain't I tellin' yer," he said. "You wouldn't understand if I didn't tell yer how he got the car and all that. So here's Henery," he went on, "with old John Bull goin' about in the fastest car in Australia, and Old John, he's a quiet old geezer, that wouldn't drive faster than the regulations for anything, and that short-sighted he can't see to the side of the road. So what does Henery do? He fixes up the speed-indicator — puts a new face on it, so that when the car is doing thirty, the indicator only shows fifteen, and twenty for forty, and so on. So out they'd go, and if Henery knew there was a big car in front of him, he'd let out to forty-five, and the pace would very near blow the whiskers off old John; and every now and again he'd look at the indicator, and it'd be showin' twenty-two and a half, and he'd say,

" 'Better be careful, Henery, you're slightly exceedin' the speed limit; twenty miles an hour, you know, Henery, should be fast enough for anybody, and you're doing over twenty-two.'

"Well, one day, Henery told me, he was tryin' to catch up a big car that just came out from France, and it had a half-hour start of him, and he was just fairly flyin', and there was a lot of cars on the road, and he flies past 'em so fast the old man says, 'It's very strange, Henery,' he says, 'that all the cars that are out today are comin' this way,' he says. You see he was passin' 'em so fast he thought they were all comin' towards him.

"And Henery sees a mate of his comin', so he lets out a notch or two, and the two cars flew by each other like chain lightnin'. They were each doin' about forty, and the old man, he says. 'I never see a car go by so fast in my life,' he says. 'If I could find out who he is, I'd report him,' he says. 'Did you know the car, Henery?' But of course Henery, he doesn't know, so on they goes.

"The owner of the big French car thinks he has the fastest car in Australia, and when he sees Henery and the old man coming, he tells his driver to let her out a little; but Henery gives the ninety-horse the full of the lever, and whips up alongside in one jump. And then he keeps there just half a length ahead of him, tormentin' him like. And the owner of the French car he yells out to old John Bull, 'You're going a nice pace for an old 'un,' he says. Old John has a blink down at the indicator. 'We're doing twenty-five,' he yells out. 'Twenty-five grandmothers,' says the bloke; but Henery he put on his accelerator, and left him. It wouldn't do to let the old man get wise to it, you know."

We topped a big hill, and Alfred cut off the engine and let the car swoop, as swiftly and noiselessly as an eagle, down to the flat country below.

"You're a long while coming to the elephant, Alfred," I said.

"Well, now, I'll tell you about the elephant," said Alfred, letting his clutch in again, and taking up the story to the accompaniment of the rhythmic throb of the engine.

"One day Henery and the old man were going out a long trip over the mountain, and down the Kangaroo Valley Road that's all cut out of the side of the 'ill. And after they's gone a mile or two, Henery sees a track in the road — the track of the biggest car he ever seen or 'eard of. An' the more he looks at it, the more he reckons he must ketch that car and see what she's made of. So he slows down passin' two yokels on the road, and he says. 'Did you see a big car along 'ere?'

" 'Yes, we did,' they says.

" 'How big is she?' says Henery.

" 'Biggest car ever we see,' says the yokels, and they laughed that silly way these yokels always does.

" 'How many horse-power do you think she was?' says Henery.

" 'Horse-power,' they says; 'elephant-power, you mean! She was three elephant-power,' they says; and they goes 'Haw, haw!' and Henery drops his clutch in, and off he goes after that car."

Alfred lit another cigarette as a preliminary to the climax.

"So they run for miles, and all the time there's the track ahead of 'em, and Henery keeps lettin' her out, thinkin' that he'll never ketch that car. They went through a town so fast, the old man he says, 'What house was that we just passed?' he says. At last they come to the top of the big 'ill, and there's the tracks of the big car goin' straight down ahead of 'em.

"D'you know that road? It's all cut out of the side of the mountain, and there's places where if she was to side-slip you'd go down 'undreds of thousands of feet. And there's sharp turns, too; but the surface is good, so Henery he lets her out, and down they go, whizzin' round the turns and skatin' out near the edge, and the old cove sittin' there enjoyin' it, never knowin' the danger. And comin' to one turn Henery gives a toot on the 'orn and then he heard somethin' go 'toot, toot' right away down the mountain.

"'Bout a mile ahead it seemed to be, and Henery reckoned he'd go another four miles before he'd ketch it, so he chances them turns more than ever. And she was pretty hot, too; but he kept her at it, and he hadn't gone a full mile till he come round a turn about forty miles an hour, and before he could stop he run right into it, and wot do you think it was?"

I hadn't the faintest idea.

"A circus. One of them travellin' circuses, goin' down the coast; and one of the elephants had sore feet, so they put him in a big wagon, and another elephant pulled in front and one pushed behind. Three elephant-power it was, right enough. That was the wagon wot made the big track. Well, it was all done so sudden. Before Henery could stop, he runs the radiator — very near boiling she was — up against the elephant's tail, and prints the pattern of the latest honeycomb radiator on the elephant as clear as if you done it with a stencil.

"The elephant, he lets a roar out of him like one of them bulls bellerin', and he puts out his nose and ketches Henery round the neck, and yanks him out of the car, and chucks him right clean over the cliff, 'bout a thousand feet. But he never done nothin' to the old bloke."

"Good gracious!"

"Well, it finished Henery, killed him stone dead, of course, and the old man he was terrible cut up over losin' such a steady, trustworthy man. 'Never get another like him,' he says."

We were nearly at our journey's end, and we turned through a gate into the home paddocks. Some young stock, both horses and

cattle, came frisking and cantering after the car, and the rough
bush track took all Alfred's attention. We crossed a creek, the
water swishing from the wheels, and began the long pull up to the
homestead. Over the clamour of the little-used second speed,
Alfred concluded his narrative.

"The old bloke advertised," he said, "for another driver, a
steady, reliable man to drive a twenty horse-power, four-cylinder
touring car. Every driver in Sydney put in for it. Nothing like a
fast car to fetch 'em, you know. And Scotty got it. Him wot used
to drive the Napier I was tellin' you about."

"And what did the old man say when he found he'd been running a racing car?"

"He don't know now. Scotty never told 'im. Why should he?
He's drivin' about the country now, the boss of the roads, but he
won't chance her near a circus. Thinks he might bump the same elephant. And that elephant, every time he smells a car passin' in the
road, he goes near mad with fright. If he ever sees that car again,
do you think he'd know it?"

Not being used to elephants, I could offer no opinion.

Town and Country Journal, 11 December 1907

3
Journalism — People and Places

EDITOR'S NOTE

I have selected several of what I consider to be the best of Paterson's pen-pictures of the celebrities he met during his various careers, as well as examples of his reporting, ranging from his visits to Australian outposts like Thursday Island to his account, as a participant, in the first motor-car reliability run from Sydney to Melbourne — an experience in which he indulged himself as the then editor of the *Evening News*.

Paterson, indeed, was by instinct and inclination much more at home as a journalist and reporter than as an editor. Claude McKay, later editor of *Smith's Weekly*, who worked as a casual reporter on the *Evening News* at the time of Paterson's editorship, recalled the latter in his rather dingy office, a roller-top desk taking up most of the space, and the desk's pigeonholes crammed with odds and ends of letters and clippings: ". . . the writing surface of his desk littered high with old proof sheets, out-of-date newspapers opened and unopened, leaving him little elbow-room at his near-submerged writing blotting-pad".[1] Paterson hated being left to himself and most visitors were treated like long-lost brothers as the editor settled back comfortably for a yarn. Thrice-welcomed was the outback visitor with his cattle dog — and usually the dog sized up the situation by curling up and going to sleep.

Paterson was greatly loved by the *Evening News* staff. Casual contributors, paid by the line, were particularly grateful that he had begun life as a lawyer, since he marked contributions for payment with a professional fee: a paragraph, three shillings and fourpence; a cross-head, six and eightpence; half a column, half a guinea; a column, a guinea. But Paterson, according to McKay, had no instinct whatsoever for news: his paper was regularly scooped by his competitors, the *Sunday Times* and *Daily Telegraph*, and it seemed he was much more interested in contributing his own articles to the paper, and in his project at the time of collecting old bush ballads, eventually published in 1905 as *Old Bush Songs,* which added considerably to his literary stature and reputation.

1. *Sydney Morning Herald*, 11 November 1952.

Journalism — People

AN INTERVIEW WITH OLIVE SCHREINER

Arundel, 21st January 1900

"Our friend the enemy"! For six weeks the New South Wales Lancers (with whom the present scribe is associated as war correspondent) had been in daily touch with the Boers. Six weeks of blazing hot days and freezing cold nights, spent in tents where the duststorms coated everything with a dull-red powder, out on picket duty lying in the scorching sun among the rocks of a kopje, or on patrol trying how near we could get to the enemy without being shot dead; six weeks of hurried movements, of midnight marches and rapid shiftings of camp, of night-long watches out in the cold of the veldt with the shivering horses standing alongside; and all with the object of killing, capturing, or dispersing the unknown and practically unseen enemy that clung so tenaciously to his heaven-built fortress of rocky kopje, and who was so ready to shoot on the slightest provocation.

We had given up thinking what the Boers were like or of considering them as human beings at all. To us they were simply so much enemy — as impersonal as the maxim-guns and the rifles that they used. For six weeks we had seen no letters, no books, and practically no newspapers. The world was narrowed down to ourselves and the enemy. All our time was fully occupied in fighting, and we gave no thought to the question of what the fighting was about. It was a great change, therefore, in visiting Capetown to call on Olive Schreiner, a bitter opponent of the war, and to hear the Boer side of the question.

The authoress of *The Story of an African Farm* needs no introduction to Australians. Born in South Africa and reared among the farmers she is an Afrikander of the Afrikanders; and while her brother (the Premier of the Cape Colony) has been very reserved in expressing opinions, Olive Schreiner has been most outspoken in denouncing the war and those who, in her opinion, are responsible for it.

She lives at Newlands, a suburb of Capetown, and no Australian city has such a suburb. On leaving the train one walks down an avenue overhung with splendid trees, and more like a private carriageway than a public road; it is hard to believe that one is not trespassing on somebody's private garden. There is no sidewalk — just the red-earth avenue between the trees. The flowers and trees grow most luxuriantly, sunflowers, box-hedges, roses, and all manner of grasses flourishing everywhere, an inexpressible relief after the miles of sunburnt karoo desert we have been staring over lately. The houses that front on the avenue all stand back in their own gardens, but instead of having a forbidding six-foot paling fence round each property there is usually a low iron-standard fence or a box-hedge as boundary, and the passer-by sees into these beautiful gardens as he goes along. If a few residences were erected in Sydney Botanic Gardens, that would be like Newlands. The trees are just as beautiful and luxuriant. In these surroundings lives the woman who made her name famous by *The Story of an African Farm*. She is married now, but still prefers to be known as Olive Schreiner. She is a little woman, small in stature, but of very strong physique, broad and powerful; her face olive-complexioned, with bright, restless eyes, and a quick mobile mouth.

She talks fluently, and with tremendous energy, and one is not long in arriving at the conclusion that she is thoroughly in earnest — deadly earnest — over this question of the Boer War. It may be news to many Australians to hear that in the Cape Colony there are more people against the war than for it, not necessarily Boer sympathizers, but people who think that the war should never have been entered upon. When our troops landed from Australia we were astonished to find that the Cape Colony was so much against the war. The local papers that were for the war were all clamouring for the arrest or dismissal of Schreiner, the Premier, but when the House went to a division Schreiner had a majority behind him, and Schreiner has always declared that England is not justified in this war. Olive Schreiner was not long in stating her views to the present writer. She talks rapidly and energetically, emphasising her remarks with uplifted finger.

"You Australians and New Zealanders and Canadians," she said, "I cannot understand it at all, why you come here lightheart-

edly to shoot down other colonists of whom you know nothing —
it is terrible. Such fine men too — fine fellows. I went to Green
Point, and saw your men in camp: oh, they were fine men —
[these were Colonel Williams's A.M.C. troops] — and to think
that they are going out to kill and be killed, just to please the capitalists! There was one officer — oh, a fine man, so like a Boer, he
might have been a Boer commandant. It is terrible — such men to
come and fight against those fighting for their liberty and their
country. The English Tommy Atkins goes where he is sent — he
fights because he is ordered; but you people — you are all
volunteers! Why have you come?

"You say that England was at war, and you wished to show the
world that when the mother country got into war the colonies were
prepared to take their place beside her! Yes, but you ought to ask,
you ought to make inquiries before you come over. You Australians do not understand. This is a capitalists' war! They want to
get control of the Rand and the mines. You have nothing like it in
your country. You have a working class that votes and that cannot
be bought to vote against its own interests; but in the Transvaal
there are just a handful of Boer farmers, a small but enormously
wealthy mine-owning class and their dependants — professional
men, shopkeepers, and so on, and the rest are all Kaffirs."

"Why didn't the Boers grant the franchise?"

"It was not really wanted. I was in Johannesburg a few months
before the war broke out, and hundreds of men there said that
they would not forego their British nationality for the sake of vot-
ing as a Boer. They are all nomads, wanderers, over there to make
money, and if Oom Paul had gone on his knees and asked them to
accept the franchise they would not have accepted it. They would
not relinquish being British subjects. But the capitalists insist on
getting hold of the mines, and all the white people are so concerned with them, their interests so depend on the mine-owners,
that they must go along with them, and now they want the franchise to take control of the mines from the Boers. It is a monstrous
war, and England will regret it; it is just to take the country from
the Boers for the benefit of the speculators. For years this war has
been worked up — all sorts of stories have been printed of the
Boers and their ignorance and their savagery. They are all lies. I

was a governess among the Boers for years, and no kinder people exist. They are clever, too. Young Boers go to England and succeed at the universities; they become doctors, lawyers and politicians. It is much like Australia from what I have read. They are such hospitable people.

"Oh, this war is a terrible thing; it will be a war of extermination. What do you think will be the end of it? There will be no end. The Boers are fighting for life or death, and they have no idea of giving in. If they are beaten back into the Free State and the Transvaal that is just the time they will be most dangerous. When the English get to Pretoria with their army they will then be in a worse position than they are now. They will have hundreds and hundreds of miles of railway line to defend, and even if the Boers are scattered and beaten they will still fight. The Boer women now are heart and soul for the war. The Boer farmer is a curious man. He marries early, usually about eighteen or nineteen, and there is not one man in the army against you but has his wife and child somewhere. And those wives and children are reaping the crops and working the farms, so that their husbands can go to the war.

"After Elandslaagte, where the Boers were defeated, one Boer went home. His wife said, 'What happened: are you wounded?' 'No.' 'Is the enemy fled?' 'No.' 'Well, back you go to the laager and fight with the rest.' Another old man, of seventy-five, when he heard of the defeat, rose up and took his rifle. 'I am going to the front,' he said. 'Why, you cannot see,' said his grandchildren. 'I cannot see at a thousand yards,' he said, 'but I can see at a hundred'; and off he went in a Cape cart as he was too old to ride.

"The small boys at school at the Capetown schools have all been brought back to the farms to fight — boys of fourteen and fifteen are in the ranks. And all of these people have their relatives all through Cape Colony; and they are to be butchered, and the English soldiers are to be butchered, to suit a few capitalists. It will benefit no one else. The effect of this war on South Africa will be everlasting; we have such a large population here who feel that the war is unjust, and they will never forgive the English people for forcing it on. Perhaps the memory of Majuba Hill had a good deal to do with it? I cannot think so — the English are not so narrow as to treasure up memories of a small thing like that. But now it is a long, terrible war that is before us, and the Boers will be more dangerous after a few reverses. A few defeats will not crush them! When the English get to Pretoria then there will begin the trouble."

Whatever may be the correctness of Olive Schreiner's views, there is no doubt of her sincerity. She says openly what most, or at any rate very many, South Africans think, and it is always well to hear both sides, so I have put down without comment exactly what her views were.

Talking on literary matters, Olive Schreiner said that though she was constantly writing she did not publish much. The cares of household life interfered much with work. When a governess in the Transvaal, after the day's work was done, she would sit in her room and work with a mind free from care. It was then that *The African Farm* was written. Nowadays she has too much to think about — household worries, and so on. She was asked to act as war correspondent for a New York paper, but the authorities would not hear of her going — in which, by the way, they were quite right. The front is no place for a woman.

It seems a pity that this woman, who is no doubt a great literary genius, should be wasting her time and wearing out her energies over this Boer War question, instead of giving us another book as good as her first one; but after an interview with her one comes away with a much more lively and human interest in "our friends the enemy". If things are as she says, if the Boers are going to make it a war to the bitter end, then England has a sorry task before her. If the Boers scatter and break to the mountains they will be practically unreachable, and the English people are too humane to care about levying reprisals by destroying their homesteads and leaving their wives and children without shelter. The result will be that even after the war is over a large force will have to be kept in the country to maintain order, and with the Cape disaffected there will be serious trouble for politicians after the soldiers have got through with their work. One is more inclined to hope that after a defeat or two the Boer, sensible man that he is, will come in under English rule and rely on the forbearance of that Power rather than maintain a hopeless straggling fight which will only prolong the misery of the present war.

Sydney Morning Herald, 17 February 1900

MARIE LLOYD*

And now, as a relief from military men, let us switch on the portrait of a stage celebrity, in her day better known, perhaps, than any general that ever lived. The judge who asked a barrister "Who is Connie Gilchrist?" would never have dared to ask "Who is Marie Lloyd?"

Sunday, October 13th 1901 — Steaming down the China coast in a P. and O. boat. Admiral Curzon Howe is on board; apparently a mild-mannered sea-dog, for, like Bret Harte's "Thompson the hero of Angels," he is always polite to the stranger. But they say that, when he gets really warmed to his work, neither Cicero nor Demosthenes could have taught him anything in the way of rugged eloquence.

An English major on board is returning from China to his duties in India, where he is in charge of the establishment of a young rajah. He is allowed to spend ten thousand a year as a sort of amusement fund to provide polo ponies, entertain visitors, preserve tigers, and to keep up a cricket team — all with the object of sweating the lust and licentiousness out of the young rajah. The Admiral says that he is sorry that he himself ever went to sea — he didn't know there were such jobs in the world! This young rajah has only one wife up to the present; but all his wife's waiting maids are his concubines, and when visiting his wife he picks out a good-looking waiting maid for future reference. He comes of a boozing and and womanizing strain, so the major makes him slog into polo and cricket and shooting. About fourteen tigers are shot in a year, and the visitor can either shoot from a *machan* (a platform in a tree) which is perfectly safe; or, if he wants some excitement, he can shoot from an elephant, where the main risk is that the elephant may pull him off and use him as a stepping-stone over boggy ground; or, if he is a genuine dyed-in-the-wool thruster, he can go out on foot with his rifle and walk up a tiger in the jungle.

Like many others of the high-caste Indians, this young rajah was a natural horseman, and in two years he and the major, be-

* Marie Lloyd, real name Matilda Alice Victoria Wood (1870-1922), a popular
  music-hall artist who made her reputation with so-called London or cockney
  low comedy.

tween them, turned out a polo team that won the championship of India. Some of these Orientals have an instinct for horses. A sultan near Singapore went in for racing, mostly with walers, and took to the game so naturally that he ran an old performer as a maiden horse; was detected, and fired out of the Singapore club. It is an education to see polo played by a native Indian team. Good horsemen, with very flexible wrists, they keep the hall in control and pass to each other almost as accurately as fieldsmen will throw a cricket-ball to one another.

At Singapore the great music-hall star, Marie Lloyd, joined the ship. A very virile lady, this, if one may use the word; a Juno of a woman, with the physique of a ploughman, a great broad face, and eyes very wide apart. She walks into a room as a dreadnought steams into a harbour, followed by a fleet of smaller vessels in the shape of sycophants and hangers-on. Her conversation consists mostly of epigram and innuendo. For instance, a lady passenger, travelling by herself, has her belongings shifted across the ship to a new cabin every time that the wind changes, and there is talk of favouritism:

"Ho, what are yer goin' to do about it," says Marie. "She sits at the purser's table, don't she?"

A wealthy Greek passenger — quite an old man — is always hanging round a very pretty young girl, who is one of Marie's entourage. Then his attentions cease abruptly. After dinner one night Marie gives me the key to the situation:

"That old Greek," she says. "Do you know what he had the cheek to do? Did you ever hear anything like it? He wanted to take the little girl a trip with him through Egypt, the old vagabond!"

"And what did you say to him?" I ask, confident that Marie must have said something worthy of the occasion.

"What did I say to him? 'Let's see your cheque-book,' I says. That's what I said to him."

Apparently the cheque-book failed to materialize, for Marie, in her primitive way, carried on a sort of vendetta against the Greek; and when a parrot, belonging to a passenger, flew overboard, she saw her chance. Beckoning to one of her hangers-on, she said:

"You go to the old Greek and say: 'What a pity that bird flew overboard! It was Hurley's bird, wasn't it?' And I'll come along and say: 'No, it was the little bad-tempered one that the butcher looks after.' That's the Greek's bird, and he won't sleep a bloody wink thinkin' his bird has flew over!''

Some officers' wives from India asked a solitary male passenger if he would mind moving a few places up the table, so that they could sit together; and Marie had a few words to say on that subject.

"They asked yer to change yer seat, did they? Well, a thing like that would kill me dead, that would — stone dead. D'yer know what I'd ha' said to 'em? I'd ha' said, 'Excuse me, but perhaps when you come out before you must have came in the steerage. You ain't used to travellin' first-class saloon.' That's what I'd ha' said."

Learning that I am some sort of literary person, Marie asks me to write her a song, and adds that she has paid as much as a pound and thirty bob for some of her song hits in London. Then she lets her eye rove over the deck where the passengers are walking in pairs, male and female, as the Lord created them.

"There you are," she says, "all you want is a good ketchline! What about 'They've all got their little bit o' muslin.' 'Ow would that go?"

No doubt Marie's vigour and vitality would have made anything go. But it appears that the difficulty is not so much in the song itself as in the business to accompany the song:

"I've sung songs," she says, "swingin' in a hammick, and leadin' a dog, and pushin' a perambulator. They'll want me to sing standin' on my 'ead next. The public is funny. I've got a beautiful song about a dyin' soldier but they won't listen to it. They like:

Didn't we 'ave a pantomime
At Folkestone for the day.

They won't listen to anything 'igh class."

A great woman, she dominated the ship. Even the captain became merely the person who was navigating Marie Lloyd back to London. The Admiral himself was impressed, and said something to her about his home in England. Marie said:

"Yes, it must be nice livin' in the country. I'll look in some time when I'm goin' past."

The Admiral, who was the soul of politeness said:

"You must come and stop with us." This invitation Marie accepted; and the Admiral, who was a married man, wore a hunted look for the rest of the voyage.

Friday, October 18th — Waiting at Aden to sail. This afternoon a lot of sharks made their appearance, grey-brown shadows lounging lazily along through the water, with the spiteful-looking pilot-fish darting on ahead. They sauntered about, smelling at the floating cabbage-leaves and melon-rinds, and then giving a swirl of their tails and flashing away into the depths.

Marie Lloyd's entourage were mostly London cockneys, and there was great excitement among them.

"Ow, 'ere's a shork! 'Arry, look at the shork! Tell Ted! Ted, 'ere's a shork! Oh, if we only 'ad an 'ook! My, there's a big one!"

A grey patriarch lounged up to a floating cabbage-head, gave it a disdainful toss with his snout, and swirled down again out of sight.

"Ho, they ain't 'ungry! 'E wouldn't eat that bit of cabbage-leaf!"

A naval officer on board had studied the ways of sharks in many waters; had fried and blistered in the survey ships in Torres Strait, where the sharks waited alongside for the ship's flotsam and jetsam until they came to be looking upon as family retrievers. To him Ted laid down the law.

"See them," he said, pointing to the pilot-fish, "them's young shorks." Hearing the captain say that they were pilot-fish, he ran after the naval officer and told him. "Them ain't young shorks," he said. "Them's pilot-fish."

"Thanks," said the naval officer. "I'm glad you told me."

Then there was a discussion as to which of the theatricals should go aft to the butcher for a hook and a bit of meat.

"Ted, you've seen more shorks than I 'ave, *you* go."

Finally, the speaker went himself and came back with a rope, a bit of meat, and a butcher's hook without any barb to it. This was thrown overboard amid the approving yells and deep-throated cheers of the chorus.

"Sling it out further, can't yer! There's one 'ere, a great big one! Bring it up 'ere, Alick, where the water's comin' out of the ship.''

"There's water comin' out 'ere, too," said Alick.

The hook was not taken at once, so the back-seat drivers got busy.

"'Aul it up to the top so they can *see* it! What's the good of 'avin' it down where they can't *see* it?''

A boat-load of Arabs came along, hoping to do great business with the crowd at the ship's side; but even the Arabs were cowed by the frenzy with which they were adjured to clear out of that. "Go away! We don't want nothin'! Go away! Can't you see we're fishin'.''

Then a big shark swallowed the bait and hook and about two feet of line. Like a Greek chorus, the supernumeraries began to give advice as to how to haul him up. The shark, however, calmly bit the line in two and disappeared with all the essential parts of the fishing tackle. The chorus burst forth again, "Ow, 'e's gorn! Why didn't you 'aul quicker?''

As nobody cared to brave the butcher for another hook, the rest of the drama consisted of explanations and recriminations; until Marie, who (like John Gilpin) had a frugal mind, made her exit, remarking: "I didn't get that 'ook from the butcher. Whoever got it 'll 'ave to pay for it." Most music-hall stars are supposed not to know the meaning of money. But Marie had worked in a rag-factory for ten shillings a week before she got to the hundred pounds a week stage; and she wouldn't part with even the price of a butcher's hook if she could see her way to get out of it.

Friday, October 25th — Left the Suez Canal and plugged through the Mediterranean. Passing a town in the distance, the Admiral said:

"That's Regia.''

But Alick, the *lion comique* of Marie Lloyd's company, said pityingly:

"No, that ain't Regia, that's Italy.''

We make some signals and a boat comes off, pulled by a lot of comic-opera Italian sailors, who clamour to know who will pay them. They are referred to the consul, but continue to talk like gramophones and to go through Swedish exercises with their arms and shoulders. Then Alick decides to give them a turn, and he says:

"Ecce signor! Bonifacio de Marco de Campagno! Si Si! Bel Giorno! Saveloy de Marconi! Corpo di Baccho!"

The old pilot looks up at Alick, taps his forehead significantly, and goes through the pantomime of drinking something out of a glass. He is the first man who has scored off any of the theatricals.

Saturday, October 26th — Land at Marseilles, and find that there are races on. A large party of us go out in a tram. Marie gives Alick a nudge, and whispers:

"You shout 'ere and then that old Greek'll 'ave to shout when we go in at the racecourse."

Alick produces an English sovereign to pay the fares of the whole party. The conductor grabs it eagerly and hands over a handful of silver in change:

"There you are," says Alick. "That's what it is to be an Englishman! They'll take an English sovereign anywhere in the world."

Drove to the races through a glorious avenue of trees, with beautiful houses and gardens everywhere. Motor cars fly past, each with a French poodle sitting on the front seat with the wind blowing through his whiskers. We pass a fat Frenchman and his wife in a little donkey-cart, drawn by an infinitesimal donkey. Everybody seems to take the racing as an amusement, while we take it as a severe mental exercise. The air is crisp and clear, and filled with the aromatic smell of dead leaves as we drive through an avenue of sycamores. About half the crowd gets in free; or rather, they sit just outside the course on a grassy slope where they have a splendid view; for it is only divided from the running by a deep ditch. Here they smoke cigarettes and drink light wines and eat things out of baskets, while their children, in hundreds, roll and play on the grass.

Arrived at the racecourse gates, the Greek somehow ducks out of sight, and Alick has to pay the admission money for Marie and himself. Then it turns out that the silver he got from the tram conductor is all bad money. They say all the bad money in the world comes here sooner or later; and this desperado has unloaded the accumulation of weeks on Alick in return for the sovereign. This ruins the day for Marie, who upbraids him bitterly.

"You call yerself a cockney," she says, "and you go and take a double 'andful of brum money. Never mind, you might shove some of it on to that old Greek tonight when we're playin' cards."

All the public stands were packed, and it was impossible to see anything. But there was any amount of room on an official stand marked *defendu*, and Marie picked on a young Canadian member of our party to escort her up into this stand. We told her that *defendu* meant no admittance; but she said she was going up, anyway. "If he tells 'em I'm Marie Lloyd it'll be all right," she said.

At the top of the stairs her escort was grappled by a gendarme about the size of a weevil, and the pair of them rolled down the stairs with the gendarme's little red legs flashing in the air every time he came uppermost. Nor was it a silent film, for the gendarme yelled, *à moi mes camarades* every time that he hit a fresh step. It took the combined efforts of three gendarmes to secure the Canadian.

The gendarmes were going to put the Canadian in the coop, but he explained that neither he nor his lady friend knew any French, so they embraced him and let the pair of them stop on the stand.

Sitting up there in comfort among the French aristocracy, Marie scorned to notice Alick or the rest of her fellow passengers milling about among the plebian crowd below. When they came down the stairs, she said to her escort:

"It's a pity you couldn't speak French, you could ha' told 'em who I was."

"I can speak French all right," he said. "I'm a French Canadian, and I can speak better French than any of these coves. But you didn't want to get locked up, did you?"

Marie was so impressed that she fumbled in her bag and gave him a card, marked "Admit one," to the stalls on the opening night of her season in London.

Happy Dispatches, 1934

TWO NOTES ON "CHINESE" MORRISON

1

We sailed for China in fine weather, but the captain was playing with the typhoonometer, an affair which the engineers said was invented by a Spanish monk at Manila. It is supposed to indicate the existence and direction of any typhoon; and ship captains will sometimes turn round and run back fifty miles to let a typhoon have the right of way. The feud between the poop ornaments and the black squad was suspended for the time being, in the same way that tigers and horned cattle will live together on an island in a flood. Even the Scotch engineers, who do not give away more than they can help, are willing to give "Typhoon Tommy" some credit for knowledge of this instrument.

September 2nd 1901 — Approaching China. The ship was in gloom today, for a very old man, a second-class passenger, jumped overboard during the night. He left his watch and chain, a few shillings, and a brief note on the hatchway. One of the grooms who shared his cabin said that the old man had been in the tea trade in England, but had been ruined by the trusts and had come out to Manila to go into the timber business. He had very little money and no "pull"; also he found that most of the timber land belonged to the Church; so he gave up the struggle and jumped overboard. His married daughter and her husband were on board. The scrap of a note said: "I have decided not to be a burden on the young people." This deserves to rank with that other great epitaph: "Here died a very gallant gentleman."

We steamed into Hong Kong harbour through a sea so crowded with junks that the Australian groom asked me, "What are those Chows holding a regatta for?" The chief engineer said they catch fish in every way known to science — and in a lot of ways of their own.

"Some of they junks are pirates," he said, "and when ye run over a junk at night, or gather up her nets in the propeller, ye don't stop, y'unnerstand. Ye don't want any nosty accidents if they get aboard."

China is a big place in which to find anybody, but by great good luck I ran against "Chinese" Morrison, *The Times* correspondent in China, and from him I got what one might call a very acute

angle on the Boxer rebellion. I had a letter to Morrison from our
Scotch engineer, who had known Morrison's father, as well as
Morrison himself, in Victoria.

"Ah wuddent say that he'll be glad to see ye," said the engineer.
"He's a nosty conceited jackass — a bit of a freek y'unnerstand.
But in his own way he's the cleverest man I ever saw. The conceit
of him! He's the only white man that unnerstands they Chinese.
He learnt the language and, when he went to a meeting of manda-
rins, an' they all rigged out in jewels an' peacock feathers, there
was a big seat at the top of the table for the boss mandarin. Morrison walks in and takes that seat an' not a Chow in the lot was
game to call his bluff. An' him the son of a school-teacher in
Victoria! Man, it'd cow ye! If they'd ha' known, they'd ha' stuck
bamboo splinters in him till he wuz like a hedgehog. But he gets
away wi' it, an' he never tells 'em a lie an' he has *The Times* at the
back of him. So the Chows run to him to know whut the Japs are
goin' to do, an' whut's the Russians' next move, and the like o'
that. Morrison's the uncrooned king o' China; and if he'll talk to
ye, ye'll know more about China than these mushionaries and
poleetical agents can tell ye in a year."

September 17th 1901 — Chefoo. Went off with a guide to visit
Morrison. This place is the flowery land all right, for flowers and
fruit are everywhere. The Chinese will sell you three pounds of
beautiful fruit in a basket for about a shilling, and throw in the
basket. Meat here is ten cents a pound, and very fair quality at
that. I bought ten silk handkerchiefs for five shillings and sixteen
yards of silk material for twelve shillings. My guide (a Russian)
talks of the probable war between Japan and Russia. He says,

"De Yappanese dey cannot fight Rooshia. Dey are leedle
apes."

Neither man nor beast in China has anything but hatred for the
foreigner. As we pass through the little villages and tumbledown
humpies of the cultivators the men scowl at us; the dogs snarl and
slink off with every symptom of terror and disgust; the cattle snort
and shiver if we pass near them; and the mules will watch us uneasily till we go away. The people hate us with a cold intensity that
surpasses any other hate that I ever heard of. A fat Chinese shop-
keeper, who speaks English, says,

"Poor Chinaman only good for chow" [is only fit to be eaten]. "what does Chinaman savvy?"

Then he adds something in Chinese which causes a laugh among his slant-eyed brethren and which, no doubt, sums up his opinion of the foreigner. The China pony resembles his owners in that he does everything grudgingly, and has to be hustled and flogged to get him to shift; and in spite of everything he refuses to fall away and get sick as any other horse would do. He keeps fat and vindictive. An owner lending a Chinese pony to a friend says,

"He's all right. He won't bite if you sneak up to him behind the *Mahfoo* [groom] and get hold of the rein over his back."

Many of them have to be blindfolded to get a white man on them, and the bad ones will kick sideways as well as backwards; will strike with either front foot as quickly as a boxer, and when they get a chance they bite savagely. They are mostly bred and broken in Manchuria; and do not come into contact with a white man till they are ten or twelve years old and well "set" in their ways. They live about as long as a donkey — and nobody ever saw a dead donkey, it is said. Before the Boxer trouble their price in Manchuria and northern China was about three pounds ten. But when the world's armies looked in on China the price went up like shares that had been sold short on a rising market.

I found Morrison at a watering-place outside Chefoo. I knew his record fairly well; for, as a young man, he had explored New Guinea and northern Australia in the days when the blacks were bad. The blacks put a spear into him. He got his black boy to cut off the shaft of the spear, but never had the head of the spear taken out till he got to Melbourne. A man like that takes some stopping.

In person, he was a tall ungainly man with a dour Scotch face and a curious droop at the corner of his mouth — a characteristic I had noticed in various other freaks, including Olive Schreiner, the gifted authoress of *The Story of an African Farm*. Morrison had with him a China-coast doctor named Molyneux who acted as a sort of Dr Watson to Morrison's Sherlock Holmes. At first Morrison talked mainly about women, and if there was any unbalance in his mentality it was probably in that direction. I plied Molyneux with questions and thus got Morrison talking. Any answers that

Molyneux gave me were annotated and corrected by Morrison, and by the time we had lunch I had got the uncrowned King of China talking freely.

It was an education to listen to him, for he spoke with the self-confidence of genius. With Morrison it was not a case of "I think"; it was a case of "I know". Of the three great men of affairs that I had met up to that time — Morrison, Cecil Rhodes, and Winston Churchill — Morrison had perhaps the best record. Cecil Rhodes, with enormous capital at his back, had battled with Boers and Baustos; Churchill, with his father's prestige and his mother's money to help him, had sailed on life's voyage with the wind strongly behind him; but Morrison had gone into China on a small salary for *The Times* and had outclassed the smartest political agents of the world — men with untold money at the back of them.

A triangular conversation between Morrison, Molyneux and myself ran on the following lines:

PATERSON. What started this Boxer trouble anyhow?

MOLYNEUX. Well, you see, the Boxers —

MORRISON. No, it wasn't the Boxers. You've got Boxers on the brain. The Boxers were just a rabble, washermen, and rickshaw coolies. Old Napoleon with his whiff of grapeshot would have settled the Boxers before lunch. The trouble was that the Chinese Government couldn't handle their job and the whole world was waiting for England to declare a protectorate over the Yangtze valley and stand for fair play and open the door for everybody. All the nations trusted England to give them fair play. You know the old song:

> The English, the English,
> They don't amount to much;
> But anything is better
> Than the God damn Dutch.

Or the God damn Russian or Turk, or Portugee either.

PATERSON. Would we have to fight anybody if we had taken a protectorate?

MORRISON. No. Everybody wanted it. You can't conceive the amount of trade there is here, and everybody wanted to have a go at it. And it's nothing to what it will be. There's goldmines and tin-mines and quicksilver and all sorts of minerals in the interior, and it's very lightly inhabited. There's all this wonderful agricultural land, on the coast, and there are hills all over blue grass, splendid grazing-land in the interior. I didn't sit on the sea-coast and write out telegrams. I went in and had a look at it. But nobody's game to put any money into the trade because there's really no government in China. The English missed the chance of a lifetime.

PATERSON. The English don't generally miss much. What made them miss this?

MORRISON. Kruger made them miss it. De Wet made them miss it. They humbugged about over this Chinese business till they had the Boer War on their hands. Then they found they were getting a lot of men shot and dying of enteric to get better terms for the Johannesburg Jews and the owners of the Kimberley diamond-mines. So they said, "Not any more war, thank you. We've had some." The next thing was that they had to send men-of-war and troops here whether they liked it or not. But instead of running the show themselves and being top dog, they just had to snap and bite along with the rest of the pack.

"They might have taken the job on only for the missionaries," he went on. "The missionaries all wrote home, and said that if the English tried to govern China the dear little converts would all get their throats cut, and they themselves would be *fan-kweid*.* But I didn't suggest that the English should govern China. I said to let the Chinese govern it, nominally, and we could have enough troops here to back them up. Then if any of these Boxers got giving trouble the Chinese would crucify them in the good old-fashioned way and everything would be as quiet as a Sunday-school."

Here Molyneux chipped in and spoke a piece.

"I have a friend on the staff here," he said, "and he got the General to write home and say that if we had twenty thousand men we could keep China nice and quiet. He got snubbed by the War Office. Then he asked his General to write and say that he refused to accept such an answer from a D.A.A.G. who had never been in China in his life. But the General had to think about his own job. He daren't go up against the brass hats. So things just muddled

---

* Cut to pieces with knives.

along until the Boxers started and besieged the legations in Peking. We thought it was just one of these comic-opera shows until we found that nobody could get out with any news. Such a thing was never known in China before. You could always square a Chinaman to go with a message. So then it was all nations on deck, to hunt the Boxers and to grab what they could by way of indemnity. You ought to have seen the claims for damages! Some of them got civil service catalogues and copied out the lists of furniture and said the Chinese had destroyed the things or carried them away. One man claimed for a mahogany sideboard, with fluted columns. He never saw a mahogany sideboard, only in a catalogue.''

MORRISON. Yes, and who pays the indemnity? Did you ever hear of a policeman arresting a criminal and then the policeman having to pay the fine? Well, that's what is happening here. The big English firms and the shipping companies, they'll all have to pay extra taxation. There's English money in every sugar-factory in the country, and in every ship that runs up the coast. One Chinese company that carries a million passengers a year — there's English money in that. There's a Russian line that trades here and their ships are all old English ships, not paid for. Those companies will have to dig into their pockets to pay the Japanese and the Germans for coming here to have a little pantomime and call it a war.

PATERSON. What was the fighting like.

MORRISON. Ask Molyneux. He knows all about war. Give him a rifle and a tin of bully-beef and he'd drive the Chinese out of China. The first man shot in Peking was the Chinese tailor, and I've always suspected Molyneux. He owed that tailor a lot of money.

According to Molyneux and other (civilian) experts on war, the allies only had to advance over about fourteen miles of contested country, and the advance was up a river with various boggy creeks flowing into it. Most of the forces had sense enough to walk round the top of the creeks, but the Germans put up trestle bridges which promptly sank in the mud as soon as anybody stood on them. The English had orders to win the war without shooting anybody, as the idea in London was to exhibit humanity and forbearance and get all the trade later on.

"Of course, that was all wrong," said Morrison. "If you want to make an Oriental think well of you you don't want to soft-sawder him; you want to kick him in the stern. The Japanese did more fighting and killed more men than anybody else because they did not worry their heads as to what the Chinese would think of them.

"There was some real fighting at the end of the march," he went on. "The Japanese ran laughing, and cheering, man after man, on to a bridge that was swept with rifle-fire, and where a mouse couldn't have lived. They ran up to a gate and laid mines against it, and were shot down, man after man, till at last they blew it down. They'll be tough gentlemen to tackle in a war. They had a field-hospital up and were treating their wounded while the fighting was going on."

Listening to this tale of woe I recalled the two English ladies of title in the Boer War, and their biting comments on that enterprise. No doubt the British people, especially the Australians, are prolific in what we got to know in after years as "back-seat drivers". Perhaps Morrison was a "back-seat driver". But before I left the China coast I got to know what national prestige means in a foreign country. Previously, I had known only Australia and South Africa. In China I saw the coast crowded with steamships of all flags fighting for trade. I saw the local lines — Jardine Matheson and Butterfield and Swire — running up the coast, and the big Empress boats pulling out from Japan. I travelled on a Russian liner (a British steamship unpaid for) and saw thousands of tons of produce coming into the China ports by river and rail. A British importer in Shanghai showed me one day's orders — windmills, building materials, stoves, brushes, locks, brooms, and every kind of hardware. I met concession-hunters, bankers and political agents of all nations, each hustling for his own hand and his own country. Perhaps Morrison was right. We should have walked in and taken the boss mandarin's seat at the top of the table.

Happy Dispatches, 1934

2

Today there arrives in Sydney one of the most notable Australians of the present day — Dr Morrison, *The Times* correspondent in China.

It is necessary to visit China itself in order to get any clear idea of the responsibilities and difficulties of Dr Morrison's position. The huge Chinese Empire has for years been jealously guarded from outside intrusion; just a few treaty ports have been thrown open, and the fringe of the country has barely been touched; and yet, so quickly has the trade grown, that in 1898 China imported over seven million pounds worth of English goods — almost equal to the New South Wales imports for the same year. Besides the English trade, there is the American, German, French, Russian and Japanese trade of China waiting to be developed; and not only is there trade development to carry on, but there are in China undreamed of sources of wealth — fertile lands that will grow anything, mines of fabulous richness, water rights for irrigation to be snapped up, permits to be obtained to make railways that will soon be carrying their millions of passengers annually; all these prizes lie in China awaiting the hardy adventurer who can get in as "first robber". In every Chinese treaty port there is a restless crowd of adventurers of all nations — English, Russian, American, German, and Jew — all scheming and struggling to secure land, to secure railway rights, to secure water rights, or to secure mining rights. There are officials to be bribed or bullied into granting concessions — officials whose oath their dearest friends would not believe, and whose written promise is a mere piece of waste paper. There are political adventurers, pulling all sorts of hidden strings, and producing all sorts of amazing gyrations among the puppets of Chinese politics. There are days when the mere knowledge that an agreement has been signed by a Chinese official may be worth ten thousand pounds in cold cash. There are rumours, lies, threats, open violence to be encountered; and among this tumult and strife there moves one man to whose knowledge all white men — Russian, American, German, and Jew alike — defer, Morrison, the Australian, who represents *The Times* in China.

It is hard to explain the secrets of his success in getting information. It is not the amount of money that he has to spend, because the utmost sum that *The Times* could allow for secret service money would be a mere fleabite to the amount that some of the concessionaries and political agents would give for early and exclusive information. And yet so marvellously does he manage that the full text of the important treaty, signed in 1901 at the conclusion of hostilities, was actually wired by him to his paper, and was being read and discussed in English homes, several days before the document was laid before the representatives of the nations for signature. This is not luck — it's a gift!

Dr Morrison lives for the most part at Peking, where he is in touch with the best-informed Chinese circles. But he moves constantly about, travelling in men-of-war, on tramp steamers, on mule-litters, on pony back, or on his feet, as occasion demands. He is a powerful, wiry man, of solid and imposing presence, and those who know him best in China say that he has mastered the secret of all Chinese diplomacy — bluff. In China you must "save your face", i.e., preserve your dignity at all hazards. He never allows any Chinaman, however important, to assume for a moment that he (the Chinaman) is in any way the equal of *The Times* correspondent in China. He has been known — so his friends say — to pull a Chinese mandarin out of his chair of state and seat himself in it, in order to impress upon that Chinaman and his friends the transcendental amount of "face" possessed by *The Times* correspondent. For the rest, a keen knowledge of men, a gift of diplomacy, and a dogged Scotch persistency pull him through his difficulties.

It needs an exceptional man to hold his own in such troubled waters; every day there is some new rumour, some new threat, some new difficulty. What are the Russians doing, what the Germans, what the Americans? He has to report, and report faithfully, every move in a game in which the stakes are millions, and the counters are the lives of men. So thoroughly do the various Europeans rely on him that when the Legations were besieged and no news came through, and it was known that Morrison was in the besieged buildings, all hope was abandoned. The general opinion all down the China coast was: "If Morrison was alive, he would manage to get some news through." As a matter of fact, the wires were never cut, and the Chinese in Hong Kong and Shanghai had news from their friends all through the siege that the Legations were safe; but no European would believe it, because it was thought that if the white people in the Embassy were alive they would be able to bribe a Chinaman to send a message somehow; the existence of an unbribable lot of Chinamen was a thing they did not believe in. And yet it was so, and for all the length of that siege the bland, imperturbable Chinaman threw off the mask, and showed his cold, uncompromising detestation of the European and all his works; and in the great Armageddon yet to come, when the Chinaman makes his next try to eject the white barbarian, woe betide those who fall into his hands.

Dr Morrison's movements are timed to take him back to China in the spring, when the gentle Chinaman, and the Russian, and the Manchu, awake from their winter sleep, and resume their game of swapping concessions and privileges; when the German once more starts to undersell his English competitor, and the river highways teem with human life, and the fishing junks go out to sea from Swatow in a cluster as thick as sailing boats at a Balmain regatta. China is the theatre of the world's chief performance for the next few years; and we may watch the unfolding of the drama with added interest from the fact that the man who is to tell us most about it is an Australian.

Evening News, Sydney, 21 January 1903

THE LATE LIEUTENANT MORANT*

Lieutenant Morant was an ardent devotee of sport. From fox hunting to riding at shows, there was nothing in the way of sport that Morant would not tackle; all his life he feared nothing but

---

*   *Morant, Harry Harbord* (1865-1902) was an Englishman who came to Australia in 1884 and worked as a drover and horse-breaker on outback properties in Queensland and New South Wales. He wrote verse and ballads under the pen name "The Breaker", and these were published in the *Bulletin*. Morant enlisted with an Australian Boer War contingent and was promoted to lieutenant after the relief of Kimberley. In 1901, Morant and another officer were convicted of murdering Boer prisoners and executed by a British Army firing squad. Controversy about this affair remains to the present day.

hard work — or rather sustained steady work, because the hardships he went through to avoid working were much more formidable than the work itself would have been. An Englishman by birth, he was an excellent rough rider, and when he was young, with a nerve unshaken, he was a first-class horse-breaker and a good man to teach a young horse to jump fences. Morant lived in the bush the curious nomadic life of the Ishmaelite, the ne'er-do-well, of whom there are still many to be found about north Queensland, but who are very rare now in the settled districts; droughts and overdrafts have hardened the squatters' hearts and they are no longer content to board and lodge indefinitely the scapegrace who claims their hospitality; even yet in Queensland it is quite common for a young fellow to ride up to a station with all his worldly goods on a pack horse and let his horses go in the paddock and stay for months, joining in the work of the station, but not getting any pay — except a pound or two by way of loan from the "boss" now and again — and leaving at last to go on a droving trip; but in New South Wales the type is practically extinct. Morant was always popular for his dash and courage, and he would travel miles to obtain the kudos of riding a really dangerous horse. He revelled in excitement and boon-companionship, and used to weary of the monotony of the bush and would constantly come to town to "see life;" as he had no money, and no means of earning any beyond a few pounds gained by very fitful work with his pen, these trips involved borrowings and difficulties that would have driven differently-constituted men out of their minds. But Morant used to manage to keep his place among his friends — and they were many — but how he managed it was always a problem. Such, then, was his life — hard and dangerous labour in the bush, given for nothing to avoid having to work, flashes of enjoyment in town so dearly bought that they were worthless. In character he was kind-hearted and good-natured to the last degree, an enemy to no man but himself. Money he never valued at its true worth; he was a spendthrift and an idler, quick to borrow and slow to pay — as many literary and other Bohemians have been from time immemorial. He would buy a young colt on credit, and ride him till he had knocked the nonsense out of him, and would then sell him and spend the proceeds — instead of paying his debts — in a visit to an orchestral concert or in the expenses incident to a day's hunting. He never saved a penny in his life, and the idea that he would take or order the taking of the life of an unarmed man for the sake of gain is utterly inconsistent with every trait of his character. Those who knew him best say that he would sooner have given a sick Boer the coat off his back than shot him for any money — especially Transvaal paper money — that he might have about him. Morant had one peculiarity, which perhaps arose from his literary propensities — he was always very untidy in his dress; and though he claimed to be the descendant of a leading English family he never affected the "swell" in his manner, and he never tried to dress himself up to act the part of the well-connected "adventurer". Such as he was, he was the same to all men. With a good commander over him he might have made a fine soldier. As it turned out he got into exactly the worst company that a man of his temperament could have met — it was always so with him. He gambled with his chances all through life, and the cards ran against him. What is it that such men lack — just a touch of determination, or of caution, maybe to turn their lives from failures to successes? His death was consistent with his life, for though he died as a criminal he died a brave man facing the rifles with his eyes unbandaged. For him Gordon's lines would made [*sic*] a fitting epitaph:

> An aptitude to mar and break
>> What others diligently make,
>> That was the best and worst of him.
>> Wise, with the cunning of the snake;
> Brave, with the sea-wolf's courage grim;
>> Dying hard and dumb, torn limb from limb.

Sydney Mail, 12 April 1902

J.F. ARCHIBALD —
GREAT AUSTRALIAN JOURNALIST

Twenty odd years ago a man who had sent anonymous contributions to the *Bulletin* newspaper was startled and surprised by seeing in the Answers to Correspondents column a brief notice saying, ''Please call on editor.'' The *Bulletin* of these days was a sort of literary chameleon that changed its aspect according to the eyes of the beholder. In the eyes of all ''right-thinking people'' — a class which its editor held in sincere detestation — it was a scurrilous rag, certain to do a great amount of harm; in the eyes of the ordinary, heedless, unthinking man in the street, it was a very good comic paper; to such few iconoclasts, uplifters, and re-generators of society as then existed, it represented a new gospel.

Figure to yourself, then, oh reader, the progress of the contributor who, by the way, was neither right-thinker, comic man, nor uplifter, down Pitt Street to the small, shabby brick building hidden away among ship-chandleries, fish shops, and wool stores, up a narrow and never dusted flight of stairs into a narrow and equally undusted passage, which hardly room for two men to walk abreast. Off this passage there opened two or three little cubicles of rooms, each about the size of, and in many ways resembling, a racehorse's loose-box — if one can imagine a loose-box furnished with a table and a chair, dust illimitable, piles of newspapers all about the floor, and its walls decorated with ink-stains and newspaper illustrations. The first loose-box contained a sallow young man who with feverish haste was writing paragraphs. That was Wilfred Blacket, sub-editor, now a King's Counsel, and man of respectability. Without pausing in his manufacture of sausage-machine literature, without even looking up from his task, he indicated with a jerk of his thumb the loose-box next door as the editor's room, and there Archibald was found.

Racially, Archibald looked like a Jew. He had the hawk nose, the open eye, and the quick movement of that Oriental people; physically he was a fairly strong and well-set-up man of medium size, long in the arms, untidy in dress, wearing a moustache and pointed beard. He was not at any time a man who had the commercial traveller's gift of making himself at home with strangers; it took him a long time to size a man up, a process in which he often made curious mistakes. At that first interview little was said except that the contributor was asked to send in copy, and was instructed in the art of cutting out the copy when it appeared, sending it in, and getting paid for it. But next day's mail brought a long letter from Archibald, a letter which contained much that is worth reading by those who aspire to journalism.

"I want you," he wrote, "to remember that Australia is a big place, and I want you to write stuff that will appeal not only to Sydney people, but that will be of interest to the pearler up at Thursday Island and the farmer down in Victoria. On all public questions the press are apt to sing in chorus. If you go to a concert you may hear a man sing a discord which is put there by the composer, and that discord catches the ear over the voices of the chorus. Well, don't be afraid to sing the discord. Even if you are wrong, you will have drawn attention to what you want to say, and you may be right. In my experience the man who sings the discord is generally right nowadays.

"For the same reason, do not be afraid to cheer for the under-dog in a fight. You will have all the cheering to yourself, for one thing, and the under-dog may come out on top."

A singular letter for a man to write in those days, when all right-thinking people got their ideas, their boots, their shirts, their titles, their jobs, their political, moral, and religious standards from England. It was looked upon as "blow", and bad taste for an Australian to talk of anything that Australians had done. We were patronized by imported Governors, insulted by imported globe-trotting snobs, exploited by imported actors and singers, mostly worn-out and incompetent. These people rode rough-shod over us, and we meekly submitted.

Archibald was about the first Australian to "call" the English bluff. In pursuance of his policy of cheering for the under-dog, he asserted that an Australian lawyer, or doctor, or inventor, or singer, or actor was every bit as good as any importation. The Governor of those days happened to be a worn-out diplomat with a hobby for fowls, so Archibald drew him — or caused his artists to draw him — as a broken down swell leading a muscovy drake by a string and carrying a broken top-hat full of eggs. Such a cartoon nowadays would pass unnoticed in the general whirligig of things but at that time it was lese-majesty; Australian irreverence, Australian ignorance, sacrilege; in that cartoon Archibald certainly "sang the discord".

"A good journalist," said Archibald once, "should be free of all trammels. He should have no family ties or connections, because they are sure to sway him and prejudice his judgement. A man without a country would be an ideal journalist, because then he could tell the truth about any place without hurting his own national pride; and he should not be tied up to any religious belief, because a man who always tells the truth must sometimes shame whatever God he believes in. In fact, the ideal man to reform the world would be a bastard atheist born at sea. Such a man would start free from ties and prejudices anyhow.''

An iconoclast, a questioner, a critic, a fearless fighter, he was all these, but had he any constructive genius? Alas, no. Your constructive genius does not go into journalism, and Archibald had all the defects of the born journalist. He could expose a wrong, detect an injustice, but he had no Morrison's pill to cure national disorders. He was a great diagnostician, but after detecting the disease he left the cure to others. To his type of mind the exposure of the Mount Rennie injustices* was of more importance than the construction of any national land or industrial policy. He could tell people when they were on the wrong road, but he could not point out the right one.

His services to Australia, therefore, may be summed up in four words: ''He made people think.'' Breaking away from traditions, holding no shams sacred, he was one of the first to make the Australian believe in himself. To that extent he rendered a service to his country, and this good at any rate lives after him: the rest of his work is interred with his bones.

Even after his death he has done something to carry on the advancement of Australia, as he has left a fairly large sum of money to provide for the purchase each year of the best portrait painted in Australia of any Australian distinguished in art, literature, or research, and this in itself speaks the character of the man's mind. Cynic and pessimist as he was, he never lost faith in the ultimate success of Australians, and when in the process of time his name is forgotten and people ask, ''Who was this Archibald who left this

---

*　In September 1886 a number of young men committed a mass assault on a sixteen-year-old girl at ''Mount Rennie'', in Moore Park, Sydney. Of eleven youths committed for trial before Sir William Windeyer, nine were sentenced to death. After a controversy on the severity of the sentences, five of the youths were reprieved; the other four were hanged.

bequest?", the question can be answered by saying, "He was the first man who believed in the home-made Australian article."

Sportsman, Sydney, 25 January 1922

RUDYARD KIPLING

One expects a great literary genius to be in some way a sort of freak: drink, women, temperament, idleness, irregularity — nearly all the great writers of the past have had one or other of these drawbacks, and some of them have had them all. Byron's life consisted mostly of purple patches; and Swinburne was not the hero of the song about the good young man that died. So, when I went to stay with Kipling in England, I was prepared for literally anything. Would he drink? Would he be one of those men who had half a dozen wives with a complementary number of concubines? Would he sit up all night telling me how good he was, or would he recite his own poetry with appropriate gestures?

None of these things happened. We have read in one of O. Henry's books of a citizen of a South American republic, where everybody was "grafting" day and night, who determined to make himself conspicuous by being honest. Greta Garbo, one of the world's great filmstars, got pages of publicity by refusing to be interviewed. Shakespeare himself seems to have dodged the publicity man to such an extent that even now there is some doubt whether he wrote all his own works, or whether they were done by somebody else of the same name. Kipling was remarkable in that his life was so very unremarkable.

He hated publicity as his Satanic Majesty is supposed to hate holy water; and in private life he was just a hard-working, commonsense, level-headed man, without any redeeming vices that I could discover. A pity, too, perhaps; for there is nothing so interesting as scandals about great geniuses. Though he was a very rich man, I found him living in an unpretentious house at Rottingdean, Brighton. The only thing that marked it as the lair of a literary lion was the crowd of tourists (mostly Americans) who hung about from daylight till dark trying to look over the wall, or waiting to intercept his two little children when they went out for a walk. By having his car brought into the garden and getting into it from his own doorstep, Kipling was able to dash out through the ranks of autograph hunters even as a tiger dashes out when surrounded by savages.

His wife, a charming and cultivated American lady, was in her own way just as big a disappointment as was Kipling. She did not seek to be a society star, nor to swagger about covered with rubies and emeralds.

"In the States," she said, "when people push their money in your face, we always wonder how they got it."

Kipling's house was a home. And it was a home of hard work, for he allowed nothing to interfere with his two or three hours of work a day. The rest of the time he roved round getting material.

"I must buy a house in Australia some day," he said. "I've a house here, and in New York, and in Capetown; but I'd like to live in Australia for a while. I've been there, but I only went through it like the devil went through Athlone, in standing jumps. You can't learn anything about a country that way. You have to live there and then you can get things right. You people in Australia haven't grown up yet. You think the Melbourne Cup is the most important thing in the world."

Motoring in those days was just in the stage when the betting was about even whether the car would get its passengers home or whether the wife would sit and knit by the roadside while the husband lay on his back under the car and had his clothes smothered in dust and oil.

Kipling, it appeared, had a new car coming on trial, and our first excursion was to be a run in this new car. One of the newly-invented Lanchester cars arrived, driven by a man in overalls, who looked like a superior sort of mechanic. He said that his name was Laurence, when he heard that I came from Australia he asked me whether I knew his brother in Sydney. It so happened that I *did* know his brother; thereafter things went swimmingly. "I have another brother," he said, "a high court judge here. When I take these cars round for a trial I generally drag in something about my brother, the high court judge, for fear they'll send me round to the kitchen. Sometimes," he added, "I would prefer to go to the kitchen."

Kipling and I piled into the back of the car, with the great man as excited as a child with a new toy. Out we went, scattering tourists right and left, and away over the Sussex downs. We were climbing a hill of about one in five with nothing much below us but the English Channel, when Kipling, possibly with a view to getting some accurate copy about motoring said, "What would happen if she stopped here, Laurence?"

"I'll show you," said Laurence. He stopped the engine and let the car, with its illustrious passenger, run back towards that awful drop. I had a look over my shoulder and was preparing to jump when Laurence dropped a sprag and pulled her up all standing. Then he threw in the engine and away we went. I said to Kipling,

"Weren't you frightened? I was nearly jumping out."

"Yes," he said, "I was frightened. But I thought what a bad advertisement it might be for the Lanchester company if they killed me, so I sat tight."

Away we went through the beautiful English lanes, where the leaves swirled after the car, and one expected to see Puck of Pook's Hill peering out from behind a tree. We passed military barracks, where Mulvaney, Ortheris, Learoyd, with their swagger canes, were just setting out for a walk. We saw the stolid English farm labourers putting in the oak bridge that would last for generations. We saw a sailing-ship ploughing her way down the Channel, and noted "the shudder, the stumble, the roll as the star-stabbing bowsprit emerges". It was like looking at a series of paintings — and here at my side was the painter.

Earnest in everything that he touched, he pulled the car up outside a butcher's shop to do a little Empire propaganda. Pointing at the carcass of a lamb hanging in the window, he asked me to guess its weight. Not being altogether inexperienced in the weight of lambs, I had a guess, and he said,

"I'll go in and buy that lamb, and we'll see if you're right; and we'll see where this butcher is getting his mutton."

It turned out that I was within two pounds of the lamb's weight. This seemed to astonish Kipling very much, and he said to the butcher,

"This gentleman comes from Australia, where they do nothing but weigh lambs all day long. You must buy all the Australian lamb you can get, and keep the money in the Empire." The butcher, not knowing in the least who he was, said,

"The Empire. Ha! My customers don't bother about the Empire, sir. It's their guts they think about!"

This unedifying incident of the butcher may be some sort of guide as to what Kipling's English contemporaries thought of him. Frankly, they looked upon him as one of these infernal know-all fellows, who wanted to do all sorts of queer things. What right had anyone to come along and suggest that some day there would be a big war, and that England should be prepared for it? Fancy advocating that we should give more time to drill, and less time to sports! The flannelled fools at the wickets, forsooth, and the muddied oafs at the goals — when everybody knew that all battles were won on the playing fields of Eton and Rugby!

Kipling, out of his own pocket, bought enough land for a rifle-range, and paid the wages of a retired sergeant-major to teach the yokels drill and musketry. Was he applauded by his neighbours? Not that you would notice it. A local magnate, stodgy as a bale of hay, looked in for afternoon tea and confided to me that Kipling was undoubtedly a clever man but too unconventional.

"All this business about drilling men," he said, "is just putting wrong ideas into their heads. I wouldn't let my men go."

Later on, in the Great War, he was to know more about it. Kipling himself lost his only son in the Great War, and was asked to write an epitaph to be put on a tablet in the centre of the thousands of war graves. He wrote: "Had our fathers not lied to us, so many of us would not be here." And who shall blame him? Needless to say, they did not use it.

So Kipling stalked through the land of little men, as Gulliver stalked through the land of the Lilliputians. He would never have made a political leader, for he was less of a quack, less of showman, and less of a timeserver than any public man I ever met. Had he been a spectacular person like Gabriel d'Annunzio he might have led a great Imperialist movement. But he had no gift of speech, and his nature abhorred anything in the way of theatricalism. He wrote of things as he saw them, bearing in his own way the white man's burden and expecting no fee or reward.

* * * * *

Kipling carried his earnestness into his work, for he must have everything right. Smoking one evening, he picked up some manuscript, and said,

"Here's something I am working on, and it brings in your country. Just see if it's right, will you?"

The verse in his hand was: "The scent of the wattle at Lichtenberg, riding in the rain." And the lines that troubled him were:

> My fruit-farm on Hunter's River
> With the new vines joining hands.

For some reason or another he was worried as to whether these lines were right.

I said that in Australia we would speak of an orchard, not of a fruit-farm; and that we called it Hunter River, and not Hunter's River. But why worry! He wasn't writing a geography or a gardener's guide. Even old Ouida, who was a best-seller in her day, once made one of her guardsman heroes, weighing thirteen stone, ride the same horse to victory in the Derby two years running — and nobody murdered her.

"They should have murdered her," said Kipling. "Writing things wrong is like singing out of tune. You don't sing, do you?"

"No. But how could you tell?"

"Nobody that has the ear for rhythm ever has the ear for music. When I sing, the dog gets up and goes out of the room."

This insistence on photographic accuracy, so unusual in a poet, may have been the one loose bearing in the otherwise perfect machinery of his mind; or it may have been that his training as a sub-editor had bitten so deeply into his system that he looked upon inaccuracy as the cardinal sin. There was no satisfaction for him in a majestic march of words if any of the words were out of step.

I said to him,

"You ought to be satisfied. You seem to get things pretty right, anyway. How did you come to get that little touch about the Australian trooper riding into Lichtenberg when the rain brought out the scent of the wattles? Inspiration?"

"No," he said. "Observation. I used to poke about among the troops and ask all the silly questions I could think of. I saw this Australian trooper pull down a wattle-bough and smell it. So I rode alongside and asked him where he came from. He told me about himself, and added, 'I didn't know they had our wattle over here. It smells like home.' That gave me the general idea for the verses; then all I had to do was to sketch in the background in as few strokes as possible. And when you're only using a few strokes you must have 'em in the right place. That's why I asked you whether it was right to talk about the fruit-farm and Hunter's River.''

All very well. But, being somewhat in the verse line myself, I knew that only a master could have written those few little verses. Possibly only one man that ever lived could have done it — Kipling himself.

He was sub-editor of a big Indian paper, and all the news of the world came through his hands to be trimmed up and cut down and put under headlines. The worst training in the world for a poet, one would think. Yet, it gave him his crisp, clear-cut style. He thought in essentials, and scorned padding, as a sub-editor should. "The Wake A Welt of Light", "He looked like a lance in rest", "Oak, Ash, and Thorn", "The Joyous Venture". These are all headlines — not a word wasted. Phil May had this gift of condensation in art, and Kipling has it in literature. Then, as to his gift of vivid description. Here are a couple of lines from the "Ballad of East and West", describing the chase of an Indian raider by an officer on a troop horse:

> The dun he leaned against the bit and slugged his head above,
> But the red mare played with the snaffle-bars, as a maiden plays with a glove.

I said, "How on earth did you manage to write that, you who say you know nothing about horses? It's just a picture of the way the horses would gallop. You can see the well-bred mare getting over the ground like a gazelle with the big, heavy-headed horse toiling after her."

"Observation," he said. "I suppose I must have noticed the action of horses without knowing that I noticed it."

It must have been the same sort of observation that made him call the pompous heads of army departments "little tin gods on wheels". The phrase was not new, but like Homer going down the road, he went and took it. Like all great artists, he was quite dissatisfied with his own work:

"If you can write a thing about half as well as it ought to be written," he said, "then perhaps, after all, you may not have written it so badly."

I asked him how he came to write *Kim* with its mass of material and its infinite (and no doubt accurate) detail.

"Oh," he said, "the material was just lying about there in heaps. All I had to do was to take it and fit it together."

And now the reader asks, hadn't the man any hobbies? Did he garden or play cards or shoot or hunt or fish? Not a bit of it. He took a great deal of interest in small improvements to his property, such as you may read about in *Puck of Pook's Hill*, but I think that was mainly on account of the enjoyment he got from watching the habits and customs of the English agricultural labourer, as set forth in the same book. His sight was too bad to allow him to race over raspers in the hunting-field or drop a dry fly over a rising trout: hence his nickname of Beetle in *Stalky & Co*. His only hobby was work. And like Goethe's hero he toiled without haste and without rest. Look at a collection of his works and you will get some idea of the urge that must have driven him to keep working. At the age of forty he had written more books than most men write in a lifetime, and not a line went into one of those books that he did not verify. True, he did once describe the Maribyrnong Plate as a steeplechase; but if he had had an Australian turf-guide at hand, he would have corrected the error. I have already quoted the Scotch engineer's objection to Kipling's description of the destroyers lying in wait for their prey in the swirl of the reefs — "and they drawing six feet forrard and nine feet aft". But did not Shakespeare once locate a navy in Bohemia or some other inland country? Apart from his literary work, he felt that the white man's burden was laid on him to advocate in every way this bringing of the British peoples under Empire council, with India as a sort of apprentice nation until it learnt to govern itself. In view of what has happened lately, he might have also questioned the ability of the white parts of the Empire to govern themselves; but he said that, when the Australians grew up, and when the young Africans forgot to be Dutch, there would be such an empire as the world never saw. By way of contribution to the debate, I suggested that the Australians would always put Australia first, and that the young Africans did not care a hoot about the Dutch — they were Afrikanders first, last, and all the time. But the only motherland he had known was that "grim stepmother", India, and he could not conceive that South Africans or Australians would study the interest of their own territories when they might be partners in a great empire. One must concede to him that he took a large view.

As to the Indians, he said that the Indian peasant could neither understand nor make any sensible use of self-government; and he wrote all sorts of nasty things about the British M.P.'s, who wandered over to "smoodge" to the Indians. He would cheerfully have seen them get their throats cut.

Happy Dispatches, 1934

WINSTON CHURCHILL

A war correspondent, in army eyes, is an evil to be tolerated, in fact he is distinctly nah-poo, as we used afterwards to say in France. Being an Australian, a steeplechase rider and polo player, I had a (possibly fictitious) reputation as a judge of a horse, and was constantly asked to go and pick horses for officers out of the remount depots.

In that way I got to know such celebrities as Lord Roberts, French, Haig, Winston Churchill and Kipling, and I attained a status in the army that I would never have reached as a correspondent. The horse may be the natural enemy of man, as some people think, but he is the key to more valuable acquaintanceships and good friendships than either rank or riches. I acquired more merit in the army by putting a cavalry regiment on to back the Australian horse The Grafter, in the City and Suburban, than by the finest dispatches that I ever sent to Reuter's. Generals, as a rule, were "off" correspondents. If they were civil to them it looked as though they were trying to advertise, and if they treated them roughly — well, the correspondents had their own way of getting back at them. One miscreant, a correspondent for an obscure Cape paper, was stopped by a railway staff officer, named King

Hall, from going somewhere or other. Probably King Hall was quite right — but look what the correspondent did to him!

He printed an article in his sausage-wrap of a paper to say that, from the top of his head to the soles of his feet, from his immaculately-fitting tunic to his beautifully-cut riding-pants and his spotless boots, King Hall was *beau sabreur*, the sartorial ideal of a British officer.

How did the army eat it up!

Wandering generals would get off the train, poke their heads into King Hall's office and say: "Well, how's the *beau sabreur* today?" Colonels on lines of communication, having little else to do, would ride up to the railway station and inquire of King Hall who made his breeches. Even subalterns, who dared not "chip" a senior officer, would look meaningly under the table at those boots, as they departed with their railway warrants. If King Hall had been made press censor, every correspondent in South Africa would have been sent home by the next day's boat — unless there was one leaving earlier.

Not that all the correspondent fraternity were casteless in the eyes of the army. *The Times* staff, headed by Lionel James, were persons of consequence. With the English passion for regimentation, they all wore a tooth-brush stuck in the band of their hats, as a sort of caste mark. If you were a *Times* man you wore a toothbrush; if you were not a *Times* man you didn't dare do it. No, sir!

Winston Churchill (afterwards to be, well, pretty well everything in British governments) was over as correspondent for the *Morning Post*. With his great social influence, his aggressiveness and undoubted ability, he was a man to be feared if not liked. He would even take a fall out of General French; and that, for a correspondent, was about equal to earning the V.C. twice over. One day, when something had gone wrong and Johnnie French was in a particularly bad temper, Churchill said to me:

"Come along up to H.Q. I am going to give French a turn. He was very rude to me last time we met."

On that particular day I would as soon have faced a Hyrcanian tiger, and said so. But Churchill insisted. So off we went, Churchill striding along in front with his chin well stuck out, while I shuffled protestingly behind. Arrived at headquarters, Churchill saluted and said:

"General," he said, "I want to ask whether I am to report to-day's operations as a success or a failure?"

FRENCH (choking down a few appropriate words that he would have liked to say): "Well, Churchill, that depends on how you look at it."

CHURCHILL: "I am afraid that my point of view would not carry much weight, sir. What I want to know is, whether from *your* point of view, the affair was a success or a failure?"

FRENCH (very dignified): "If you apply to Major Haig, he will let you see the official report. Good morning."

It was a victory for the Press, but one felt that a few such victories would mean annihilation. Churchill was not then in parliament — in fact, he had been hooted and badly defeated at his only attempt; but he expounded his plan of campaign.

"This correspondent job," he explained, "is nothing to me; but I mean to get into parliament through it. They wouldn't listen to me when I put up for parliament, because they had never heard of me. Now," he said, "I am going to plaster the *Morning Post* with cables about our correspondent, Mr Winston Churchill, driving an armoured train, or pointing out to Lord Roberts where the enemy is. When I go up for parliament again, I'll fly in."

All of which things he did. Persons burdened with inferiority complexes might sit up and take notice.

Churchill was the most curious combination of ability and swagger. The army could neither understand him nor like him; for when it came to getting anywhere or securing any job, he made his own rules. Courage he had in plenty, as will be shown later on; but, like the Duke of Plaza Toro, he felt that he should always travel with a full band. As one general put it:

"You never know when you have got Churchill. You can leave him behind in charge of details and he'll turn up at the front, riding a camel, and with some infernal explanation that you can't very well fault."

Even his work as a correspondent jarred the army to its depths. When there was nothing doing at the front, he always managed to get himself into the news. The Duke of Norfolk's horse fell with him in an antbear hole (everybody's horse fell with him in an antbear hole at some time or other) and the matter was too trivial for comment. But the *Morning Post*, when it arrived, had a splash heading: "Our Mr Winston Churchill saves the Duke of Norfolk from being crushed by his horse." As the Duke of Norfolk was the great Catholic peer, Churchill no doubt reckoned that this would be worth thousands of Catholic votes to him at the next election.

Churchill and his cousin, the Duke of Marlborough, each drank a big bottle of beer for breakfast every morning — an unholy rite that is the prerogative of men who have been to a certain school or college. It was like *The Times* tooth-brush or the I Zingari colours — only the elect dare use it.

Marlborough, by the way, was just as retiring as Churchill was aggressive. He could not get much higher than the House of Lords, so he had no necessity to advertise himself; but he was a duke, so he had to act up to it when under public observation. He was riding one day on the flank of an Australian patrol, when it was found that the Boer bullets, fired at extreme range, were just about able to reach the patrol. The common or garden Australians swerved hurriedly out of danger; but the Duke rode on impassively, while the bullets whipped up the sand in front of and behind his horse. Said an Australian trooper:

"If I had that bloke's job, I wouldn't do that."

Churchill, on the other hand, had such a strong personality that even in those early days, when he was quite a young man, the army were prepared to bet that he would either get into jail or become Prime Minister. He had done some soldiering; but he had an uncanny knack of antagonizing his superior and inferior officers. As he said himself:

"I could see nothing in soldiering except looking after the horses' backs and the men's mess-tins in barracks. There's not enough wars to make soldiering worth while."

Happy Dispatches, 1934

PHIL MAY

Bohemia, the land of lightheartedness, where everybody borrows money and buries trouble. Bohemia, where the inhabitants live by backing one another's bills, and discounting them with the *bourgeois* and the Philistine. There was a Bohemia in London at the end of the last century, and Phil May was its prophet.

I had known Phil in Australia, where he worked for the Sydney *Bulletin*. I found him living at St John's Wood and firmly established as one of the leading artists on London *Punch*. There are Bohemians of the beer and back-biting variety, but Phil was the genuine article. He earned about two thousand a year and spent three thousand. An extraordinarily skinny man, with a face like a gargoyle, he was a self-taught artist, a self-taught actor; could give a Shakespearian reading as well as most dramatic artists, and could dance a bit if required. He knew everybody in the artistic, literary, and theatrical world, and his Sunday evenings at St John's Wood gathered together the brightest and best of the Bohemians.

Phil welcomed me with open arms, mainly because he had bought a horse which he hadn't seen for a year, and he wanted somebody to ride it. Phil was for ever buying things that he did not want; and he would have bought (on credit) anything from an elephant to an old master when properly approached. Also, like most comic artists, his life was one long and wearisome search for jokes suitable for illustrations. He told me that he kept a locker at the *Punch* office, and went down every week and bought away a hand-bag full of suggestions sent in by the public. Only one suggestion in each bagful was any good at all.

"One chap starts his suggestion by saying, 'Draw a Scotch humorist,' and another says, 'Draw an elephant sitting on a flea,' and I'm supposed to draw the agony on the flea's features."

He thought I might have some new Australian jokes. I fired one off at him with the warning that it had probably been done before:

"Never mind if it has, dear boy," he said. "*I've* never done it."

The theatrical profession, for some reason or another, looked upon Phil May as a kind of Aladdin — he only had to rub a lamp and he could get them jobs. So they flooded his Sunday nights and asked him to see producers, managers, concert promoters, etc., for them. It appeared that half the leg-shows in London were run by wealthy men, who had nothing to do with the theatre business, but who put up their money for female rather than financial reasons. One such show was being floated at the time, and May said:

"There's a syndicate at the back of this show, and every one of the syndicate has a lady friend on the payroll. They thought they'd boost it up by getting Arthur Roberts as producer. Arthur's a great joke as a comedian, but he's a bigger joke as a producer. What with the women fighting, and their gentlemen friends interfering, he could get nothing done. At last he tackled a johnnie who was sitting on a table in the centre of the stage, swinging his legs, and talking to a delicate damsel in a domino. Arthur, for once, in a way, was too angry to be funny, so he said: "Get to hell out of here, will you! How can I rehearse them with every loafer in London hanging about?' So the chap said: 'Well, you can't rehearse them anyhow. I've got a thousand pounds in this show, so I'm going to stop here and talk to it!' "

Phil's guests were as various as the animals that Noah took into the Ark. Van Biene, the 'cellist, of "Broken Melody" fame, might be seen talking to a little American *siffleuse*. Lewis Waller, the tragedian, and his offsider, Mollison, were heavily important for the benefit of three Australian girl singers, all with colds.

Mollison told us that he had arranged with a capitalist to finance a show that he was going to produce, with Lewis Waller in the lead. The capitalist, after weeks of judicious handling, had just been led to the sticking-point. Then an interview was arranged, at which papers were to be signed and cheques handed over. Waller lost his head at the feeling of careless swagger of having five thousand pounds to play with; and when they met, he said to the capitalist:

"Five thousand pounds! It's all very well, you know, but hardly *enough*, you know. You can lose five thousand in a fortnight. I produced *Bouncing Belle* — lost three thousand in a week. Lost four thousand in three weeks of *Midsummer Madness*. Five thousand's only a flea-bite, you know. You want fifteen thousand really. Then you can hang on! Then you can stand a siege!" The capitalist's jaw was dropping all this time, and as each fresh loss was mentioned he went whiter and whiter.

Then Waller made a dignified exit. The capitalist drew a long breath and said:

"Mollison, I don't think I'll go in for this."

At these Sunday night shows, nobody did his own specialty. Instead of doing lightning sketches, Phil May sang sentimental ballads in a pleasant tenor voice. Florrie Schmidt, an operatic soprano, played the accompaniment of "There'll be a hot time in the old town" for a tragedian, who was making his audiences flood the pit with their tears every night. Back of it all, there was a strain — the strain of the wanted job, of the thousand and one worries of the hard-up professional. Bohemia hid its troubles as well as it could, but there were many little anxious colloquies in corners of the room and many faces that looked a lot brighter after a talk with a manager or a concert promoter. Phil's Sunday nights got many a poor mime or musician a job.

Phil's proudest possession was a prize bulldog that somebody had given him — the cheeriest, kindest, slobberiest bulldog that anyone ever saw. When we proceeded to sally out at night, Mrs May would always insist that Phil should take the bulldog, hoping that the sense of responsibility and fear of losing the dog would bring him home before daylight. In our peregrinations from pub to pub everybody knew Phil and everybody wanted to shout for him. Americans who recognised him by his portraits would introduce themselves and say:

"Ah must have a drink with Mr Phil May."

While I was arguing the point, and saying that he did not want any more drinks, the bulldog would brush against somebody's leg; and the owner of the leg, looking down into the cavern of ivory and red flesh which the bulldog called a mouth, would go faint all over. Then there would have to be drinks to bring this man round, and to insure the others against a similar collapse. After a couple of hours of this, Phil would call a cab and say:

"Take this dog home to St John's Wood for me, will you?"

The dog loved riding in cabs, and evidently had the idea that when he entered a cab he had bought it; for if there happened to be nobody at home when he arrived there, he would refuse to leave the cab and the cabman had to sit on the box and wait, perhaps for an hour or two, until Mrs May came home. No wonder that Phil was chronically hard-up!

One night, after the theatres had shut, we went for supper to a restaurant much frequented by the better-paid of the theatrical world. The place was wreathed in smoke; the jabber was incessant, and there was much hilarity as each celebrity came in. Louis Bradfield, with some of the beauty chorus from the Gaiety Theatre, got perhaps the best "hand". Then Phil May started to do little caricatures on the backs of the menus. The next thing was the appearance of a waiter, bearing a silver salver, on which lay a ten-pound note:

"The Duchess of So-and-so's compliments, and she would like to buy one of Mr May's little sketches."

Phil took up the tenner and drew a sketch on the back of it — about the sketch the less said the better — and handed it to the waiter.

"Mr Phil May's compliments, and he has much pleasure in presenting the duchess with one of his sketches."

"Blast her impudence," said Phil. "She'll never be able to change the tenner, anyhow."

Happy Dispatches, 1934

Journalism — Places

THE CYCLOON, PADDY CAHILL, AND THE G.R.

Far in the north of Australia lies a little known land, a vast half-finished sort of region, wherein Nature has been apparently practising how to make better places. This is the Northern Territory of South Australia. Britain, it is said, thinks of establishing an Imperial naval station at Port Darwin. But let Britain beware! The Northern Territory has "broke" everybody that ever touched it in any shape or form, and it will break Britain if she meddles with it. The decline and fall of the British Empire will date from the day that Britannia starts to monkey with the Northern Territory.

This vast possession, which extends half way down the Continent of Australia, is not, strictly speaking, a part of the S.A. province. It is a Crown possession, handed over to the Adelaide folk to manage and work for their own loss, and for years they have poured their capital like water into this huge sink. And still, after swallowing two and a half millions of Government money, and Heaven only knows how much private capital, the place is steadily going seventy thousand a year to the bad. Year after year the South Australians have swallowed the same old wheeze about the immense undeveloped resources of "our magnificent Northern Territory", and have hung on pluckily, in the hope of one day getting some of their money back — and possibly also in the fear of the N.T.'s resumption as a Crown colony, an event which would at once be followed by an influx of cheap Asiatics from Britain's Eastern possession. And, in fact, the Territory itself is now clamouring for the introduction of the cheap and nasty Chow, notwithstanding that it is breeding its own Chinky fast enough, in all conscience. The Territory people want more Chows, and would gladly cut loose from South Australia to get them. As for the trifle of two and a half millions that they owe, they would attend to that small matter after the wet season. In the Territory everything good is always going to happen after the wet season.

The capital of the Northern Territory is Palmerston on Port Darwin, a harbour little, if at all, inferior to Port Jackson. Palm-

erston is unique among Australian towns, inasmuch as it is filled
with the boilings over of the great cauldron of Oriental humanity.
Here comes the vagrant and shifting population of all the Eastern
races. Here are gathered together Canton coolies, Japanese pearl-
divers, Malays, Manilamen, Portuguese from adjacent Timor,
Cingalese, Zanzibar niggers looking for billets as stokers, frail
(but not fair) damsels from Kobe; all sorts and conditions of men.
Kipling tells what befell the man who "tried to hustle the East",
but the man who tried to hustle Palmerston would get a knife in
him quick and lively. The Chow and the Jap and the Malay consider themselves quite as good as any alleged white man. In Jap-
town (the Easterner's quarters) Chinese children by the dozen play
about all day long in the dusty streets; gaily-dressed cheerful little
barbarians, revelling in the heat. The goldfields are all worked by
Chinese fossickers about the old alluvial claims; fifty pearling luggers go out every tide, carrying seven hands each, practically all
coloured men — 350 yellow, brown, and brindled vagrants moving backwards and forwards with the tide. And more boats building and more brindle-coloured Japanese arriving every month. To
supply the needs of all these, there are stores of every kind in Jap-
town, and the storekeepers all deal with the East for their supplies.
There is an Eastern flavour over everything; when the Pal-
merstonians went to gamble at the annual races they do it by Cal-
cutta sweeps, an Eastern form of betting little known or practised
elsewhere in Australia.

Palmerston is supported by the pearlers, the goldmines, and the
Government officials. The Overland Telegraph ends at Palmerston and employs a large staff known as the O.T. men; and the
Singapore cable which there leaves Australia, also employs a large
staff of British and Australasian Telegraph ("B.A.T.") officials.
These, with a publican or two, the Government Resident (always
referred to as "the G.R."), a couple of lawyers, a doctor, a few
storekeepers, customs and railway officials and Paddy Cahill, the
buffalo shooter, pretty well make up the white population of a
place upon which the Government has nevertheless squandered
money madly. The huge jetty cost £70,000 and ere it was well finished the teredo had eaten the piles away, and a gigantic crane,
that had just been erected, fell into the water with a mighty splash.

It is there still, but they will get it out "after the wet season". Also, the little tin-pot railway to Pine Creek cost a million and doesn't pay working expenses; and yet S.A. Parliament talks of spending nine millions in prolonging this useless railway down the centre of the continent.

There's a curse on all N.T. undertakings. Private enterprise, as represented by Fisher and Lyons, Dr Brown, and many other "big" men of the past, has poured into it hundreds of thousands of pounds in cattle stocking and so on. What is there to show for it all? When not dead, the cattle are unsaleable, because there are no markets. Not a station in the Territory today would fetch at auction half the money it cost; not a mine in the Territory pay steady interest on its capital. Sugar planting and quinine planting have failed; the blacks now hunt for wild-goose eggs on the lagoons at Sergison's abandoned sugar plantation and the wild buffaloes wallow in the swamps below Beatrice Hills where the quinine was. Once, though, a ray of hope broke the gloom when ruby-like gems were discovered in the MacDonnell ranges. These stones look exactly like rubies, which at their best are far more valuable than diamonds, and as they lay about in any quantity it was thought for a while that the Territory was Saved. A few three-bushel bags were hastily filled with "rubies" and sent to England. Alas, the English experts on examination pronounced them no more than worthless natural simulacra of the ruby. The goldmines were rich down to waterlevel; but there the ore became refractory, and now all the mining is surface. A few market riggers bought a lot of mines from the Chinese for about £17,000 and then, subdivide and water as they like, they are still the same £17,000 worth of Chinese goldmine and apparently not likely to pay interest on even that modest capital. Out in the ranges are all sorts of prospectus claims — some of them good shows; but no one does any work in the Territory. They put everything off till "after the wet season". It is the land of Later On. If a Northern Territory man knew that his mine was full of gold, he would not dig it out. He would sit down and wait for a Chinaman to come along and take it on tribute. If no Chinaman came, he would "send it Home to float". Said one miner, "I'd sooner be in W.A. on one feed a day than be on good gold here. They don't 'elp a man to do nothin' here. If the G.R. would only let us have a Guv'ment battery we might get some stone out and have a crushin'." And there he sat waiting for a Government battery. Waiting — always waiting, that is the typical Northern Territory attitude. The old brisk days have gone; the pushing men have departed; and those who have stayed have got the white-ant in their systems. If the wet season is past, they wait "till the ground dries"; and by the time it is dry they think the next wet season might come early, and they wait!

The government sent up a buoy to mark a dangerous reef. The buoy was taken out with great ceremony, and anchored over the reef, and immediately sank. They didn't get it up again. It is at the bottom of the sea now, and the reef is unmarked. Another buoy got adrift from a dangerous reef; this buoy was cruising about Vernon Straits for some time, but no one fetched it back. When some lepers were discovered at Palmerston once, a leper station was formed at a little island in the harbour, and the lepers were landed there with great precaution, but as soon as the tide went down (it falls 24ft) the lepers calmly waded ashore and returned to town. Nobody bothered any more about them.

There is only one great landmark in Palmerston history — the cyclone which some years ago blew the town down. A lot of it isn't rebuilt yet. This atmospheric disturbance, locally known as "the cycloon" is one of the three topics of conversation in Palmerston; the second is the Government Resident (the G.R.). He is an English barrister, and, in his own person, Supreme Court, Head of the Mining Jurisdiction, Protector of Blacks, and Police Magistrate. No wonder they talk about him. Good man for the position too as he doesn't care a damn for anybody, and, starting from that safe basis, discharges his varied duties with a light heart. The third subject of discussion is Paddy Cahill, the buffalo shooter; he is popularly reported to pursue the infuriated buffalo at full gallop, standing on his saddle, and dressed in a towel and a diamond ring, and yelling like a wild Indian. The trinity of the N.T.; the cycloon, the G.R., and Paddy Cahill! The inhabitants sit about the shady verandas and drink, and talk about one or all of the three. They start drinking square gin immediately after breakfast, and keep it up at intervals till midnight. They don't do anything else to speak of, yet they have a curious delusion that they are a very energetic and reckless set of people. But it's all talk and blasphemy. There is an Act compelling a publican to refuse drink to an habitual inebriate. This is locally known as the "Dog Act" and to be brought under the Dog Act is a glorious distinction, a sort of V.C. of Northern Territory life.

To sum up, the Northern Territory is a vast, wild land, full of huge possibilities, but, up to now, a colossal failure. She has leagues and leagues of magnificent country — with no water. Miles and miles of splendidly watered country where the grass is sour, rank, and worthless. Mines with rich ore that it doesn't pay to treat. Quantities of precious stones that have no value. The pastoral industry and the mines are not paying, and the pearling, which does, is getting too much into Jap hands. The hordes of aliens that have accumulated are a menace to the rest of Australia. Nevertheless, the white folk there are hospitable to a fault. The strangers within their gates never have a dull moment — nor a sober one — if the inhabitants can help it. And, after all the hard things I have written about it, I would give "my weary soul" to be back at Palmerston in that curious lukewarm atmosphere and watch the white-sailed pearling-boats beating out; to see the giant form of Barney Flynn, the buffalo shooter, stalking emu-like through the dwarfish crowd of Japs and Manilamen; to be back once more with the B.A.T. and O.T. and Paddy Cahill and the G.R., while the Cycloon hummed and buzzed on the horizon; or to be in the buffalo-camp with Rees and Martin, shooting big, blue bulls at full gallop, or riding home in the cool moonlight with the packhorses laden with hides.

If you've heard the East a-callin' you don't never heed naught else. And the man who once goes to the Territory always has a hankering to get back there. Some day it will be civilized and spoilt; but up to the present it has triumphantly overthrown all who have attempted to improve it. It is still "the Territory". Long may it wave!

Bulletin, 31 December 1898

THIRSTY ISLAND

Travellers approaching a bush township are sure to find some distance from the town a lonely public-house waiting by the roadside to give them welcome. Thirsty (miscalled Thursday) Island is the outlying pub of Australia.

When the China and British-India steamers arrive from the north the first place they come to is Thirsty island, the sentinel at the gate of Torres Strait. Newchums on the steamers see a fleet of white-sailed pearling luggers, a long pier clustered with a hybrid crowd of every colour, caste, and creed under Heaven, and at the back of it all a little galvanized-iron town shining in the sun.

For nine months of the year, a crisp, cool south-east wind blows, the snow-white beach is splashed with spray and dotted with the picturesque figures of Japanese divers and South Sea Island boatmen. Coconut palms line the roads by the beach, and back of the town are the barracks and a fort nestling among the trees on the hillside. Thirsty Island is a nice place — to look at.

When a vessel makes fast the Thirsty Islanders come down to greet the newcomers and give them welcome to Australia. The newchums are inclined to patronize these simple, outlying people. Fresh from the iniquities of the China-coast cocktail and the unhallowed orgies of the Sourabaya Club, newchums think they have little to learn in the way of drink; at any rate, they haven't come all the way to Thursday Island to be taught anything. Poor newchums! Little do they know the kind of people they are up against.

The following description of a night at Thursday Island is taken from a newchum's note book:

"Passed Proudfoot shoal and arrived at Thursday Island. First sight of Australia. Lot of men came aboard, all called Captain. They are all pearlfishers or pilots, not a bit like the bushmen I expected. When they came aboard they divided into parties. Some invaded the Captain's cabin; others sat in the smoking-room; the rest crowded into the saloon. They talked to the passengers about the Boer War, and told us about pearls worth £1000 that had been found lately.

"One captain pulled a handful of loose pearls out of a jar and handed them round in a casual way for us to look at. The stewards opened bottles and we all sat down for a drink and a smoke. I spoke to one captain — an oldish man — and he grinned amiably, but did not answer. Another captain leaned over to me and said, 'Don't take any notice of him, he's boozed all this week.'

"Conversation and drink became general. The night was very hot and close, and some of the passengers seemed to be taking more than was good for them. A contagious thirst spread round the ship, and before long the stewards and firemen were at it. The saloon became an inferno of drink and sweat and tobacco smoke. Perfect strangers were talking to each other at the top of their voices.

"Young MacTavish, who is in a crack English regiment, asked the captain of a pearling lugger whether he didn't know Talbot de Cholmondeley in the Blues.

"The pearler said very likely he had met 'em, and no doubt he'd remember their faces if he saw them, but he never could remember names.

"Another passenger — a Jew — was trying to buy some pearls cheap from the captains, but the more the captains drank the less anxious they became to talk about pearls.

"The night wore on, and still the drinks circulated. Young MacTavish slept profoundly.

"One passenger gave his steward a sovereign as he was leaving the ship, and in half an hour the steward was carried to his berth in a fit — alcoholic in its origin. Another steward was observed openly drinking the passenger's whisky. When accused, he didn't even attempt to defend himself; the great Thursday Island thirst seemed to have communicated itself to everyone on board, and he simply *had* to drink.

About three in the morning a tour of the ship disclosed the following state of affairs: Captain's room full of captains solemnly tight; smoking-room empty, except for the inanimate form of the captain who had been boozed all the week, and was now sleeping peacefully with his feet on the sofa and his head on the floor. The saloon was full of captains and passengers — the latter mostly in a state of collapse or laughing and singing deliriously; the rails lined with firemen who had business over the side; stewards ditto.

"At last the Thursday Islanders departed, unsteadily, but still on their feet, leaving a demoralized ship behind them. And young MacTavish, who has seen a thing or two in his brief span, staggered to his berth, saying 'My God! Is *all* Australia like this place?"

When no ships arrive, the Islanders just drop into the pubs, as a matter of routine, for their usual evening soak. They drink weird compounds — horehound beer, known as "lady dog", and things like that. About two in the morning they go home speechless, but still able to travel. It is very rarely that an Islander gets helplessly drunk, but strangers generally have to be put to bed.

The Japanese on the island are a strong faction. They have a club of their own, and once gave a dinner to mark the death of one of their members. He was shrewdly suspected of having tried to drown another member by cutting his air-pipe, so, when he died, the club celebrated the event. The Japanese are not looked upon with favour by the white islanders. They send their money to Japan — thousands of pounds a year go through the little office in money-orders — and so they are not "good for trade".

The Manilamen and Kanakas and Torres Strait islanders, on the other hand, bring all the money they do not spend on the pearling schooner to the island, and "blow it in", like men. They knife each other sometimes, and now and again have to be run in wholesale, but they are "good for trade". The local lock-up has a record of eighteen drunks run in in seven minutes. They weren't taken along in carriages-and-four, either; they were mostly dragged along by the scruff of the neck.

Billy Malkeela, the South Sea diver, summed up the Japanese question — "Seems to me dis Islan' soon b'long Japanee altogedder. One time pa-lenty rickatta (plenty regatta), all same Isle of Wight. Now no more rickatta. All money go Japan!"

An English newchum made his appearance there lately — a most undefeated sportsman. He was put down in a diving dress in about eight feet of water, where he bubbled and struggled about in great style. Suddenly he turned, rushed for the beach, and made for the foot of a tree, which he tried to climb under the impression that he was still at the bottom of the ocean Then he was hauled in by the life-line.

The pearlers thought to get some fun out of him by giving him an oyster to open in which they have previously planted a pearl; he never saw the pearl and threw the oyster into the scuppers with the rest, and the pearlers had to go down on all fours and grope for that pearl among the stinking oysters. It was funny — but not in the way they had intended.

The pearlers go out in schooners called floating stations (their enemies call them floating public-houses) and no man knows what hospitality is till he has been a guest on a pearling schooner. They carry it to extremes sometimes. Some pearlers were out in a lugger, and were passing by one of these schooners. They determined not to go on board, as it was late, and they were in a hurry. The captain of the schooner went below, got his rifle and put two bullets through their foresail. Then they put the helm down and went aboard; it was an invitation almost equivalent to a royal command. They felt heartily ashamed of themselves as they slunk up on deck, and the captain of the schooner eyed them reproachfully.

"I couldn't let you disgrace yourselves by passing my schooner," he said; "but if it ever happens again I'll fire at the deck. A man that would pass a schooner in broad daylight is better dead."

There is a fort and garrison at Thirsty Island, but they are not needed. If an invading fleet comes this way it should be encouraged by every possible means to land at the island; the heat, the thirst, the horehound beer, and the Islanders may be trusted to do the rest.

Bulletin, 5 April 1902

PEARLING INDUSTRY AT THURSDAY ISLAND: A DAY ON A LUGGER

The schooner *Tarawa* is lying at anchor in Endeavour Straits, just opposite the place where Captain Cook landed. Around her, like chickens round a hen, are anchored her fleet of a dozen pearling luggers. The sea is as smooth as glass, and there is a constant clatter of rowlocks and splash of paddles as the black boys row the little dinghies from lugger to lugger, laughing and chattering with their countrymen; "go walkabout" they call it. The sun strikes down dazzlingly on the white sand of Possession Island, and the hills of the Australian mainland are wrapped in a blue haze; on the beach a crowd of black men are disporting themselves, swimming and racing and shouting with laughter.

On the luggers the Japanese divers — serious little men — are overhauling their gear, and round the schooner there is a cluster of small boats, because it is refitting season, and every lugger wants something — either a new diver's dress, or a new sail, or a new anchor, or a new meat cask, or some other item. The clerk of the stores on the schooner consults with the captain as each demand is made, but no reasonable thing is ever refused, because a diver will not work with bad gear; so that to be sparing of stores is false economy. By degrees some of the luggers are fully fitted out ready for work, and they are ordered to go out and fish until the rest of the fleet are ready, when they will all move off together to the pearling grounds out by Radhu Island or down the coast. A slight breeze springs up, and at once there is a clinking of pawls, a rattle of chain, and the creaking of blocks as the anchors are got up and the sails set in the luggers that are ready for sea, and away the little white-sailed vessels go, each with its crew of happy black faces forward and its serious little Japanese diver at the helm. The diver is always the captain of the lugger, and there are matters of etiquette in connection with pearl-diving which the outsider finds it hard to grasp. The diver, for instance, never rows a dinghy. If he wishes to visit the schooner or another lugger one of the crew has to pull the dinghy for him; also the diver and "tender" sleep aft in a tiny little cabin the size of a dog kennel, while the crew live forward under the half-deck. Among the luggers ready for sea is the *Pearl*, commanded by Billy Makeela, a South Sea islander who has been diving for 25 years, and on this lugger the stranger is sent out to see how the pearl oyster is obtained.

On coming aboard he finds the lugger to be a 10-ton vessel of beautiful yacht-like lines, and, indeed, some of these luggers are designed by the best designers in Australia. The sails are white and the gear in good order. Billy Makeela makes us welcome in a stately way. He is very black, and his only clothing is a dirty loin cloth, but that is his service equipment. When he goes ashore in parade order he is majestic, and Solomon in all his glory is not arrayed like Billy Makeela. As this is only a short trip to kill time till the other luggers are ready, Billy has taken with him his wife, Balu, a native of the Torres Straits. Balu is very black, but very comely; she is about 30 years younger than Billy, and is clothed in a white print dress which she got at the mission station. She can read or write English, but the unaccustomed surroundings make her shy, and as the lugger moves off the old primeval instincts overcome her civilised training, and as Billy squats down by the helm she crouches submissively behind him, holding on to his shoulders, with her nose buried in the small of his back, and all that one can see of her is the back of a round, woolly head. As the boat "goes about" and Billy shifts across the deck she shuffles over with him, never looking up and never letting go his shoulders. It is the primeval woman trusting blindly the skill of the primeval man. The lugger bends over to the breeze till her lee rail is under water and the spray comes flying aboard. The crew forward consists of four Torres Straits Islanders — fine specimens of humanity. The Torres Straits islanders are a compound of the Australian black, the Malay, and the South Sea islander; they are born natural boatmen and as much at home in the water as the dugong which they occasionally hunt to death. They have great contempt for the "Binghies", or Australian aboriginals. These boys on the Pearl are missionary-trained boys, but as soon as the lugger is fairly under they go below and begin to play cards. Two of them are brothers of Balu, so that it is quite a family party.

They are dressed in cheap pyjama trousers, "*et preterea nihil*".* Aft with Billy and his wife sits Joe, the Portuguese tender, who has to attend to Billy's life-line. Joe has been a steward on various vessels, and has been in more parts of the world than the Wandering Jew. He confides to us that "Dis Billy'e altogether good diver. 'E get shell on de reef. Dose Japanese dey walk over it; dey do not see it." As a matter of fact, the Malays and islanders have more natural hunter-craft than the Japanese, and they can find shell in the reefs and under rocky ledges; but for sheer hard work the Japanese is their master, and he will out work them on open bottoms.

We thresh our way to the "old ground" — a large area of open sea about eight fathoms deep — and here Billy studies his land-

---

* [Latin]: "beyond that nothing".

marks by the neighbouring islands and studies the look of the water. At last he orders, "Stan' by foresail. Down foresail. Down mainsail. Down jib. Let go!" and the anchor goes over with a couple of turns of chain round the fluke, so that it will allow the lugger to drift. Billy dresses rapidly with the assistance of Joe, the tender. The dress is canvas and indiarubber, with great heavy lead-soled boots, a corslet of great weight, gun-metal helmet and two lead weights to hang over the shoulders. A man can only just move with this gear on him. Billy stands on the ladder, half in the water, two of the black boys set to work at the pump, and the plumb line is thrown over. This is sent down so that the diver may keep hold of it and see what sort of bottom he is coming to. If he chanced to find that he was descending just over a big valley in the bottom of the sea, or among jagged rocks likely to foul his line, he could hold on to the plumb line and reconnoitre the bottom before finally descending.

Joe screws the face-plate into the helmet and Billy suddenly throws himself backward with a loud splash into the water, and sinks slowly — a grim, uncanny object descending through the blue water. Joe, the Portuguese tender, holds the life-line, one of the boys holds the air pipe to prevent its drifting and fouling, and a smother of white bubbles coming up in the lee of the lugger shows where Billy is walking along beneath us. Balu, his wife, is not concerned at her husband's peril; she takes little interest in the dress or the descent, but stares fascinated at her two brothers, who are methodically turning the air pump. The revolution of the handles and the rise and fall of the cylinders seem to her much more wonderful than the diving dress. Meanwhile from below Billy is talking through the rope to Joe, the Portuguese tender. Two sharp vicious pulls come, and Joe calls over his shoulder to the two boys at the pump, "More air," and the boys make the handles fairly spin for a few moments, to Balu's great admiration. Then four distinct tugs, and Joe calls to the forward hand, "Haul up; li'll piece more chain. Dat'll do." For Billy has seen a shell out of his reach, and wants the lugger to drift over to it. Then a shake on the line, and Joe calls sharply, "Slack up chain"; for evidently Billy has got on to a patch and wants the boat's pace retarded. Thus the lugger drifts for nearly an hour, the signalling going on all the time, when suddenly there comes one sharp pull, and Joe calls, "Haul up"; it is curious what a different tone is impressed into the "haul up", because if the other orders are muddled it only means the loss of a shell or two, but "haul up" may mean that the diver is in trouble, and "haul up" must be obeyed at once. Down below, Billy, having been down long enough, has decided to come up, so he closes the escape valve of the helmet, and the confined air fills his dress, and as Joe and the boy with the air pipe haul away, Billy suddenly floats to the top about 20 years from the lugger, a ghastly, sprawling, bloated sea-monster; his huge uncanny helmet is face down, half buried in the water; the air has filled his dress till it looks as though his body were swollen out of all proportion of humanity; his legs and arms sprawl feebly like the limbs of some wounded animal. This gruesome object is hauled alongside, and the stranger is quite sure that some accident has happened and the diver is dying. Once alongside he clutches the ladder and hands up his little open basket full of shells. Then the face-plate is unscrewed, he is helped on the deck, and the lugger sails away, with Joe at the helm, to another ground, while Billy sits on deck in his diver's dress and smokes and tells stories of the old days "before dem Japanese come".

Arrived at the new ground Billy dives for another hour or so, and while he is down the shells are inspected by the strangers. They are the size of a fruit plate, covered with weed and coral growths. The smaller oysters are always attached by a strong green ligament to some object — a piece of rock or piece of coral — but this ligament dies as the oyster gets older. The shells are opened in the lugger on this occasion only — by rule they should be brought to the schooner unopened. Inside each shell is a fish more like a squid than an ordinary oyster, and with the fish there lives on terms of great amity a small reddish-coloured lobster about an inch long, and a small crab about a quarter of an inch in diameter. These there seem to agree well with each other. The pearls, if any, are visible among the fringe of the oyster's beard, but occasionally they are hidden among the oyster's anatomy.

On the long cruises, when the schooner and her fleet are out for months at a time, it is the rule for the schooner to send her collecting boat, a half-decked 20-footer, round the luggers every second

day at least, if it be at all possible. But sometimes the weather is
bad, and the luggers have got a long way from the schooner, and
the shell may be a week or more on the luggers before it is collected. Then the heat of the sun makes the oysters open and the
deft little Japanese fingers soon pick out any pearls that may be
visible. Sometimes an oyster is induced to open by being held near
the galley fire on the lugger, and once open is kept open by the in-
sertion of a piece of cork, while the pearl, if any, is hooked out by
a piece of wire. Then the cork is removed and the oyster closes
again as good as ever. Sometimes the bumping in the collecting
boat shakes the pearl out of an oyster that is just a little open, and
when these boats are washed out a careful search for pearls is always made among the bottom-boards. Fancy getting a pearl worth
a thousand pounds drifting about among the slime and rubbish at
the bottom of a dinghy!

One great difficulty is keeping the boats in water. In the tropics a
lot of water is wanted, and it is always carried in canvas bags . . .

By great persuasion, Billy Makeela is induced to allow the
stranger to go down in eight fathoms. Billy is not encouraging. He
says, "I frighten let you down. S'posin' anything go wrong; you
die queek!" At eight fathoms the pressure is severe for a beginner;
the blood is crushed out of the body into the head, but the severe
feeling of oppression vanishes after a time. The floor of the ocean
lies level and flat, studded with knobs of coral and patches of grey-
ish weed. Here and there are clusters of marine growths, and a few
shells lie about on the bottom. The diver can see some 10 or 15
yards apparently, and beyond that all is an opaque mist; small fish
come and look in at the eye holes of the helmet; the novice feels
oppressed by the weight of the water, and blunders along, feeling
as though he were held back by some invisible power as he tries to
walk. The mud rises as he moves, and beyond him stretches always
the level sand floor and all round him the oppressive opaque mist.
He feels like a very small and insignificant fish in a very large
aquarium. After 10 minutes' search, he finds one shell, and is
hauled up by the anxious Billy. Then the lugger is headed for the
schooner; the dress is turned inside out and hung up to dry. Joe
and the black boys lie down and smoke, while Balu makes a fire in
the little iron fire-place bedded in some earth in a box in the well of

the lugger and makes tea, while Billy sails the lugger back. One boy goes up in the rigging to look out for reefs, and thus we get back to the Straits just as the soft tropical darkness shuts out the islands and the mainland, and leaves only the schooner's lights to show the way.

Billy will have to leave Australia under the new legislation but it does not trouble him much; he and his wife are simple people, and back in his own island he can get "plenty banana" without any such arduous work as diving; but having once risen above the savage scale of existence he is not likely to go back home; he is most likely to go to New Guinea and get employment on Dutch boats, and become a South Sea Dutchman — a sort of coloured Van Tromp of the ocean bed.

Sydney Mail, 17 May 1902

HUMOURS OF A HORSE BAZAAR

The business of the bazaar begins at daylight. Overnight the stalls have been cleaned up, fresh straw put down, and neat tan rides laid on the ashphalt, and at daylight the stable hands are off to meet horses arriving by trains and steamers — terrified, bewildered horses, rushed hurriedly in from their grass paddocks and hustled on board of coasting craft, with the long swell of the ocean swaying before their astonished eyes, and a chattering, old-fashioned steam which making a terrifying din just alongside them. Or else they have been crushed and jammed into a railway truck, bumped off their feet each time that the engine shunted, and frightened half out of their lives each time that a screaming, flying monster of a passenger train rushed past with a dizzying, nerve-destroying roar and rattle. No wonder that by the time they arrive in Sydney the country horses have become dazed, and the stable hands go in among them in the yards or on the steamers, pushing them about in a style that makes the uninitiated wonder how it is that some of those men don't get their brains kicked out every week. But the men know that to be afraid is the surest way to make the horses afraid, so they push them about like so many old cows, and before long the string are clattering up to the bazaar, each horseman riding one horse and leading two or three others, each

horse being tied to his mate's neck. Then they are hosed and
cleaned, a process that would startle the life out of them, only that
they have been through so much already, and then they are put
into the stalls ready for the day's sale.

After breakfast the town horses begin to arrive — the dealer's
horses, who are passed from hand to hand; "swell" horses, who,
perhaps through overfeeding, have become too flash for their
owners, and are sent in to be sold for what they will fetch;
carthorses, sold by hard-up men, who have given up any hope of
making a living at their work; race ponies that cannot race fast
enough to win, or else that have got themselves so much up in the
weights that they are no longer valuable; gigantic draughts and
small boys' ponies, all come threading their way in, and take up
their positions in the stalls. The vehicles, too, begin to arrive — the
sulky of the broken-down sport, with the flash trotting pony in the
shafts; the four-wheeled buggy, with lamps and hood, and a
sturdy old slave attached to it; the traveller's waggon, with two
road-worn, wiry, long-distance horses in the pole, and the
splotches of the Darling River mud still on the wheels and under-
gear.

All sorts and conditions of horses and vehicles find their way to
the bazaar; and as they arrive the regular attendants at the sales —
the dealers and exporters, and buyers with commissions to execute
— drop in, too, and walk round the stalls scrutinising each horse.
Some they dismiss with half a glance; while others are carefully inspected, their legs felt, their mouths opened, their eyes looked at,
and their feet picked up. As each possible buyer examines a horse
there gathers round a little group of the bazaar hangers-on, the
human flotsam and jetsam that attend each day at the sales. They
never buy anything; they never even bid for anything; but day in
and day out they are there scrutinising the horses, watching the
sales, and criticising the wisdom or folly of each purchase. They
are mostly broken-down men that have been in racing stables or
have been horse dealers or coachmen.

From long practice they can tell to within half a sovereign what
each animal should fetch, but if they see a novice examining a
horse they always make out that the animal is first-class and
should be secured at all risks. This is known as "bearing up" for

the owner of the horse, and is done in hopes that the owner may come along and reward them with a beer, though it sometimes has quite another effect, as the following anecdote will show. A dealer was trying to sell to a novice a pony for saddle work, and was talking hard, trying to convince him that the pony was all that could be desired, but the buyer thought that the pony was too heavy, and said, "He'd make a nice buggy pony." A casual passer-by happened to hear this last sentence, and seeing that a "deal" was going on, he dashed into the fray with enthusiasm. "Buggy pony," he said, "why, o' course he's a champion buggy pony! What else is he but a buggy pony? He ain't one of those all-sorts-no-sort 'orses! He's a buggy pony and nothin' else." "That's just it," said the buyer. "I want a saddle pony." The dealer was naturally, a bit put out, and he turned on the "casual" in style. "Why can't you keep your mouth shut?" he said. "What business have you comin' puttin' your oar in?" "Well, Bill, I was only bearin' up for you," said the poor casual humbly, and the deal was declared off.

As the forenoon wears on, a good crowd has collected. The casuals, the dealers, the sporting men who buy for India, have gathered together. The auctioneer mounts his box, and after hammering on the sides of it for a time to attract attention, he starts the sale.

The earlier lots are nearly always equine derelicts, poor old worn-out horses shifting uneasily from one infirm limb to another; "radicals" that have been starved and bullied into some kind of submission, eyeing the crowd with hostile glance; showy cripples that surprise the onlooker by their apparent cheapness. All these are offered at the start of the sale, and are dealt in almost exclusively by a few dealers who know where they can place their purchases at a profit — possibly with rabbit-oh vendors. Now and again among those cast-offs one sees an old horse of good type, whose strong constitution and iron limbs have been proof against all the assaults of starvation, overwork and ill-treatment. Such a one only wants feeding and fair working to become once more a valuable horse; but, as a rule, the early lots do not contain many of this description. The saleyard crowd do not pay much attention to these derelicts, but when a start is made with the advertised lots there is a closing in, and dealer and loafer, swell and bearer-up, all alike gather to inspect, to criticise, and perhaps to bid. Then it is that the *cognoscenti* get in their fine work. A horse is brought out and ridden up and down at a great pace, with much shouting, whip-cracking, and general flourish. A small group of buyers stands looking on, and from the moment that the animal appears, each buyer's eye at once fastens on his weak spot. Perhaps it is a slightly enlarged fetlock; perhaps the mark of an old blister; perhaps an incipient curb on the hock. Whatever it may be, it is safe to say that ninety out of every hundred in the bazaar will have noticed it before the horse has gone ten paces. The odd ten will be the non-professional buyers who have just dropped in to see if they can pick up a twenty-pound horse for a tenner — a thing that they invariably persuade themselves they have done till they try to realise their bargain. And it is this anxiety on the part of the public to get twenty-pound horses for tenners that leads to all the lying and chicanery of the horse trade. A dealer always says his horse is worth double what he is asking for him, because he knows that the would-be-sharp purchaser will not buy unless he thinks he is getting twice the value of his money. To the expert, the bazaar value of each horse is as definite as the value of a bale of wool to a wool buyer, and the guileless novice must remember that if he likes to go to the bazaar and buy at the dealer's price, he must also take the dealer's risk. The auctioneer will tell him what the owner represents the horse to be, the trials promised must be performed, and from then on the buying is easy, because, as a sale ring Solon put it: "You've only to nod your head, and you can find out afterwards what you've got."

Evening News, 3 December 1904

OVERLAND TO MELBOURNE

1

We're away! And the wind whistles shrewd
    In our whiskers and teeth,
And the granite-like grey of the road
    Seems to glide underneath;

As an eagle might sweep through the skies,
    We sweep through the land,
And the pallid pedestrian flies
    When he hears us at hand.

We outpace, we outlast, we outstrip.
    Not the fast-fleeing hare,
Nor the racehorses under the whip,
    Nor the birds of the air
Can compete with our swiftness sublime,
    Our ease and our grace;
We annihilate chickens, and time,
    And policemen and space.

There is nothing very granite-like about the roads in Australia — worse luck. Ruts and loose metal, sidelings, and sand-drifts, washed-out creeks and heart-breaking hills — these are the items on the bill of fare before the cars that start on the reliability trial to Melbourne tomorrow. If an English or French automobilist were told that a "reliability" trial in Australia consisted in running six hundred miles in five days on a main public road between two capital cities, at sixteen miles an hour, running time, if he were told that this constituted a "reliability" trial, he wouldn't see where the "trial" came in. On English or Continental roads such a trial would be a mockery, as every car would get full marks, and as for sixteen miles an hour, they wouldn't call that motoring; they would only call it oozing along. They would tell you that a good motorist ought to be able to get out and push the car as fast as that. But if the same English or Continental motorist had a look at our roads he would whistle softly and would withdraw his car. In those old-fashioned places they don't care about racking a car to pieces by teaching it to jump down the side of a hill from one rock to another.

And right here it is worth while to say a little about motoring in England. The roads in England require to be seen to be believed. Even narrow little country lanes, overhung by great oaks, and littered ankle-deep in leaves, even these have a surface as smooth as glass, whereon the motorist can let her out to his heart's content, drawing the leaves and dust in a whirlwind after him. Down about Brighton, which is the happy hunting ground of the London motorist, in dry weather each car flies along, raising a cloud of dust that moves like the pillar of fire that guided the Israelites, but a trifle faster. And it is just the excellence of the roads that has made the motorist so unpopular in England. When a man has got a machine under him that can travel at thirty miles an hour and a good road to run her on, it isn't human nature to throttle her down to six miles an hour. So they let her out, and the Bumbles and Parish Council prosecute and fine them relentlessly, planting policemen in hedges to take the time of the flying motors from one milestone to another; and the motor clubs pay men to track out these policemen and to stand outside their hiding places and wave a red flag, so that the motorist can see where the danger lies and can slow up in time.

In rural England they do not love the motorist. The local squire, who has never been hurried in his life, is condescending to cross the village street at his usual leisurely strut, when "Booh! booh! whizz!" — a motor is all but over him, and he has to skip in a very undignified way for the sidewalk if he wishes to save his precious life. Giles Jollyfowl, the farmer, taking a load of maure home, sleeps peaceably on top of his load as usual, and lets the old horses go their own way. Next thing there is an appalling whizz, and a racing Panhard or Gladiator tears past like a long streak through the atmosphere, the old horses wheel round, and rush off the road, and Giles Jollyfowl finds himself in the ditch, with his load of manure on top of him. That is why the English papers are full of complaints against motorists. They don't like being hurried in England. But the motorist is a good deal to blame, for a sort of professional pride exists among gentlemen motorists and their chauffeurs, and it considered de rigueur to drive full speed just where the traffic is thickest, to cut corners by the merest hairbreadth, to graze vehicles as closely as possible in passing — just to teach them to give a bit more room another time — and, above all, always to pass a traffic constable so close as almost to shave the buttons off his uniform. They are great people for "the correct thing" in England, and "the correct thing" in motoring is to make all created things step lively when you are on the road.

And how will it be with the overland to Melbourne trip? The Australian is not so conservative as the Englishman, and the only objection to the cars is that they frighten horses; but the Australian looks upon a race of any sort as a sacred thing — all business and public interests must be suspended in favour of a race, so that the cars on the reliability trial are being warmly welcomed, and a country Mayor is actually going to entertain the motorist in his public capacity. In England, he would take all their names and "summons" them.

A Sydney car had a trial run as far as Picton and back last Saturday. Roads were not bad; but how they will be for eighteen or twenty cars, if it is dusty, goodness only knows. However, sufficient unto the day is the evil thereof. It's no good anticipating trouble, as they told the steeplechase rider who wanted to know whether the horse he had to ride could jump the fences or not. "You will find that out," they said, "as you go along." So we will, no doubt, find out a good deal between here and Melbourne.

Cras ingens iterabimus aequor. Tomorrow we start on a reliability trial, as our old friend Horace used to say.

2

When a friend asked me to go in a motor-car trip to Melbourne, and said that over twenty cars were going, I had an idea that the whole commando would go together, and visions arose of a horde of motors flying along in clouds of dust, hooting like fiends in torment. But such expectations were agreeably disappointed. The cars were dispatched at intervals of three minutes or so — enough to put about a mile between each car — and there seemed to be little or no closing up in the running. The motor-cycles started first, and went spluttering and shaking their way along at a great pace, each rider's head nodding over the handles like the head of a Chinese Mandarin. Every man to his taste, of course, but I am of opinion that the man who would ride a motor-cycle for pleasure, would go to the infernal regions for pastime. Anyhow, these get away first each day, then the light cars, and then the heavy cars. After a few miles, one begins to come up with the motor-cyclists — mostly camped by the roadside, mending something.

One such unfortunate hailed us with a frenzied appeal for petrol, and he was so pathetically anxious to get along that our driver stopped and gave him a lot, though he risked losing points by delay. This is written at Goulburn after the first day's run, and at time of writing only about half the motor-cyclists have showed up. The rest are scattered far and wide, by mount, and stream, and gully. One of the first to get in was so elated with his success that he told us, ''it was dead easy; he had time to have stopped at every pub if he'd liked''. The others, who have not arrived, would probably have a different tale to tell.

As a rule, one sees very little of the other cars. Sometimes on climbing a hill there appears far ahead a little doll-like vehicle climbing the next hill, flying for dear life, with two little bunched-up figures sitting in it. Then after a hill or two the big horse-power begins to tell, and though all cars can go much the same pace down a hill, the up-hill grades bring back the low-powered cars, and while a twenty-four horse-power will stride up a hill without turning a hair, the little cars have to use their lowest speed and go up slowly, clattering like threshing machines.

As one car overhauls another the leader is bound to give room to pass, and so far there has been nothing but the best of good-fellowship over it. The car that is leading, if it carries on to a bit of dangerous road, will signal to the car behind, the signal being given by a vigorous waving of arms. Whether this brotherly love will continue all the way remains to be seen. The amateurs who are competing do not particularly care whether they are in first or not, so long as they get in by the specified time, but the agents of various cars are anxious to get in first, and there may be a little more rivalry later on.

Though it is all right overtaking a car, it is a different thing when you hear ''toot, toot'' behind you, and you have to pull to one side to let a car go by. It was much more annoying to us than to the surprised swagman upon whom we came suddenly. We had to let the French (Brasier) car with the French driver go by, and he was letting her spin, too. He is said to have won a Grand National, or something equivalent to it, in France. But nothing could catch the Darracq that is driven by the Melbourne agent for those cars. He said he came through with his spark retarded (I think that is the right expression) but the other drivers don't altogether accept the statement. In fact, the motorist is just like the hunting man that always jumps the biggest fence. Each motorist, by his own account, has used less petrol and less spark, and has been in bigger ruts and his car has jumped higher and side-slipped more than any other car. It is quite a new language that has to be learnt — something like golf language — when one goes motoring.

There is an awful bit of luck about it, too. The car that the writer was in hit nothing, jumped nothing, and picked up nothing. Another car picked up two nails — punctures each time, and blew out a tube once by plunging into an unexpected washaway. Next day the luck may be reversed. At time of writing, it is said that the only car driven by a lady, is stuck in a river, about four miles from anywhere; but this, like many other rumours, may be disproved later on.

In a previous article, reference was made to the sacredness of a race in Australian eyes. We had abundant evidence of it in this run. Everywhere the people cheered the cars on, even though their children and poultry were snatched by hairsbreadths from untimely graves. Men ran to show us the turnings, and volunteered the information, "He's just ahead of you! Go at him! You've got him!" as if they were cheering on a friend in a foot race. None of the cars did any racing — the road is too bad for that, but occasionally, in stretches of good road, one could "let her out" a bit, and then it really was enjoyable. Occasionally a horse will object to us, but nothing serious in this way has so far happened.

It is only now and again that you get the full advantages that motoring can offer. When you get a bit of really good road, clear away as far as you can see — smooth gravel for choice — and the car is at her best, the engine working with a rhythmic hum, but everything else as noiseless as the tomb, and you feel her answer to every least touch of acceleration, while the milestones slip past one after another in surprisingly rapid fashion, and you put the watch on her and find she is doing thirty miles an hour, and only sauntering along at that — then one knows for a few brief minutes what motoring really is. But when the smooth-looking stretch of road is constantly crossed by the apparently harmless waterways that rack and jolt the car two or three feet in the air, if you let her rush into them; or when the hills are long and steep, and dusty, and loose metal lies thickly, and she doesn't seem to answer properly when you liven her up a little, that is the depressing side of the sport. But one gets a glorious rush through fresh air, laden with scent of half-dry gum-leaves, and sees the homesteads flying past, and catches glimpses of far-off blue hills and deep gullies, that make the ride worth having, even if there were no race or trial at all. The car is like an untiring horse, that breasts the hills gallantly and then flies away again as fresh as ever on each stretch of smooth road.

There is not much intercolonial jealousy among the competitors, though three States are represented. Motorists are cosmopolitans and the only rivalry is as to the make of the car. American, German, English, and French workshops have turned out their best work to enable us to fly through Australia a little faster than we could otherwise do. And the various owners — Australian, English, or foreign — think only of their cars. It is a contest of foreigners. The chauffeur is more important than the driver. To compare it with horseracing, the driver is the jockey, while the chauffeur is the trainer. The driver must take the risk of sending her along, must save every bit of bad road, and let her out on the level, and a lot depends on his skill, nerve, and judgment. But the chauffeur has to know by the slightest sound if anything is wrong, and he must know what is wrong. If any stoppage occurs and he takes an hour to find out what is the matter, then the best driving in the world can't serve him. Anyone with a little skill in steering, or fair share of pluck, and a quick decision, can drive and perhaps drive well, but it takes years of training to make a man a really first-class chauffeur.

By common consent, breeches and gaiters similar to those used for riding, seem to be adopted as the correct motor costume. Add to these a high-peaked cap, a white macintosh, a pair of awful goggles, and possibly a mask with a false leather nose, and you have some idea of the visitors who are stirring up the City of Goulburn at the time of writing.

There is a famous expression used by Mark Twain in the *Innocents Abroad* — "We made Rome howl." That is just what the motorists are doing here. They are making Goulburn howl. From 11.52, when H.L. Steven's Darracq car rushed into Goulburn ahead of the ruck, up till 4 p.m., the main street has been blocked by a singing, jabbering, mass of small boys, agriculturalists, and local oracles, all explaining to each other all about motor-cars. As each fresh car comes in there is a wild rush, and the small boys push each other nearly under the wheels, and just as the throng is thickest a Yankee driver, with a face like granite, sends two thousand pounds' weight of priceless mechanism in amongst them, and the mob scatters and drifts up and down the street, fingering the cars that are waiting by the roadside filling up and making adjustments before being handed over. Each fresh chauffeur is a thing of less beauty than the last, and Goulburn has not got reconciled to their peaked caps, their goggles, and their iron features. One hears of bicycle face. Motor face is the same, but a good deal harder. Concentrated watchfulness is the essence of the motor face — the watchfulness of the man who may hit a drain, or take a side-slip and spin off the road at any moment and land in the ditch with a lot of nearly red-hot machinery on top of him. They say the crack drivers in the old country have to be in full training to do one of their long speed runs, and when one sees the wreck that can be made by the hundredth of a second's carelessness, one can easily believe it.

So far everything has worked all right, and the officials are in high good humour. Tomorrow we strike worse roads, deeper washaways, and steeper grades. We go through Gunning and Yass. At the former town the residents asked that the cars should be allowed to go through full speed, so that they might see a race. But the only Yass resident yet met with said cautiously, "Well, look out yer don't run over some of my crossbred ewes!" But, undismayed by bad roads, big hills, and crossbred ewes, we point her nose for Gundagai in the morning, and only hope that she will eat up the miles till we get there.

3

It is a "reliability" trial sure enough. The second day's run was enough to fix that in the minds of the competitors. Eighteen miles an hour over bush roads tries the best car, and there is a lot of luck needed to get through. The extra speed necessitates driving for all she is worth on the level, and if the level happens to be bisected by a drain, you haven't time to step out; must just bump over it. The result is that constant bumping and straining weakens the axles, and the wheels begin to lean in towards each other. Quite three-fourths of the competing cars are "developing bowed tendons" as the racing men would say. The axles are all bending a little. And coming round sharp curves through loose metal causes a side strain that sooner or later tells on the wheels. Two cars today — Messrs Rand's and Langford's — pulled their wheels right off. Of course, an occasional "interesting adventure with cattle" is met with, but nothing of a serious character.

In fact, disasters began early, as the lady competitor — Mrs Thompson — got into difficulties soon after leaving Goulburn. The French demon driver, who has so far formed the chief topic of conversation on the trip, came to some sort of grief at Gunning. We passed him, but, as Mr Jorrocks says, the pace was too good to inquire. From Goulburn to Yass you get the best bit of road we have seen so far; and being delayed soon after the start, we had to make the most of that bit of road.

In an English magazine lately appeared a picture of a car going at full racing pace. It is called the delirium of speed. The last car to leave on each day has some such sensation. With all the others ahead, and with a perfectly clear road and good grades, the driver bends over his wheel, and, so long as the road is clear ahead, he lets her rip. Hill after hill, level after level, we flying behind, till at last a car is sighted in front, and then the driver knows that he is holding his place. it is a good deal like "picking up the wheel" of a racing cyclist; but when once the cars have settled to work it becomes a terrible nerve-straining contest against time. The motorist must have one eye on the watch and the other on the road. The other cars are almost sympathized with, as they, too, have their struggle against the common enemy. And as the bad roads are met, signals pass from car to car, and warnings are shouted as cars pass each other.

During the run the people whom we have met have, as a rule, taken an agreeable interest in the race. There was one exception, who cursed us with great fluency.

Gunning went by like a flash. Yass, full of people, had a lovely road for eight miles or so on either side of it, and the Victorians, who had driven their cars over, had a big advantage, as they knew where they could safely "let her out". At Jugiong they were holding a race meeting, the march of civilization having as yet made no mark on Jugiong. The Murrumbidgee was running yellow, probably with melted snow-water from the mountains. And then we plunged again into the stringybark ranges. By the way, though the guide-book issued by the Dunlop company says that there is a "nice drop down" to Jugiong, the road we struck nearly landed us in Jugiong in one jump from the top of an adjoining hill, as the metalled road suddenly ceased, and the unmade track nearly led to disaster. But after Jugiong we got out into the good flats about Colac, and so on to Gundagai, all good country and good road.

Incidents were few and far between today. J.M. Arnott's big Innes car passed all the small cars on the hills, and as she is fitted for touring and carries three passengers and a lot of luggage, it is a good performance for the Sydney-owned haste wagon. The next stage they say will try the cars more thoroughly than anything yet met with. Stevens, in his Darracq, again headed the procession, and as things now are, with the Frenchman and Rand out of it, looks like a well-deserved win for the Darracq. But there is a lot of road between here and Melbourne, and already the drivers are offering to bet that not half-a-dozen cars finish.

Gundagai to Albury was the hardest of the three days in the New South Wales ride, and it was hard enough for any one. The metalled road ceases soon after Gundagai, and the track is an ordinary bush affair, rusty and dusty, and the bushfires had burnt nearly all the culverts.

The Sydney cars did badly on this part of the run. Mark Foy's Panhard car got along all right, but he is only out for an airing, and is very indifferent whether he scores full points or not. J.M. Arnott's big Innes car, being new, ran hot, and two of the four cylinders ceased work. This stuck us up for hours, and we lost 68 points. Trying to make up points was the fun; during the afternoon we had seventy miles to do in under two hours — a quite impossible task on such roads, but the car was sent headlong into such dust and holes as we would have pulled up for on the first day.

Once she took charge in a sand-drift, and spun away to one side like a skidding bicycle, and picked up a log and did a sort of waltz with it, and then regretfully dropped it again, and was coaxed back on to the road. The rest of the journey was run in a duststorm that nearly hid the front of the car, and nearly blew the chauffeur out of it; but no amount of hard driving would pull up the deficient points.

H.R. Arnott, the third Sydney car, just saved his points by steady and careful handling of his car; but the advantage of knowing the road is very great, and Stevens, the Victorian, again did fast time; while his rival, the Frenchman, lost several points.

The French driver, who knows no English but the two words — "bad road" — was asked how our glorious highways struck him. He said there are no roads in all France anything like as bad as what we saw here, but there are some in Scotland nearly as bad, which is rough on Scotland. He does not despair of getting to Melbourne, as he considers the pace nothing — in fact, his great trouble is to go slow enough. The other drivers predict that he will snap an axle doing some of his steeplechase driving; but his car seems to stand anything.

Mrs Thompson, the South Australian lady, had an awful time. Her car is one of the slow but sure order, and her great ambition is to do the run irrespective of what points she gets. All hope that her pluck will be rewarded. Her car stuck in the sand, and was towed out by "yokels" who seemed to spring up out of the ground. She arrived in Albury a lot late, but undaunted. Another Melbourne car dropped out, Mr Stewart not having showed up.

Friday's run is only set at fourteen miles an hour, so the road must be awful. The contestants are all pretty tired of it, half blinded with dust, and bruised and shaken by being jolted about in the cars like a pea in a pod. It is really hard work to sit in a car on some of the most jolty places; but those who have got full points, or near it, mean to see it out, unless they break something. One chauffeur said: — "I reckon it's worth five pounds a minute to drive over such roads." The result of the hard knocking about is that no one feels equal to attending the entertainment very kindly arranged by the Mayor of Albury.*

Evening News, Sydney, 24 February 1905

* The leading cars in the trial arrived in Melbourne on the afternoon of Saturday 25 February 1905. The winner was the young American H.L. Stevens in a 14-h.p. Darracq.

4
War Dispatches and Army Poems

EDITOR'S NOTE

I have already commented on Paterson's abilities as a war correspondent and have selected those dispatches that seem to me to illustrate best his capacities for observation and description.

His war poems are rather less distinguished but are interesting as examples of how Paterson viewed the wars he saw firsthand. In all, Paterson wrote twelve poems from his Boer War experiences. Ten were published in the years after his return to Australia in 1900 — "Driver Smith", "Jock", "Johnny Boer", "Right in Front of the Army", "That V.C.", "On the Trek", "The Last Parade", "There's Another Blessed Horse Fell Down", "The Scottish Engineer" and "With French to Kimberley". "Reveille", the first poem he sent back from South Africa, was published in the *Sydney Mail*. It was a jingoistic, cliché-ridden affair. Paterson, like some of the English poets laureate of years past, was hardly himself on formal poetic occasions, which inhibited the natural ease and flow of his versifying. His twelfth poem, "Now Listen to Me and I'll Tell You My Views Concerning the African War", was published in London in *Reynold's News* towards the end of 1901 and reprinted in the *Bulletin* of 29 March 1902 under the heading " 'A Bit of War Verse' by Australian Banjo Paterson in *Reynold's News*".

In passing one wonders how "That V.C." ever found its way into the *Collected Verse*. Paterson wrote few lines worse than these:

A wounded soldier on the ground
  Was lying hid behind hummock;
He proved the good old proverb sound —
  An army travels on its stomach.

He lay as flat as any fish;
  His nose had worn a little furrow;
He only had one frantic wish;
  That like an ant-bear he could burrow . . .

From his World War I experience, mainly in Egypt with his remount command, Paterson wrote ten poems, some of which were only discovered after the publication of my Paterson biography,

The Banjo of the Bush, in 1966. Edward Fisher of Surrey Hills, Victoria (formerly No. 1878 in the 6th Light Horse Regiment in World War I) wrote to tell me of poems by Paterson buried away in the regimental magazine, the *Kia-Ora Coo-ee*, which was written and edited by troops of the Australian and New Zealand Light Horse units on desert duty. Happily these included Paterson's best war ballad, "The Army Mules", written with his customary verve and vigour, and which, according to Fisher, his fellow soldiers recited with as much gusto as they did "The Man from Snowy River". Indeed one of them commented, "Someone must have sent Banjo a niner* laced with water from the Snowy River."

One should not judge Paterson out of context for elements of imperialistic jingoism and indeed racism that occasionally occur in his writings and especially in his war dispatches. Shooting Boers like rabbits and pumping Fuzzy-Wuzzies (Kaffirs) full of lead were accepted colloquialisms in the Boer War campaign. Although repugnant to a modern reader, terms like "nigger" and "Chinks" were commonly used in Australia at the turn of this century (the *Bulletin* was notorious in this regard), part of a hard-line White Australia policy and a resentment, especially among the working classes at the prospect of an influx of coloured races who would deprive them of their jobs. Most abhorrent was the idea of "mixed races". Needless to say, Aborigines fared badly under these attitudes of white supremacy. Without excusing Paterson, he was nevertheless representative of his times and to expurgate his racism and imperialism would be to misrepresent him.

* A nine-gallon (about forty litres) keg of beer.

War Dispatches

ARRIVAL OF THE NEW SOUTH WALES TROOPS

Off Capetown, 30th November 1899

After thirty days of weary steaming we at last sighted the South African coast. We saw a line of low, scrub-covered hills, without any sign of habitation. At the edge of the sea were sandhills, snowy white, with streaks of white sand running back among the low timber — a barren uninviting coast. There was no sign of life anywhere, no houses, nor any traces of settlement. The great African continent lay sleeping in the sun as peacefully as if war had never been heard of.

The first sign of life that we saw was the sight of two big ocean-going steamers coming down the coast at great speed side by side — one a great four-master, the other a passenger boat. The big vessel had a number painted on her bow, showing that she was a transport. They slid grimly along, side by side, and on each the British flag went up. We were frantically anxious for news of the war, and on the signals going up, "Constant fighting going on", our men broke into loud cheers. We gave our name, and stated that we had troops on board from Sydney. They were not impressed. When we hoisted "Troops on board" the big vessel thought we were asking whether she had troops on board, and promptly replied "No". When they gathered our message they did not make any reply — they did not signal "Hooray" or "Glad to hear it" or anything like that. There were others troops along the coast, hundreds of them, thousands of them. Our handful did not make much difference in that multitude. The two vessels hurried on their way, and were soon hull down on the horizon.

Next morning at grey dawn we steamed into the roadstead of Port Elizabeth. We saw a big town, clean and white-looking — a town looking larger than Newcastle — covering the hills over the harbour. The buildings were large and solid-looking. Here and there the spire of a church rose through the blue haze. By the water's edge two large railway stations marked the starting point of the line to the Cape. The whole town had an air of solid endurance about it; there were no small rubbishy-looking buildings to be seen. As we steamed up the harbour we discussed our prospects. Would they know we were coming? Would there be a staff officer to give us our orders? Were the New Zealanders here? Would they land our horses, or would we be landed at all? It can easily be understood that on arrival in a distant land on such a mission as ours we were very excited to know what sort of a reception we would get. We went to our anchorage without attracting any attention. Behind us a bigger vessel than ours came looming out of the mist; behind her again came another, bigger and more important than ours. Further out was the dim smoke of yet another great big vessel; all hurrying down the African coast.

In the harbour were many fine vessels, and one, the size of a P. and O. liner, got up her anchor and went out with as little fuss or ceremony as a North Shore ferry-boat, taking no notice of us. We were beginning to realize our position in the general scheme of things.

The pilot came on board to take us to the anchorage. He was a half-bred Dutchman, and we eyed him with interest. We thought that perhaps he was a Boer sympathizer. We badgered him with questions about the war, about the town of Port Elizabeth, about the troops, and about ourselves. He told us of the fighting. He knew in a vague way that there were Australian troops expected; but he said he thought that they had gone past in the *Medic*. Poor benighted heathen; he didn't know that Australia was divided into many colonies. In his eyes one Australian was just as good as another. We gathered from his talk that we would not set the harbour of Port Elizabeth on fire. We asked him if he thought the town would have facilities for landing 180 horses in lighters, and if it could be done in a day, and we pointed out that 180 were a lot to handle. He smiled indulgently, and said, "Dey landet one dousand mules here on Monday by half-past dree o'clock in de afternoon." So they had, too, and done it without killing a single mule.

This made us rearrange our ideas a little. We had thought of Port Elizabeth as a little doghole of a place, and that when once we were landed we would straddle all over it, so to speak; but a place that could land a thousand mules in one day evidently wasn't going to be astonished by 130 Australians. We asked were there any other soldiers there? He said, "Yes," a thousand men of the Welsh Fusiliers landed on Monday as well as the mules. Besides these there were Brabant's Horse and the Prince Alfred Guard, a local regiment. A thousand landed in one day — and we were 130 of all ranks! The Kangaroo began to think that he was not such a very large animal after all.

The pilot had a local daily paper, and there we saw that, in addition to all that troops that had already landed, there were over sixty transport ships to arrive, all loaded with soldiers. He reckoned that there were thirty thousand men yet to arrive. Thirty thousand men on the water! It sounds easy to speak of sixty transports on the water — it's not much when you say it quick; but when you come to think of a fleet of sixty vessels each as big as a P. and O. liner, and each swarming with soldiers as an anthill swarms with ants, one begins to get one's ideas enlarged. We asked the pilot whether there were any refugees here, and he said, "Yes, thousands". They were living in big camps out on the racecourse — the blacks in one camp and the whites in another. There were plenty of refugees that had money, but they were living on the Government relief funds — there seemed a familiar ring about this, it sounded like home somehow. A couple more great big steamers came shouldering into the bay as he talked and out to each of them went a tug with lighters, and in a few minutes each vessel was hard at work discharging cargo. They don't waste any time here. The pilot drifted on with his talk; he said it would take a long time to kill the Boers as they would not come out in the open to be shot at.

After we anchored we waited an hour or more for the health officer. He was boarding some of the other vessels, and when he reached us he merely steamed past, and shouted out that he would not come aboard till the transport officer came out, and away he went, leaving us very disgusted. But we didn't feel big enough to say much. We waited a couple of hours, and then the launch came back with our orders — "Go to Capetown at once"! We were given an hour on shore, and off we went.

The first thing we saw on landing was a shambling, bandy-legged, flat-footed old nigger — one of the niggers one sees in the comic papers. He looked farcical and overdrawn. We expected him to say, "Be seated, gentlemen", and to ask us a conundrum or two, but he shuffled sadly past us with his absurd coat nearly down to his heels. The next thing we saw was another similar nigger, and then we realized that we were in the home of our coloured brother, and before long we saw such a lot that we failed to take any notice of them.

We found the town quite a large place, apparently larger than any New South Wales town, except Sydney or Newcastle. Electric trams run up and down the streets; and two-horse vehicles run as cabs at a low tariff. The town is all up and down hill, and the cabmen drive little Basuto ponies, wiry little things, that shamble up and down the hills at a great rate. The town is very like Adelaide, only that it is built on a steep hill. What struck us most were the long bullock teams of about twenty oxen, all black, or black and white, driven by a large nigger, while in front of the bullocks walks a small black boy, who tows the whole concern along by a rope attached to the two leading bullocks' heads. The small boy takes this rope over his shoulders, and drags away as if his sole efforts were fetching the thing along. As a matter of fact, when he appears to be pulling his hardest, he is simply leaning all his weight on the ropes to rest himself. The rate of progress is about .05 of a mile an hour. The shops are all small and unenterprising. All English illustrated papers were sold right out before we came. One local photographer had taken no views of the landing of the Fusiliers. He had not thought it worth while.

We drove up to the principal hotel, a pretty place, very neat and tidy, with coloured waiters dressed in spotless white with flaming coloured sashes round their shoulders. We met men attached to the various regiments in the town — Brabant's Horse, the Welsh Fusiliers, the local Guards — but they were not enthusiastic. Australians will be eager to know, "What did they think of the Australian troops?" Well, in Port Elizabeth, they did not think anything about us one way or the other. The British Army man adopts a very nil-admirari attitude towards strangers. He is not necessarily narrow-minded, but his ideas are all fixed for him by centuries of precedent. He has his own work to do, and he does it in his own way. He is so absolutely sure that his is the best way that it never enters into his head to look outside it. He assumes that you also have your work to do, but he doesn't bother to inquire what your work is or how you do it.

The very day before we arrived our Lancers had made a successful debut in action at a place called Grasspan. We went to the club at Port Elizabeth and said we were Australian troops. The English officers were politely indifferent. We explained who we were, and where we came from, and conveyed no impression; but when we said that we were the same regiment that had been in action the day before that made all the difference. We were no longer outsiders, no longer a handful of Australian refugees crawling along the coast in a disconsolate tramp steamer; we were of the brotherhood, and could hold up our heads with the best. The Kangaroo was himself again! And once we have gained an entrance to the Briton's scheme of the universe we will not lose our position. Once a Britisher learns a thing he never forgets it, and he never unlearns it. He will say, "The New South Wales Lancers are a good regiment", and he will hold on to that idea till death. This morning we were nobodies; now we are full-blown soldiers, and can ruffle it with the best of them.

After visiting the town we returned to the wharf, and found that the Mayor had hurriedly gathered a few friends and was coming off to read an address of welcome which had been prepared under the impression that only one body of Australians were coming, viz, those on the *Medic*. The *Medic* did not call at Port Elizabeth, so we scored off the Victorian and got the address which was meant for them. There was great work getting the Mayor and suite to and from the ship. The harbour is an open roadstead, the tenders are little flush-decked affairs with no shelter, so we all got wet going out. Then the Mayor delivered the address, champagne was opened, speeches were made, and "God Save the Queen" was sung. The tone of the speeches showed that the burning question in the Cape is not Boer rule *v.* the British rule so much as Afrikander rule *v.* British rule. The speakers were careful in their utterances. But it was evident that there was a lot of feeling at the back of what was said. There are more Boer sympathizers in the Cape than one cares to talk about. One is never sure of one's next-door neighbour.

Having done with speeches the next thing was to get the Mayor and his following off the ship again. The wind had freshened, and the tender was surging alongside the *Kent*, leaping up at her side like an angry dog. Sometimes she rose till she touched the gangway; then she sank down far below it again. The Mayor clung to the gangway and quaked with fear till Private Lewis (a gigantic Double Bay fisherman) went down into the tender, and as she rose on a wave Lewis reached out his gaunt arms and plucked the Mayor from his perch, detaching him limb by limb from the ladder, to which he clung like a young native bear. As the Mayor had a tall hat and a light frock coat the spectacle was very humorous. Then the anchor was hoisted, and off we went to join the procession of big black silent vessels that are ceaselessly racing up and down this coast, each so intent on his own business that we waste no words on anybody. ''Who goes there?'' ''Welsh Fusiliers.'' ''Pass, Welsh Fusiliers, and all's well. Get on with your business, we also have ours to attend to, and in fact have been attending to it lately, not without results.''

Talking of Welsh Fusiliers, that regiment is at Port Elizabeth now. They landed with a goat, their regimental pet. We had no chance to go out and call on this regiment, which is camped a mile and a half out of town. I don't suppose they missed us much. It takes a lot to startle the British Army, and the Fusiliers have a great fighting record to live up to. We may meet them again. To-night (30th November) we are off Capetown. We were told at Port Elizabeth that a reception awaited us here. We can do without the reception if they will let us get to the front.

Capetown, 1st December

We steamed into the harbour and saw towering above us the flat-topped eminence of Table Mountain. In the harbour we saw transport after transport, all great big vessels with the big white numbers painted on their bows. There was the *Kinfanns Castle* that brought out three-thousand men; the *Scot*, that made the quickest passage on record; the *Spartan*, a hospital ship, with the red cross on her bows, and loaded with wounded. Ashore we saw the city of Capetown nestled in under the big mountain, and, away to one side on the cleared ground, rows and rows of white tents, where the Canadians and Victorians were camped. We went ashore to find that the Victorians were just on the move, as also were the Canadians. The New Zealanders had gone some days ago.

Hardly had I landed when I met an old New South Wales resident, who has been surveyor at one of the big mines on the Rand. He described the situation as full of difficulty, as the majority of the townsfolk of Capetown were disloyal, and he was of opinion that England was building up for herself a new Irish question at the Cape. When the Canadians marched through the streets they were loudly cheered by sympathizers, but there were a great many glum and silent faces. Schreiner holds power here by a majority of eleven in a House of about ninety members. Once landed, I had a good look round. The first thing I saw was a Highland regiment drilling. It was very machinelike in its drill, and its non-coms were fine men, but their rank and file did not impress me much. Our men are quite as good. We are to land this afternoon, and our horses will be glad of the relief.

When the British Artillery regiments landed here their horses marched off the wharf to the sound of the bugle, halting and wheeling to the bugle calls, and this after being three weeks on the ship. Our horses are not educated quite up to this standard yet. I have just seen the Victorian Mounted Rifles march through the streets on their way to the front. They were a glorious contrast to the riding of the regular troops I have seen. Our men looked more workmanlike, and also, if the truth must be told, a more "hard-faced" lot than the English. The crowd cheered them liberally, and flags were flung out here and there, but a stolid Dutchman drove a traction-engine with a string of trucks attached right through their ranks.

I got my pass as a war correspondent today from a polite military official, who informed me in a bland voice of the pains and penalties I would undergo if I misbehaved myself in any way. The hotels are full of officers; the staff headquarters are besieged by a multitude of weeping women and children asking for news of their relatives reported killed. Orderlies gallop to and fro, and bells are ringing all over the place, and yet everything is done with machine-like precision. You see, if an order is given in any of these quarters it is obeyed literally, and so nothing has to be done twice over. The streets are full of mules, traction-engines, and niggers. Either you pass a cart drawn by a mule and driven by a nigger, or a string of wagons drawn by a traction-engine, and conveying the baggage of a regiment with some Tommy Atkins smoking in great state on the top of the bags.

Capetown, 2nd December

We made our formal landing on South African soil today. The *Kent* arrived early in the morning, and during the day I went ashore to prospect. The first thing that struck us was that the boatman (a half-bred black) took us ashore in an oil launch — a novel kind of waterman's boat to a Sydneyite. We landed on a wharf very much like a Sydney wharf, and marched up the wharf through a line of steamers discharging hay, forage, stores, and every kind of war material. It was all just like Sydney, except that the unloading was done by coloured men of every shade, from ebony black to faint yellow, and the goods were put into lorries drawn by great big mules. I saw mules here as big as any horse one would care to ride.

Threading our way through the niggers and mules we came on a cab, a hansom cab of ordinary type, except that it was driven by a huge black nigger, and was painted white, with its name, the *Pride of Limerick*, painted boldly on the side. I asked the *Pride of Limerick*, what his fare was, as we had heard so much of "war prices" that we were cautious. "Half-a-crown an hour, sah," he said. A hansom cab, drawn by a good sort of an Arab pony, and driven by as fine a specimen of a nigger as one would wish to meet, for half-a-crown an hour! And these were war prices. We closed with the *Pride of Limerick* at his own figure, and started up town. We expected to meet a sentry every four yards, and we fumbled nervously to be sure that we had our passports ready. We turned into a long street full of mule wagons, cabs, electric trams, and traction-engines. These latter go thundering through the traffic like an elephant through a brood of chickens. There is no rule of the road in Capetown traffic, anyhow. You go either side of the man in front of you, or right fair over him, according to circumstances. Every now and again we were nearly leaping out of the cab as the

Pride of Limerick tried to maintain him full in the face. So we navigated up the street.

Plenty of the business houses, insurance offices, and advertisements were the same as at home. I only knew one man in all South Africa, and I had last heard of him at Johannesburg. He did not know I was coming to Africa. By the curious decree of chance I met the man in the street before I had driven half a mile. He got into the cab and proved a perfect mine of information, and while he talked we drove to the headquarters staff office. So far we had seen an ordinary civilian crowd, with a fair sprinkling of coloured persons, very few soldiers, and no one that we could recognize as a typical Boer. We turned into the gate of a barracks, and at once came into a different atmosphere. Soldiers, soldiers, everywhere, all khaki-clad, all sun-blistered and dirty with long sea-voyaging. Some were on duty, standing sentry with solemn immobile faces; others idly lying in the sun; others holding officers' chargers and letting them pick at the grass. The chief staff office was a big stone building and a perfect rabbit-warren of rooms, every room full of soldiers acting as clerks. Typewriters were clicking, bells ringing, and a hurry, din, and bustle going on like a beehive; but everyone was cool and methodical through it all. I stopped a staff officer and asked him where the press censor was. One would expect it to be sudden death to speak to a staff officer in such a state of affairs; but he was as bland as though in a drawing-room. He even offered to draw a plan of the way to the press office, and there were a dozen wailing women round him all the time, beseeching him for news of the killed and wounded, for the great battle of Modder River had just been fought, and the news of the killed and wounded was beginning to trickle through. We went over to another barracks and saw the press censor. He, like every other officer we met here, had only one ambition, to be let go to the front.

Then we went out into the road and met a regiment just disembarked — the 6th Dragoon Guards and Carbineers. They landed in full marching order, every man walking by his saddled horse with all his gear on the saddle — sword, carbine, picket-peg, everything read to go on to the field. I was anxious to see how they compared with our men and our horses. The men were nearly all fresh-faced young Englishmen; fine big men, and a more

even-sized and solid-looking lot than any body of colonials I have
seen together. One hears so much nowadays of the puny physique
of the British army. If there are puny regiments among them, I
haven't seen any specimens. At the camp here there are many of
all sorts of regiments, men left at the base for various purposes,
wounded men, Army Service Corps men, Highlanders, Gloucester
Regiment, Guards, every kind of regiment; and as they are all
dressed in khaki it is very hard to tell one from another, and very
hard to tell our men from the rest. Shortly after the Carbineers
marched in, the Victorians marched out. They rode through the
streets, each man leading a spare horse. Seeing the two forces so
closely one after the other, I was able to form a good comparison.
The Victorians looked more smart and wide-awake than the English. To use a slang expression, they were more "hard-faced".
The English troopers, as a rule, had a heavy, vacant, chaw-bacon
look about them, while our compatriots looked smart enough to
steal a policeman's watch if they were given half the chance.

The Carbineers landed fully satisfied that the eyes of the world
were upon them. They evidently thought their arrival would create
a sensation in South Africa. All regiments think that. We did. But
when one gets there and sees the great troopships rolling in and the
troop-laden trains rolling out every day, and sees the bustle and
hurry everywhere, the newly arrived trooper soon finds that he is
not the centre of the whole show, and drops into his place accordingly. The Carbineers marched up the streets looking proudly
from side to side at the crowded traffic on the footpath. But the
people only paused a second or two, and a few enthusiasts
cheered, and just as they reached the main crossing a huge half-
caste engine-driver phlegmatically drove his traction-engine right
fair through the ranks, and went clanking away with his train of
cars after him, while the troopers' horses snorted with fear, and a
couple of officers who were directing the march on polo ponies
had much ado to keep their seats. Polo ponies are the correct thing
for officers' use, and some beautiful little animals are landed, but
for wear and tear work I have not seen anything of the class of the
black pony presented to me by Mr T. Watson, the well-known
starter of the A.J.C.

As to the horses — the English troop-horses are much more

solid than ours, and are bred on stouter and heavier lines. They are more what we would call "gun horses". They lack quality, and one can quite understand, after seeing them, the accepted idea in England that Cavalry can only charge once. The class of animals they use can carry any weight you like, but if they have to go fast they crumble up in no time. These Carbineer horses landed very stiff, sore, and jaded after only about eighteen days at most on shipboard. When our horses came ashore after five weeks' solid travelling they walked as briskly as possible, and not one of them showed the slightest signs of wear and tear from the trip. They were very terrified on landing, the long spell at sea having apparently frightened them for all other purposes.

The first that was landed promptly kicked a trooper, but without doing any harm. Then they were led off in pairs up the wharf and out to the camp on the common. There they were led about and had a roll, and a saddle was tried on one or two, and lo, and behold, before the day was out they were all doing slow exercise without seeming particularly stiff. And this after thirty-five days' standing on a ship's deck, sometimes in a very heavy sea. One or two were inclined to play up, but did no harm. They looked light and wiry alongside the English horses, but the authorities here pronounce them the finest lot of horses yet landed. These, it should be explained are mostly police horses, and no better advertisement for the Australian horse could possibly have been made. They are the sort that are known as "walers" in India, and are first-class walers at that. The mounted police get the pick of Australian horseflesh, and these are very good specimens. They elicited warm praise everywhere, and should do well in the field.

On arrival with the horses at our camping ground the men were put to hold them in sections of four, a guard tent was erected, and then ensued one of those long delays that defy human exertion. It appears that a lot of our stores were ready to land, but could not be put over the ship's side, as the wharf was loaded with a previous ship's cargo. Messages went to and from headquarters, to the ship's agents, the stevedores, and so on, and all the while the men sat and waited round the tent holding their horses, looking like a circus of which the proprietor had run away. Colonel Williams got a few carts out and harnessed up his ambulance horses, and they pulled the camping gear and fodder out through heavy sand to the camp, and a rough camp was pitched and picket lines put down.

Our landing was watched by two men and a boy. By the time the camp was pitched and lines put down it was dark, and when the heel-ropes were put on the 130 Lancer horses the scene that ensued baffles description. The horses had never been picketed before, and most of them kicked valiantly. The Army Medical Corps' horses were experienced hands and gave no trouble at all, but the others surged and swayed at their ropes and did their best to kick themselves free. There were not nearly enough men to handle that number of horses, and in addition to the care of the horses they had to pitch tents. The A.M.C. detailed a body of men to pitch tents for them, and by degrees the tents were got up, but all the time the men were running up and down the lines clearing horses out of the entanglements they had got themselves into. Some had got themselves into a regular network of heel-ropes of the other horses, and as the land was very sandy and the pegs drew out in spite of everything, the Lancers had a very hard time. They stuck to it resolutely, Warrant-officer Fisher being up and down the lines practically the whole night long, and all the men were as much on their feet as lying down that night.

It was a weird sight. The camp allotted to us was on the common adjoining a large camp of Imperial troops, and the sound of revelry came to us in fits and starts, but there was no revelry in our camp. There is no fuel to be got in this country, and our only fire was made of fragments of a case that had contained stores. By the dim light of this fire we could see the long lines of struggling, plunging animals. Every now and again one would kick himself loose, or throw himself down, and the men would have to rush to the rescue. Sometimes eight or nine of them would make a simultaneous charge forward, and we fully expected them to stampede the camp. While feeding they were fairly quiet, but after feed they got struggling, and suddenly eight or nine broke loose and made a dash out of camp at a frightful pace, with their heel-pegs flying loose around them. They went past the British lines, going great guns, and disappeared into the night. They cleared the road all the way, too — nothing short of a traction-engine would have faced them. The men redoubled their watch over those that were left, and about midnight a policeman came into camp to say that a police station seven miles out of town had reported that the horses had passed at full speed with heel-pegs flying, and that one had jumped into a tram. The policeman explained that the road on which the horses were going was circular, and that if we waited by the roadside they would be due to pass the camp about once an hour so long as their wind held out. The camp is divided into Lancers and A.M.C. lines. The latter are all right, having plenty men and a quiet lot of old horses; but Major Lee, with a handful of men, and a big lot of unruly horses for them to look after, has a hard time. All the men that can be spared from the Army Medical Corps are lent for Lancer purposes, but an annoying delay has taken place in the unloading of the *Kent*, and we have a big fatigue party at work there getting up stores.

At date of writing (3rd December) we are in a state of preparation for departure, the Lancers having orders to go to the front tomorrow. How we are to load the horses with our small number is a mystery. There is very little help to be had here. While men and horses are landing by the thousand they have to let small units such as ours fight their own battles. Our A.M.C. unit has triumphed over all difficulties, having their own supplies and transport, and they only wait orders to march at once, except that some of their wagon gear is still on the ship. Our experience here teaches one lesson. All camps of instruction should be moved from day to day, as the mere pitching of tents, selecting a camp, and so on are things that must be known for active service. The staff officer in charge of the line of communication, Colonel Winter, expressed his opinion that our unit had shown more ability to shift for itself than any previous colonial troops, and with that we must be satisfied. While making ready to proceed to the front we got letters from the Mayor welcoming both Army Medical Corps and Lancers.

After landing was finished I went up the town and met my first Boer. I heard that a Boer prisoner on parole was at one of the hotels, and a mutual friend introduced us. He was not long and wild and hairy. He was a refined and educated man, a doctor of medicine, and had seen several battles. He at once offered to play me billiards, and said he had occasionally made breaks of over fifty. I thought it wise to decline. He says that the Boers are having a long way the best of it as regards the fighting. They lose positions but they save men. They shoot till the last moment and then run. All the talk about the Boers being savages is nonsense. They treat the wounded well. I saw a man today who had four bullet wounds, and he had nothing but good to say of the Boers. They assisted him in every way they could. Here the ultimate success of the English is looked upon as assured; but there is a deep political question underlying it all. The Cape Ministry is looked upon as pro-Boer, and the British organs call them all sorts of names. But the fact remains that they hold office by a vote of a majority of the local House. There are more locals against the war than for it; and the extremist papers on the English side here are urging that after the war the franchise should be taken from the pro-Boer party.

This seems strange in view of the fact that the war itself is undertaken solely to get the franchise for the Uitlanders. The fact is that the Cape is very Dutch, and it cannot be expected that these people will look kindly on a war in which their own kinsfolk are engaged. After England has beaten these Boers she will still have a sullen and discontented population to deal with, not only across the Vaal but in the parent colony. All classes of the community are impregnated with the Dutch element, not that they profess any preference for Dutch over English, but their sympathies naturally are with their kinsmen in the Boer Republic. One never knows, even in a club or an hotel, who may be a Boer sympathizer. Very little feeling is openly expressed. People are frightened to make any open declaration of hostility to England or of opposition to the war, lest they or their relatives should incur punishment when the day of reckoning comes. That the Boers will have to pay that reckoning is looked upon as beyond a doubt. Boer money is already advancing in price in the expectation that there will be no more Boer coinage after the war.

The war makes little difference in the town. The townsfolk seem to stand aloof from it. Theatres, bicycle races, cricket, and all such sports go on just the same as ever. You can still get quarters at a good hotel for twelve shillings a day, and can have the best entertainment that the city affords for a pound a day. The English regiments land like an invading army. They are hurried into depots for a day or two, and then hurried on, and the town knows nothing of it. The press are told nothing, or next to nothing; the people know nothing. The war is quite apart from the life here, so far as one can see outwardly, but under the surface matters are otherwise. There is a long reckoning to look forward to before this matter is settled.

To the Tommy Atkins landing here none of these difficulties present themselves. His simple creed is, ''The Boer won't stand a charge'', and in that faith his only one idea is to get to close quarters. They won't stand the cold steel. The Tommy on active service proceeds to get himself as dirty as he possibly can, as soon as he can. Our men have the knack of keeping themselves clean.

4th December

We hope to get away today. The mail closes tomorrow. General Forestier-Walker inspected our lines today, and expressed great surprise at the style of horses we had. The A.M.C. are a new idea in military matters here in that they have their own transport. The Imperial A.M.C. depend on the Service Corps for transport, and judging by our experience of the Army Service Corps they have a good deal of disappointment. At time of writing we are waiting for the carts to shift our baggage. We had to send men to unload the *Kent*, as the contractor gave up the job apparently. We had A.M.C. Australians working winches, unloading cargo, and carrying stores as wharf-lumpers, and first-class lumpers they made.

We are out in camp here, and very few people visit us. The town does not approve of the war. The bicycle races and everything else go on just as usual. The war correspondents are catching it hot this war. There are too many of them, and very little news is given them, and they are not let see anything. Here, on the spot, we know as little, or less, then you know how things are progressing. I saw the Carbineers start yesterday. All the men were anxious to get to the front, and the British Tommy is a fighting man sure enough. They haven't sense enough to know fear when they see it.

I inspected some Argentine horses yesterday. They are much like ours, but a little more solid. They are worth about £5 to £7 in their native land, and we have not got the same class at the same price. The Cape ponies here are small, wiry little things, very good for their size. The remount agents are buying them, but the locals are putting the price up and making hay while the sun shines. They get £20 a head now.

My next letter should be from somewhere near the front. Our medical officers have been inspecting the Boer prisoners. They are very Dutch, and not many of them speak English. They were playing Association football, and playing it fairly well too. They had never heard of Australia. We might have come from Timbuctoo for all they cared. One Boer assured Dr Fiaschi, on his honour as a gentleman, that they had not fired from ambulances in the field. We think of the Boers as semi-savages. We have plenty people just as rough as they are. We have 150 Boer prisoners, here, and thirty more coming in. They are square sturdy men, much the type of our bushmen. They look upon it as a civil war. In some cases brother and brother are on opposite sides.

Our horses have all cast up but one. Major Lee gave the first man that brought one back a half-sovereign, and half the coloured population are looking for our horses now. The missing one must be the one that jumped into the tram.

I can close this letter by saying that our contingent so far have quite satisfied the Imperial authorities. Colonel Williams moved all our gear down on his ambulance wagons or we would still be on the *Kent* waiting for the Army Service Corps. The traffic in the harbour is congested owing to army requirements. A horse speculator that came here with ponies has them on a ship in harbour, and can't get them ashore. When he asked if there was any chance of getting to a wharf to land them, they asked was he mad to ask such a question.

We have not had any parades or inspections so far. There is no time for parades here, and General Walker's hurried visit is the only official visit we have had. The great chief of all the veterinary surgeons came here yesterday and inspected our horses with a supercilious air. "Nice horses," he said, "very nice horses; but they'll all die. They're eating sand!" "How long will they live"? we said. "Half an hour," he said in an authoritative tone, and off he went. So far they are as fit as fiddles. They have three days in the train now to face, and we can hope they will survive in spite of the great man's prediction.

Sydney Morning Herald, 28 December 1899

AUSTRALIANS RUSHED TO THE FRONT

Naauwpoort, 13th December 1899

My last letter was written from Capetown, on the eve of our start for the interior. We were played to the station by a band of the local Highland Regiment, and a few residents of the town had subscribed to present us with tobacco, cigarettes, water-bags, and sherbet. The train is a narrow-gauge affair and very slow. The livestock are travelled in little narrow trucks that will only just hold them, and all the way up our horses were trying to kick their boxes to pieces. The journey by train began on Monday evening, 4th December, at about 6, and we did not get out of the train till 5.30 p.m. on Wednesday, 6th, so that we had a good chance to see the country.

All the way up we passed through open country, not a tree to be seen, except what were planted in rows on a few farms and the gardens round the homesteads. The soil is fairly good, but there is no water to be seen, and the herbage is a sage-like brushy scrub a few inches high. Looking out of the train windows we saw a series of low stony hills, separated by big stretches of rolling land, covered with this low stunted herbage. A few sheep (merinos) may be seen from the train, an occasional flock of goats, and here and there an ostrich farm. All day long it is as hot as the hottest day in Bourke, and at night the temperature falls to about 50^0, so we require a light khaki suit in the middle of the day and two or three blankets at night. We found Naauwpoort to be in full occupation by the division under General French, to which we were attached.

We met Captain Cox here and about forty of the Aldershot trained men. They had been out patrolling and had been fired at several times. They showed us a letter from Lieutenant Osborne, who was at Modder River, to say that the men under his command had been in three engagements and had had some horses shot under them, but there had been no casualties. We found here also the 6th Dragoon Guards, a regiment of Cape Volunteers, and the New Zealanders, all very eager to get to the front.

Naauwpoort is a frightful place — just a lot of small galvanized-iron houses and a duststorm. Sometimes whole mule wagons drive into each other in the dust, not being able to see a yard ahead. The heat is intense. We were ordered to move to the front the day after we arrived, but General French inspected the horses, and found that they could not fairly be asked to move so soon; so he granted a day's respite. I found two other press representatives here; and as they had been waiting for weeks, but had now suddenly decided to go out, I thought it worth while to follow them, lest I should miss anything, and as I thereby got separated from our men for a little, I had better describe what I saw, and then say what happened to the men till we met again.

Well, I left the camp with a saddle-horse and a packhorse, and rode out about fifteen miles and camped on the railway line. If the reader looks at the map he will see that Naauwpoort is a junction, and that a line runs north to Colesberg, about thirty miles off. This town is held by the Boers, and we knew that they were in force some miles this side of it, but how far we did not know. The Carbineers and New Zealanders went out by train and landed at a little place called Wildebeestfontein, and set to patrolling the country. The country is just the same as all the rest — high rocky hills, with big level stretches in between. No Boers were seen or heard of, except that one mounted man was found by the Carbineers prowling in an aimless way across the veldt, and as they said he was a Boer general he was promptly arrested. No one else was heard of, and my companion and I camped with the New Zealanders that night, and went on next day in the full idea that the Boers had retired beyond Colesberg, and that we could promenade as far as that town at our leisure. The bulk of the New Zealanders were left to patrol the line, and only about fifty went on.

We rode with the troops to a place called Arundel, and here we heard that there were Boers about, and the New Zealanders pushed on across a big plain, and pulled up under a steep hill. Here the men dismounted and went up the hill to reconnoitre. The Carbineers went to one flank and the Mounted Infantry to another. My acquaintance and I decided to follow the New Zealanders, and it was just as well that we did, as in a few minutes there was a roar from a big hill about one and a half miles off, and a shell fell between the New Zealanders and the Mounted Infantry, and at last we knew that we were face to face with the enemy. A hurried search with the glasses showed that there were dozens of them visible on the big hill, and no doubt hundreds that we could not see. We climbed up the nearest kopje (a hill about 150 feet high, consisting mostly of rock and heather) and we found it simply alive with New Zealand infantry crouched in among the stones, their khaki uniform blending perfectly with their cover. Away about a mile and a half to the right of us were another dismounted party of Cape Rifles, and some Carbineers were patrolling the hillside further away. A messenger was sent there, and as he rode across the flat between the two hills the guns boomed and a shell fell about a hundred yards from him. The spurting of the sand showed where the bullets were falling, though we could not hear the musketry.

He cantered leisurely on, and all through the morning anyone crossing that plain was fired at, and it got to be quite the "thing" to pull up and look at the place where the shell struck, if you happened to be near enough. The shells did not explode and no harm was done. I was snug in among the rocks in the kopje with the New Zealanders, and though we were in range they only sent an occasional shell towards us by accident. A nasty screaming sound a shell makes coming through the air, too! The Boers had a splendid position, as they were on a very big hill, and commanded all the lower kopjes and the plains in between.

Our men made no advance, except that the Carbineers kept up their patrol, and the Boers were quite contented to stay where they were. I went back to the field telegraph, and there heard that the Sydney Lancers were on the road, but they had left their lances at the station, so I did not see them go by. They went on to patrol business, and were told to go towards the Boer position till they drew a shell or two, and then retire at once, and as fast as they liked. The idea of course was to locate the Boer guns. I didn't see what followed, but from what the men tell me it appears that they were riding along stretched over about a mile of country. Their right wing got within easy rifle range of the enemy, and a fire of both musketry and shells was opened on them.

Having found the guns they retired as expeditiously as the most exacting commander could wish. One horse was shot, and Staff-sergeant Winch had a severe fall by a collision with a trooper, but he was not seriously hurt. They returned to camp at the foot of the small hill, and waited further orders. Meanwhile I had been waiting for them, and had seen no end of excitement as the Boer guns were tried on the small parties crossing the open. It was quite interesting to watch them, and one forgot the risk the men were running. We would sit up there in the kopje, and say, "My word, that wasn't a bad one!" "That bullet nearly hit that fellow on the bay horse", and so on. Then as the Boers got the range a bit better the different parties had to canter across, and sauntering was done away with. Suddenly an order came that we were to relieve the Carbineers, who were patrolling the country at the back of the hills on our right; so we had to go across the open plain, and the matter suddenly assumed a much less sporting aspect. There had not been any firing for some little time; and I suggested to Veterinary Lieutenant Mellhuish that perhaps the Boers were tired of wasting shells, but he said he thought they were just those profligate sort of people that would fire a shell at a party like ours on spec. We moved out across the open, the vet. and I riding behind; and sure enough, before long, away on our left came the well-known coughing bark of the seven-pounder, and we heard the shell screaming towards us and a few bullets began to kick up the dust near us.

The nearest shell was quite up to the average of the days shooting, say thirty yards off; but we forgot to note this fact at the time. We were wondering how it was that it seemed such a long way over to the cover. It had not seemed any distance from the kopjes. We got the order to canter, and went across pretty briskly, but keeping good order, though our horses are not trained troop-horses, and we had to keep in line. After leaving the cover we came out on another plain, and found the Carbineers waiting for us. We heard a shell or two fired, and were speculating how near they were getting to the men crossing behind us, when suddenly as we neared the Carbineers the gun spoke again, and whew-w-w-w the shell came whirring its way over towards us, and pitched very close indeed, while a lot of bullets went over us, showing that we were well in range. The Carbineers at once moved off in one direction, and we went to take up the ground they had left, and we had hardly moved off when the Boers pitched a shell right on to the spot we had left. This made us move off to a safer place, where we took up our patrol duties, and so ended the first day of our lot under fire, creditably enough, though the retreat from the first rifle fire appears to have been more enthusiastic than orderly, but after all that was in obedience to orders.

We got back to camp and found quite a good meal for us — a great surprise these times. The rule is when you see a man eating anything to ask him, "What meal are you having, Bill?" "The day before yesterday's tea", is about the average answer. On 9th December we were to accompany the guns into action, but a change was made at the last minute, and the guns were sent back. Our men, who had been in the saddle all day before, were sent out on picket duty, and did not get back till three o'clock in the morning. Lieutenant Heron had the pleasure of this experience. As soon as they got in they had to take off their greatcoats and go straight out again. At time of writing a train has arrived with maxims and infantry, and we expect to see these people in action. So far we have only had cavalry and mounted infantry on the field. We have lost two or three horses, one shot by the Boers, one that broke his leg by a fall, and a third is said to have got away from the lines; but no man is any the worse, except that Staff-sergeant Winch after his fall was taken back to Naauwpoort in the train.

This is written from a Boer homestead. The owner is arrested as a sympathizer with the enemy. I have got the use of the stable for my horses. It is absurdly like an Australian homestead in every way. Sheepyards, horseyards, cultivation paddocks — everything reminds one of Australia. There is a spring here of lovely water and a grand garden. The troops keep great discipline. The crops are untouched in the fields, the sheep go out with their shepherd through the middle of the camp. One can buy milk at sixpence a pint, and forage, very good hay, at sixpence per bundle. The farm people are much put out, though. A boy who speaks a little English, a smart little chap of about fourteen, is the head of the family while the father is away. He says the Kaffirs won't do any work — they sit down and play all day long — and the cows are frightened of the troops, and keep coming up to the yard to see what the matter is.

At the time we landed severe fighting was going on at Modder River, and we had hoped to be sent there. When we heard that we were to go to Naauwpoort we consoled ourselves by thinking that anything was better than guarding lines of communication, a spiritless job which we were very much dreading. All the way up the line we passed camps of men "guarding lines of communications", i.e., sitting in the red hot sun by the line, and bemoaning their fate. While we (the Lancers) were travelling, P.M.O. Williams and his comrades of the knife and bandage were parading and displaying themselves at Capetown, and bothering all officials they could reach to send them somewhere; and the mounted infantry were just arriving, and had got orders to go to De Aar, a central depot which would enable them to reach several fields of action.

At Naauwpoort we found Captain Cox fit and well, with a few men. It seems that only about eighty of his original hundred had stayed with him at the Cape, and out of these thirty-five had been sent under Lieutenant Osborne to Modder River, where they had done well. We saw a letter from one of the troopers saying that they had been in three battles, and had had horses shot under them, but none of the men were hurt. This fired our men with much enthusiasm, and the orders to march from Naauwpoort were anxiously awaited. While the new contingent were coming up Captain Cox and his men had done a lot of patrol work, and had been out nearly every day, so that when we were ordered to go out it was looked upon as an ordinary bit of patrol work.

Suddenly, however, we found that the whole camp was on the move, and lo and behold we were actually on the way to the front. We landed at Arundel camp on Friday, 8th, and found everything in a great state of excitement. The Boers were defending a big hill a few miles from the camp, and we were to go to the front at the trot. All the way over in the ship we had been wondering whether we would be allowed to go under fire, and now we found that we could not get to the front fast enough to suit the authorities. It was only a small skirmish that was going on, but quite exciting enough for beginners such as ourselves. The battleground was a great big plain (called veldt in this country) with a circle of irregular hills round it. These hills are very rugged and stony, and are called kops if of a great size and kopje (pronounced coppy) if small.

All Africa so far as we have seen it is either veldt or kopje; and the reader must get this thoroughly in his head to understand the difficulties which beset our army in attacking the Boers. No better fighting ground for cavalry could be found than the veldt, and no worse ground for them could be found than the kopje. A kopje in full working order is as good a fortress as can be imagined — a great heap of loose stones, with a little covering of sage-like brushwood. No horse in the world could get up it, and the most daring infantry would hesitate to attack it. Still our infantry do attack these kopjes, but it requires to be seen to be believed. The Boers hide among the stones in these kopjes, and if they have a succession of them to retire on it is very hard to do them much damage. Shell them out of one, and they scamper across to the next. If they were to be caught on an isolated kopje, matters could be made warm for them, but our friend the enemy is no fool, and usually has some safe place to retreat to at a pinch. When we arrived on the scene of action a Boer cannon was sullenly blazing away from the top of a far-distant hill, and the shots were kicking up the earth near the various parties passing in range.

We were ordered to patrol a fine big open veldt, a stretch of open country about four miles wide with kopjes all round it. We opened out in review order and marched along, feeling that the eyes of the Australias were upon us. Suddenly out of a small kopje on the right there came a most unhallowed din — a gun going, shells flying, and bullets whistling all round us. Our duties were simply to reconnoitre and retire, and we retired — and lost no time about it either. Later on in the day we passed across a big flat and met a party of the Carbineers patrolling. As the two bodies of troops passed each other the Boers let fly again, and a shell struck very close to us, while bullets rattled all round. It is marvellous how so many bullets can be fired without hitting anybody.

We retired again. Our horses got nervous when the shells burst near them, but we kept fair order this time; and when later on we met another reception in the shape of bullets we felt that we were getting quite used to it. On Saturday morning we were to have accompanied our guns to a trial attack on the enemy's position, but we were late on the scene, and earned a reproof for our delay. There is no "later on" about this business; if you get an order it has to be complied with at double quick time. We spent Saturday on patrol work, locating the enemy; and a ticklish job it is. One

never knows whether the Boers are on a kopje or not till the guns
start shooting. All day we manoeuvred and rode about just out of
range of the enemy's guns. Our commanders were evidently anxious to ascertain the Boers' strength; but we could not draw much
fire from them, and their guns were silent. Now and again, as we
drew near a kopje, a snarling crack from the rifles would send us
back to the plain, and the day closed without much done so far as
we were concerned.

Sunday was a *dies non* so far as fighting was concerned. Johnny
Boer does not fight on Sunday. Everyone slept the sleep of the
dead tired. On active service there are no parades and no swapping
of compliments. Out all day in the hot sun, out all night on picket
duty or patrol, small wonder the men sleep when they can. Everyone gets as dirty as a badger with the dust that is flying, and we had
a storm one night that flooded the tents and stained everything
with muddy water. We have no time to think of appearances. I
have averaged fourteen hours a day in the saddle since I came
here. We thought we were being put in a little quiet out-of-the-way
corner, where we could do no harm; but ever since we came here
we can have a fight any hour of the day that we happen to want it,
and it is supposed that a really big battle must be fought before we
take Colesberg.

On Monday, 11th, our patrol went out at daylight, and while
going round some hills they heard shooting, and found a party of
Inniskillings being chased by the Boers, who were running after
them from kopje to kopje. Our party was commanded by Captain
Cox, and included Lieutenants Allan, Heron, and Roberts, and
about twenty of the private soldiers. Our men joined in a rifle fire
at the Boers, who withdrew to their hills, but whether any were
killed we cannot say. Captain Cox's horse was shot in the shoulder
but the bullet was pretty well spent, and did not do much damage.
The reader may not understand why our combined forces did not
attack the Boers, but it would be much like marching up the side
of the Great Pyramid to attack a force of unknown strength. It
might be magnificent, but it wouldn't be war.

The combined parties came into camp with the news of the Boer
position, and after breakfast two guns of the Royal Horse Artillery went out under Lieutenant Lamont, with Major Burton com-

manding R Battery as a looker-on. They were escorted by a squadron of Carbineers and some West Yorkshire mounted infantry. I went with their force and saw the operations. Captain Cox acted as guide. The Lancers were not taken out, as they had been on patrol duty at night. We rambled along steadily over a lot of veldt, with kopjes on either side, and on coming across a big plain we saw a little white Boer farmhouse with a round kopje at the back. There was nothing about the farmhouse to show that it was occupied. The guns were hidden behind the squadron of cavalry, and the whole was advancing at a sharp trot. Suddenly, when we were about a mile off, a swarm of men ran out of the cottage, jumped over a low wall, and then reappeared on horseback. Their horses had been tied up behind the house. Our cavalry swung aside left and right, the gun was wheeled round, the artillerymen jumped to their places, and before the Boers could cover the quarter of a mile of ground that separated them from the kopje bang went the cannon, and once of the horsemen went down; the rest rode wildly for shelter but before they could reach it two more shells fell just behind them.

It was a magnificent bit of work: it was the first shell fired by a Royal Horse Artillery gun in Africa, and the major and subaltern were in great glee at such a successful start.

The Carbineers rode up to reconnoitre the kopje, and the Boers let them get within half a mile, and then they opened a heavy fire on them. The Carbineers withdrew as steadily as if on parade, each horse's head being in line with the next, although the bullets were dropping all round them.

Then the guns set to work to shell the kopje, but soon found that they were within rifle range, and the bullets came pattering unpleasantly close, so the guns were moved back, and then the shelling began. It is marvellous with what accuracy these guns shoot. They pitched shells exactly on the skyline of the kopje, they pitched shells just over it, they fired shells that went over the kopje and burst on the other side, and practically every shot landed exactly where it was intended it should land. The Boer rifle fire was soon silenced, and under cover of the guns a trooper rode up to the dead Boer and had a look at him. Then he inspected the farmhouse and got a lot of cartridges that the Boers had left in their flight.

After well shelling the kopje we came home, and found that the Lancers and New Zealanders, a combined Colonial Contingent, under Major Lee, were to go out and reconnoitre, and, if possible, capture a farmhouse which it was thought the Boers were using to sleep in. The start was made at midnight, a bitter cold night, and slowly the procession of three hundred men filed across the plain, the horses shivering with cold. A medical man had been told off to accompany us, and he looked upon the whole affair as a forlorn hope, and cheered us with gloomy prognostications of the number of Boers we would meet. Our guide was a Kaffir boy, and as we rode along he coolly informed us that the Boers had fixed a big cannon by the farmhouse, and had formed a camp on the only available pass. This put a different complexion on matters, and, before proceeding, Major Lee sent a report back to the camp, and we waited in the bitter cold till an answer came; we were not to attack, but to get round the Boers if we could. In the dark this was not a very feasible matter, and dawn found us close to a range of hills which had not up till then been occupied by Boers. Matters had changed in the night, however, as the moment we were seen a fire was opened on us. Captain Cox's horse was hit in the shoulder, and one of the New Zealand horses was shot through the hind leg. How none of the men were hit is a mystery. We withdrew out of range, and were ordered to keep horsemen off the ground and observe the movements of the enemy. This put us in for a long, dull, hot day, riding about or resting the horses by a dam of water. Meanwhile the Carbineers had gone round this house by another road. At first they saw no Boers, but just as they were turning away a fire was opened on them. A sergeant was killed and a private wounded, so that if we had blundered on to this nest in the night we should have found things very warm.

Two guns were sent out to shell the place, but the Boers had a surprise packet in store for us as they opened on us with a 40-pounder gun, and our 12-pounders had to be taken home. The discovery of this big gun made our commanders very anxious to know his whereabouts next day, and very early in the day a force went out, and sure enough before long the big fellow spoke up and sent two shells scattering among our horses. It is a marvel how few men get hit. Our 12-pounders answered with great alacrity, and no more was heard of the big fellow. Whether he was silenced or merely shifted we could not tell. All forces have been under arms all day long ready for a rumoured Boer attack; and in fact they are moving along our flank. This takes me up to Wednesday evening, 13th December.

Sydney Morning Herald, 12 January 1900

THE ADVANCE TOWARDS COLESBERG

Rensburg Camp, 4th January 1900

I closed my last letter just as the Lancers were starting for the front on Saturday night, 30th December, to take up a position in expectation of a big fight next day. They went out with the horses loaded up with forage and men's feed for two days and bivouacked for the night at the foot of a big hill known as Porter's Hill, after Colonel Porter, who commands the Carbineers, and is commander of the brigade to which we are attached. On arriving at the hill they found the Boers strongly posted on a big range to the right.

The range formed, roughly speaking, three sides of a square, with the town of Colesberg, which we are going to take, on the fourth side. The hill they occupied was steep and rugged on all sides and ended abruptly at all the corners; it was more like a great fortress than a hill. In fact, all these kopjes seem naturally designed as forts. They are simply great piles of boulders, and a few resolute Boers can hold them against any force. This particular hill was a beauty to defend, and as we expected that it would be attacked in front a big engagement was looked for. The Lancers lay down in among the rocks and stones under Porter's Hill with horses tethered beside them, and so the night passed away. There is no luxury in sleeping among the stones of a kopje, while the cold South African wind reaches every nook and corner of the hill, and the horses shiver and cough all round. It takes a lot of the dash and glamour out of war.

At dawn all expected to advance, but orders came to wait, and all day long they waited in the broiling, shadeless heat, the rocks reflecting every ray of the sun till they were nearly roasted, and still no orders to advance. All sorts of rumours went round the troops. The Boers had all run away; they were all at church; they were in overwhelming strength; they had moved down our flank, and might pour shellfire into us at any moment. All these various stories found more or less credence among the Carbineers and the mounted infantry (Yorkshire Regiment) who were waiting beside the Lancers. Sunday night found them still on Porter's Hill, and again they slept as best they could beside their saddled horses ready to move at any moment.

At grey dawn troops began to arrive from the camp at Rensburg; guns rumbling vaguely through the darkness, clattering and bumping over the rocks, and masses of infantry dimly seen in the darkness and dust, tramping past the Boer position, and evidently moving on to the back of Colesberg. The Lancers were standing to their horses expecting to move at any moment, when they received the dismal news that they were to go back to camp; having been out two days and two nights, it was thought best not to use the horses during that day's engagement. The disgust and disappointment of the troopers may be imagined, but, as things turned out, it was about the best thing that could have happened. Major Lee asked the brigadier if some of the men might remain, so that the Lancers might take some part in the engagement, and permission was given for Lieutenant Roberts and eight men to remain. The rest rode sadly back to camp, about three miles away.

I was in company with Lieutenants J.B.N. Osborne and Heron, who were not on duty that day, and we considered ourselves a roving commission to see all we could of the battle. We first waited at Porter's Hill in front of the Boer position, and business was commenced while it was still dark by four guns of the Royal Horse Artillery coming into action at the foot of Porter's Hill, and sending shell after shell crashing in among the rocks and stones of the front of the Boer position. It was very fine to watch the gunners spring back as they fired, and the flash of the gun and the long scream of the shell as it went on its mile-and-a-half journey to the top of the opposite hill, and then to watch for the crash as the shell exploded. But we could not form any idea of what effect was being produced. The Boers treated our shooting with dignified indifference, though we had seen plenty of them on the hill at nightfall, and we knew that they had a big gun up there. The Carbineers and the few Lancers left in action were stationed at Porter's Hill as a guard to the guns, and to be prepared to charge if any Boers should come out into the open. Meanwhile the rest of the forces under Colonel Fisher, of the 10th Hussars, went on past the Boer position unseen.

Our forces that went on past Porter's Hill were the R Battery of Horse Artillery, the Inniskillings, the 10th Hussars, the Yorkshire Mounted Infantry, and five hundred Berkshire Infantry. With Colonel Porter there were the Carbineers, the New Zealanders, mounted infantry, and some guns and our few Lancers. We left Porter's Kopje, as things were not very exciting there, and rode along the open country direct for Cole's Kop, following up the column that had already gone on. It seems that the advance guard of this column, pushing along in the dark, came right under the big hill known as Gibraltar Kopje. The first thing that they knew was a challenge in good English by a Boer picket, "Who are you?" Then there was a scurry of hoofs into the darkness, a voice shouted some sentences in Dutch, and a volley came from Gibraltar Kopje that whistled around our guns like hail. If the Boers had waited a few minutes and let the brigade get a little closer they would have cut them up terribly. As it was two gunners were killed, two or three horses were shot dead, and one gunner's helmet was shot through without any injury to the man. The escort were ahead of the guns, and nearer the Boers, but they seemed to shoot at the sound of the gun-wheels. This caused a rapid withdrawal of the guns and cavalry to Cole's Kop, the guns coming into action at the foot of it and shelling the Gibraltar Kopje while the escort withdrew behind the shelter of Cole's Kop.

It was just at this time that Lieutenants Osborne, Heron, and myself arrived on the scene. We saw a splendid artillery duel going on.

Our guns under Cole's Kop were blazing away as fast as ever they could be served, and the summit of the Boer position was white with the smoke of our bursting shells. The Boers answered with a 15-pounder shrapnel, a shell that sends a hail of bullets tear-

ing along the ground when its bursts. As we rode across the long
flat between Porter's Hill and Cole's Kop we could see far ahead
of us our gunners working like mad in the dust caused by the
bursting shrapnel falling near them. From a long distance off it
seemed as if every shell was right among them, but, as a matter of
fact, the Boer shooting was nothing like as accurate as ours. The
line of guns kept its position with the black mass of the cavalry
waiting behind the big hill, when suddenly the Boer fire slackened;
our cavalry dashed up from behind the big Cole's Kop, half the
guns were limbered up, and on they went at full speed, skirting the
foot of Cole's Kop, and working round towards the Gibraltar
Kopje. It was one of the finest sights one could wish to see, the
steady swing of the cavalry in front and rear of the guns, while in
the centre of the column the guns bumped and rocked madly over
the stones and deep water-channels, now and again crashing into a
waterway and up the other side at full speed, while the gunners
clung to their seats and the drivers plied their whips to keep the
pace going.

As soon as they began this rush we saw at the top of the hill at
the end of the Boer position nearest to us a flicker of five or six
small flashes of light, and there burst out the most appalling sound
one could wish to hear — the angry clatter of a quick-firing gun, a
Maxim-Nordenfeldt gun of some sort; the noise was like a quick
succession of small thunderclaps, and when we saw the dust fly up
as the shells burst just behind our guns, we saw what Kipling
means by "the hail of the Nordenfeldt". When the shells burst
they tore up the ground like a storm of iron hail. The Boers have
plenty of these guns, both here and at the Modder, and everyone
who has heard them admit that the noise of their discharge is the
most terrifying sound on the battlefield. It seems such a terrible
thing, this constant repetition of explosion, and the storm of small
shell that follows. Men who will joke when they hear an ordinary
shell coming their way turn white when they hear the devilish clatter of the "thunderbolt-gun", as it is called by the troops. It
throws a succession of shells, each weighing a pound, and bursting
into iron fragments on landing.

We watched our guns and cavalry holding their way headlong
past the foot of Cole's Kop, while the shrapnel and the

Nordenfeldt shell tore up the ground just in front, just in rear, just over them, or just short of them. Every time the thunderbolt gun spoke we watched in suspense while the shell flew across, and every time we gave a sigh of relief as we saw the duststorm rise clear of the flying guns and horsemen. We could not divine what the object of their rush was, but evidently it gave the Boers much uneasiness from the desperate way in which they worked their guns.

All of a sudden we saw the reason of the manoeuvre. From the far side of Cole's Kop there emerged from the outlying hills a stream of our infantry, about five hundred men, and these all began to run as fast as they could towards the Gibraltar Kopje, from which the Boer riflemen were now shooting with great energy. It takes a lot of lead to kill a man. Our guns, cavalry, infantry, and mounted rifles all advanced under heavy rifle fire, but not a man fell. The guns that we had left behind at Cole's Kop kept up their fire on the Boer position, but it was a shot from Colonel Porter's guns that silenced the clamouring Maxim-Nordenfeldt. A shell went whizzing from one of our guns and landed right on the Boer gun, making a general distribution of the gunners, and we heard no more of the thunderbolt gun for a while.

The mounted infantry threw themselves from the horses, and together with the infantry they charged up the steep, rocky sides of the Gibraltar Kopje. The Boers fled at once from that end of the kopje, and in five seconds our infantry had seized the western end of the kopje, and the whole of our force was under shelter of the hillside, while the Berkshires and the mounted infantry perched among the rocks at the top opened a vigorous fire on the enemy at the other end of the hill, while our guns went out into the open and opened fire on the Boer position. The Boer guns were not long getting the new range, and the shrapnel and Nordenfeldt shell flew across from gun to gun, and two of our artillery horses fell dead in their harness in rear of the guns. Then a gunner dropped in his tracks, and was swiftly carried to the rear. Then another followed. All the while from the top of the kopje 200 feet above the guns our infantry and mounted infantry kept up a rattling fire, which the Boers returned from the far end of the hill.

Our troops were lying hidden among the rocks, and as both

sides used smokeless powder, there was nothing to be seen on the Boer end of the hill, but plenty to listen to as the rifles cracked and the bullets flew overhead or flattened against the stones, behind which our men lay. A lieutenant of the Berkshires stood up in a spirit of bravado, or to encourage his men, and was at once shot dead. The stretcher-men clambered up the steep rocks and fetched his body down. While this rifle firing was going on the guns kept up the artillery duel, but one after another the Boer guns ceased to shoot, and before long we got no answer from them at all. Still our guns had to keep at work to prevent them shifting their disabled guns, and every now and again a shell was thrown into the hills at the north to prevent the Boers working round that way.

It was wonderful how soon the dash of the thing was over. After the first excitement of the rush subsided we found the artillery mechanically blazing away at an unresponsive hillside while up on the top of Gibraltar Kopje the officers of the infantry regiment slept peacefully, while the men fired steadily at every sound that came from the other end of the hill. The fact is that everything is done at such long range nowadays one hardly ever sees anything in the way of results till a battle is over. Our shells burst among the rocks from which the Boers were firing, but with what result we could not tell. The bullets rattled away to the other end of the hill, but we could not tell if any single man was hit by them. So the shooting went on all through the long, hot summer afternoon, and men slept beside their horses, horses that had not been unsaddled for two days and nights. All that day, all that night, and all next day the shooting and artillery fire went on, and not a man came back to camp. Horses were worked four days without unsaddling, and on two days few men had more than one meal a day, sometimes not that; we had secured this good position, and dared not leave it for a moment, for fear the enemy might retake it.

A battle is a slow business — there are flashes of brilliancy, but as a rule it consists of long-range firing, and dodging from position to position. The days of bull-headed attacks on the kopjes should be over so far as our generals are concerned. They cost too much in human life. General French in his operations against Colesberg profited by the lessons of Magersfontein and Tugela, and fought the Boers at their own game. Except this dash on Gibraltar Hill all the rest of the firing was done at long range or by men under cover, and we kept quietly pushing more men out past the Boer position. We saw the firing settle down till dark, and then returned.

Meanwhile at Colonel Porter's end of the battlefield, we shelled away at the Boers till they were supposed to be driven from their positions, and then he sent a reconnaissance consisting of New Zealanders, Carbineers, and mounted infantry to go up to the foot of the Boer hill to see if any were left alive. Lieutenant Roberts begged hard to be allowed to take his men with this force, but permission only came when the troops were half-way across the open to the foot of the Boer Hill, and were receiving a fire of musketry that sent them to cover as quick as might be. Even then young Roberts wanted to go out and join them with his men, but he was told that they would infallibly have to retire and that he must not expose himself and his men for nothing. Sure enough they did retire, and under very severe fire too. Where the Boers had hidden themselves during all the shellfire that we treated them to is a mystery; they showed no sign of life at all, but the moment we advanced they proved to be as lively and as venomous as ever. The New Zealanders behaved very steadily in this retreat, and they are earning great praise in all quarters. Meanwhile, the bulk of our Lancers and Australian Horse, after enduring the disappointment of return to camp, went comfortably to bed on Monday night bewailing their bad luck and little knowing what fate had in store for them.

About midnight on Monday night, while the bulk of the troops were still out on the field, an orderly came at hot haste to the Lancer tents with the extraordinary news that two or three trucks loaded with supplies for the camp had run down the line accidentally, and were believed to be at Plowman's Siding, somewhere near the range of the Boer guns. The Lancers were to furnish a patrol at three o'clock in the morning, and to go down to see where the trucks were, if they were in range of the Boers, and in fact report generally on the state of affairs. Accordingly at three o'clock Lieutenants Heron and J.B.N. Osborne, with twelve men, went down along the line to Plowman's Siding, a railway stopping-place about three miles from the camp. A small cottage does duty for a station-house, and as our men rode up to this cottage a few men were discerned on the veranda. Lieutenants Heron and Osborne, dismounted, drew their pistols, and marched up to the cottage, but found no one there, though a half-eaten meal was on the table, and the late occupiers had evidently taken a hasty flight. They went over to the line and found that in place of three trucks no less than thirty-six had run down the line, and what was most extraordinary of all was that twenty of the trucks were standing safely on the line, while on one side of them the other sixteen trucks were piled in a confused heap off the line, and with the contents scattered all over the place. These trucks had evidently run along the line, though how they were started no one knows, and the first lot had exploded some concealed mine laid by the Boers on the track. This blew up the line, and the latter part of the train was sent flying. The leading part went on for about a quarter of a mile before it stopped. Thus there were two lots of trucks about a quarter of a mile apart, with a big railway smash in between. The runaway trucks contained supplies for the camp for four days, and as we have four thousand men in camp and about as many horses it can easily be understood that there was a fine haul waiting for whoever could get it. Biscuit tins, beef, demijohns of rum, and boxes of chocolate were scattered about in lavish profusion.

There was no sign of any Boers, so the patrol went on towards the Boer position to fulfil their mission of finding out whether the trucks were in range, i.e., they had to ride on till they were fired at. They spread out as wide as possible, so that if bullets did come they would not present too easy a mark, but no fire came. They ventured right up in range of the hills, but drew no fire. Then they returned to camp and reported what had happened. Later on in the day Captain Cox and Lieutenant Dowling, with twenty-five men, went down again to guard the tracks and found them full of Boers, who were looting the trucks. The British guns at Porter's Hill were firing on the Boers in the trucks, but they were not daunted in any way, and when Captain Cox's troops came up they were received with rifle fire from the trucks and shellfire from the Boer gun. This combination made them withdraw for a while, and they sent a heliograph message into camp to say that the trucks were in range of both Boer and British guns. The rest of the squadron was sent out to their support, and a hundred infantry also accompanied them. An engine was also sent down the line to see if any trucks could be recovered from the smash.

As our squadron advanced on the trucks the Boers fired a few bullets, but seeing that our men meant to have the trucks they fled, and the Lancers advanced to take the trucks. The moment that the Boers had cleared out of the wrecked train the Boer gun on the hill and the riflemen at the base of the hill opened fire on our squadron in great style. Our men made a dash up to the line, and the troop under Captain Cox and Lieutenant Dowling got to the row of trucks nearest the Boers, while Major Lee and his subaltern occupied the wrecked trucks; and Lieutenant S.F. Osborne with his troop was put out as a guard by the side of the line. A most singular cross-firing business then began.

The Boers kept their gun going on the trucks, and their riflemen pushed out from the kopje as far as they dared, and kept up a steady rifle fire on our men, while the British guns kept pelting at the Boers, and our men in, or rather under, the trucks, fired their carbines whenever they saw a chance. It was a ticklish corner, and for five hours they held the trucks while shell after shell came down among them, and the bullets kept spattering on the wheels. The horses were removed to a gully, where they were fairly sheltered from fire. A shell hit the end of one of the trucks and burst, smashing the bogie of the truck, but luckily no one was under that particular truck. The Australian Horse contingent behaved particularly well, though it was their first experience under fire.

When the shelling first began and orders were given to close in on the train, the troops came in as steadily as a parade, the horses were dismounted and removed, and the men went to their places as coolly as possible. Trooper Ford, an ex-policeman and a member of the First Australian Horse, was one of the steadiest under fire, and he shot away fifty rounds of ammunition — shot it away steadily and quietly without any fuss. He was wounded in the face by a shell bursting near him. After some hours of this Major Lee sent in word that he could hold the trucks, as while the men kept under them the shells could not reach them, and the Boers dared not come down close again. As night drew on the Boers left the hills and came down closer and closer, sniping away at short range, and they came up fairly close on the flank. Five horses were shot dead, but none of the men were hit. At last it grew quite dark, and our men still held the trucks, but a lantern signal came that they were to retire, and to our unutterable disgust, after all the risk we had run, the Boers for the next three days were calmly allowed to loot the escaped train, though our artillery on Porter's Hill occasionally sent a shell down amongst them. It is hard to estimate what a godsend the trainload of provisions was to them. The shells set some of the trucks on fire, but the Boers got most of the stuff away. Our men were willing to go down and take the trucks again, but no orders were to be had to that effect.

This closed the battle so far as Australian troops were concerned. We ran a big risk, and brought off a successful attack, only to see our efforts wasted and the trucks lost; so of course we got no thanks for it. Some Boer prisoners captured a day or two afterwards said that our fire disabled two men. At time of writing the fighting is still going on. Millbanks, A.D.C. to the general, was shot through the leg today. We expect to make a big attack tomorrow, and start at 2.30 with that object in view. For the next few days I may be camping out, so I close this letter now. By the time it reaches you you will know whether we have got Colesberg or not. One thing is certain, our troops have no reason to be ashamed of their display at the railway-trucks, and if another chance occurs there is no doubt they will make the most of it. This is written hurriedly preparatory to a daylight start.

Sydney Morning Herald, 5 February 1900

THE PERSONALITY OF KIPLING

Bloemfontein, 25 March, 1900

We are still outside this place, camped on the side of a big green hill, with a maize and melon field alongside, and we have nothing to do but try to cure our horses' backs and ride into the town buying clothes and listening to the absurd rumours that always spring up in a camp after a day or two's idleness. No one knew for some days where Buller's force had got to, and it was reported to be in Johannesburg, in Pretoria, and in fact in all sorts of impossible places. Then at last a man came in from Buller and said that the latter had not left Ladysmith; consequently, when we heard that four officers of the Guards had been sent in wounded by the Boers, we thought it was another camp lie, but it turned out to be true.

While in town inquiring into a certain matter I had the luck to meet Kipling. He has come up here on a hurried visit, and partly in search of health after his late severe illness. He is a little, squat-figured, sturdy man of about forty. His face is well enough known to everybody from his numerous portraits, but no portrait gives any hint of the quick nervous energy of the man. His talk is a gabble, a chatter, a constant jumping from one point to another, and he seizes the chief idea in each subject unerringly. In manner he is more like a businessman than a literary celebrity. There is nothing of the dreamer about him, and the last thing one could believe was that the little square-figured man with the thick black eyebrows and the round glasses was the creator of Mowgli the jungle-boy, of "The Drums of the Fore-and-aft", and of "The Man Who Would Be King", to say nothing of Ortheris, Mulvaney, and Learoyd, and a host of others. He talked of little but the war and its results, present and prospective. His residence in America has Americanized his language, and he says "yep" instead of "yes". After talking for some time about Australian books and Australian papers he launched out on what is evidently his ruling idea at present — the future of South Africa.

"I'm off back to London," he said, "booked to sail on the eleventh. I'm not going to wait for the fighting here. It's in London I'll have to do my fighting. I want to fight the people who will say, 'The Boers fought for freedom — give them back their country!' I want to fight all that sort of nonsense. I know all about it. I knew this war was coming, and I came over here some time ago and went to Johannesburg and Pretoria, and I've got everything good and ready. There's going to be the greatest demand for skilled labour here the world has ever known. Railways, irrigation, mines, mills, all would have started years ago only for this Government."

I asked what sort of Government he purposed to put in place of the Boers.

"Military rule for three years, and by that time they will have enough population here to govern themselves. We want you Australians to stay over here and help fetch this place along."

I said that our men did not think the country worth fighting over, and that all we had seen would not pay to farm, unless one were sure of water.

"Water! You can get artesian water at forty feet anywhere! What more do they want?"

I pointed out that there is a vast difference between artesian water which rises to the surface, and well-water which has to be lifted forty feet. When it comes to watering a hundred thousand sheep one finds the difference.

"Oh, well," he said, "I don't know about that; but, anyhow, you haven't seen the best of the country. You've only seen five hundred miles of Karoo desert yet. Wait till you get to the Transvaal!"

"Will there be much more fighting, do you think?"

"Well, there's sure to be some more, and the soldiers want to get their money back."

"How do you mean, get their money back?"

"Get some revenge out of the Boers for the men we've lost — get our money back. The Tommies don't count the lot captured with Cronje at all. They're all alive, and our men are dead. We want to get some of our money back. You Australians have fought well," he went on, "very well. Real good men. Now we want you to stay here and help us along with this show. I can't understand there being so many radicals in Australia. What do they want? If they were to become independent, what do they expect to do? Will they fork out the money for a fleet and a standing army? They'd be a dead gift to Germany if they didn't. What more do they want than what they've got?"

I didn't feel quite equal to enlightening him on Australian politics, so I said, "What are you going to do with the Boers if you take their country?"

"Let 'em stop on their farms."

"Won't they vote against you as soon as you give them the votes back? Won't they revert to their old order of things?"

"Not a bit. We'll have enough people to outvote 'em before we give 'em the votes. There'll be no Irish question here. Once they find they're under a Government that don't commandeer everything they've got, they'll settle down and work all right. They're working away now to the north of us, entrenching away like beavers; we'll give them something better to do than digging trenches."

One could almost see the man's mind working while he talked, and yet all the time he was talking with quick, nervous utterance of the great things to be done in those unsettled countries I seemed to see behind him the heavy, impassive face of the man I saw in Kimberley — Cecil Rhodes. Kipling is the man of thought and speech, Rhodes the man of action. Cecil Rhodes seems to own most things in these parts, and when our Australians reached the promised land of which Kipling speaks so enthusiastically, they will be apt to find the best claims already staked out by Cecil Rhodes and his fellow-investors, at least that is my impression. There are no fortunes "going spare" in this part of the world; but anyhow this is not a political letter, and Kipling is big enough to draw his own rations, and if he choose to temporarily lay aside the pen of the author for the carpet-bag of the politician, it is his own look-out. He expressed great interest in the Australian horses, and promised to come out to the camp and see them, and he gave us a graphic account of the way in which an Australian buckjumper had got rid of him in India. "I seemed to be sitting on great eternal chaos," he said, "and then the world slipped away from under me, and that's all I remember."

He looks pale and sallow after his illness, but seems a strong man, one that will live many years if his brain doesn't wear his body out.

Let us return now to our muttons, or at any rate our Australians. I rode over and saw Colonel Knight's men and horses yesterday. Captain Antill's men are attached to Knight's command now. Antill's troop have been a long time here, and have settled down, and their saddles are fairly good, so that the whole force are fit for action; but Colonel Knight's men were sent from Australia with saddles I wouldn't put on a mule, and many of the horses are dying, weakened by hard work, under-feeding, colds, and sore backs. The question of saddles and sore backs is the great cavalry question from one generation to another. Books have been written on it, speeches made about it, kingdoms have risen and fallen on the question of cavalry saddles; and the thing is as far from a settlement as ever. It isn't the bullet of the foe that the cavalry has to fear, it is the sore-backed horse that cripples the regiment, and leaves hundreds of men on foot useless.

While I am writing this in Bloemfontein Club, most of the original members of that club are digging trenches around Kroonstad, and it is freely rumoured that they are holding a Volksraad there to decide whether they shall fight on or not. We don't care how soon they surrender, we are not like Kipling's soldiers, wanting any "money back". And talking of "money back", I may as well close with a little incident, in which an Australian and a Boer figured as follows:

When Cronje surrendered, and his men came bundling out of the trenches, each man with a carpet-bag in one hand and a rifle in the other, a great many of them were leading horses laden with all their goods and chattels. One Burgher had a very fine, creamy pony, and on this animal he had at least a hundredweight of luggage of various sorts, rugs, blankets, a sugee-bag, a carpet-bag, some boots, and innumerable other things. One of our Lancer officers took a fancy to the pony, and offered the Boer a pound for him. As he was sure to lose the pony as soon as he became a prisoner he was willing enough to take the pound. But the trouble was — how was he to shift his luggage? He was solemnly assured that Lord Roberts would be certain to send a cart for his luggage, and on this idea he took the sovereign, unloaded the pony, and handed him over, and sat down cheerfully smoking beside his pile of luggage. He had hardly got comfortably seated when a Tommy came up with a fixed bayonet, and said, "Now, then, move off your hank! Don't you see the others movin' off! Come along! Where's the — what? The cart for your luggage! Leave it 'ere, mate, leave it 'ere, and I'll tell Lord Kitchener about it." By dint of dividing it up among his friends, he got it along somehow, and the pony, with an English shrapnel bullet in his jaw, is now an officer's servant's charger, and a very good little animal he is.

We expect to move north in ten days. The corps from New South Wales has been given charge of the main hospital building

here, and is doing great work. Majors Scot-Skirving and Mac-
Cormick are just in time for plenty of hard work. We have no
tents, and the weather is getting bitterly cold at night. Curiously
enough, we are probably the only English-speaking people that
have never heard ''The Absent-minded Beggar'' sung or recited.
When we get back and hear the tune, we will wonder what it is.
The English papers are full of ''Absent-minded Beggar'' concerts.
Probably you are just as full of it.

29th March

Since closing my letter of yesterday all the Australians have been
ordered to the front, and ordered in no end of a hurry, too. I have
only stayed for the correspondents' dinner to Sir Alfred Milner,
Lord Roberts, and Kipling. It was a memorable event that dinner.
Though a private affair given by certain of the correspondents, it
had a semi-public flavour, in that it was the first occasion in which
any speeches had been made by the men who have fought this battle all along — Milner and Roberts. The former is a tall, thin, care-
worn man, but obviously a cool-headed diplomatist. He made an
excellent speech when responding to the toast of his health. He
said, with a grim smile, that he had already visited Bloemfontein
under very different circumstances — alluding, of course, to the
time when he came up to negotiate with Kruger. Since then, he
said, we had all gone through a time of stress, strain, and anxiety,
which he trusted was now over. Now the fact that the anxiety of
the Empire had been relieved was due, under God, to the skill and
courage of the great commander, Field-Marshal Lord Roberts.

Lord Roberts made a very fine speech in reply. He speaks slowly
and precisely, and makes every word tell. He has grown younger
during the campaign, and is as alert as posible, showing no sign of
his age in spite of the stress of campaigning. He has a lot of dry
humour. He said that he was delighted to be the guest of the correspondents, though he could not always make things very pleasant
for them on the field. He always felt towards the correspondents
much as a prisoner in the dock feels towards the jury, as they were
the men who pronounced on his work for the millions of newspaper readers, and he always awaited their verdict with anxiety —
guilty or not guilty. The correspondents shared in the hardships

and the dangers of the soldier's life, and he felt that he could call them his comrades on the field. The army had behaved in a manner which had no parallel; although they were marching through a hostile country, there had been no robbing, no pillage, nor any kind of crime. The men had been through great hardships, but he had heard no complaints, even though he had asked, not only among the healthy men, but among the sick and sounded. He had visited all the wounded men, and found them cheerful and determined to make the best of things. He was heartily glad to meet so many comrades in arms that night on such a momentous occasion, and finally, in thanking the correspondents, he said that he had no hesitation in saying that if he had to submit his work to any tribunal he knew no body of men more fitted to give an accurate, skilled, and impartial decision than the body of correspondents who had accompanied his army to Bloemfontein.

Kipling was next in order. He speaks very humorously, and made a great hit by proposing an unexpected toast, the "Health of Paul Kruger". He said that Kruger had done more to knit the Empire together than any man that had ever lived. He had been consistent throughout in his refusal to budge an inch from his position, and he had enabled us to make a white man's country of South Africa. This toast was not responded to, and he went on to propose the health of the Press Censor, Lord Stanley.

General Hector Macdonald also spoke. He proposed "Canada and Australia", to which Colonel Otter (Canada) responded. Macdonald was a great surprise to me. I had expected from descriptions I had read, and from photographs, to see a dour, hard-faced, weather-beaten Presbyterian-looking general, with the brand of the sergeant-major all over him. Instead of this, I saw a quite young-looking, pleasant-faced man, with quick eyes and a mobile mouth, and a general expression of light-heartedness — a man with a regular devil-may-care look in his eye, a man who looked as if he would fight a policeman on the way from the dinner, and think nothing of it. He yarned away about the Australians at a great rate, and obviously thinks that our troops are quite as good as any for the work here. Macdonald is as little of the "Muckle Sandie", i.e. the typical Scot, as any man I have ever seen, and I had thought he was the embodiment of all that eat burgoo. He must be a wonder to have risen from the ranks to the position he holds while still so young a man. He might be Lord Roberts's son to look at him, so far as age goes. I was seated next to Kipling at dinner, and if any man wants a better neighbour to sit next to, he is hard to please. There were twenty-four people at the dinner: Lord Roberts, Sir Alfred Milner, Gonard (Railway Staff Officer), Hanbury Williams (A.D.C. to Sir Alfred Milner), Generals Colville, Pole-Carew, and Macdonald, Colonel Otter (Canada), Earl of Kerry (Staff), Kipling, Gwynne (Reuter's), the correspondents of *The Times* and other journals being amongst them. We had songs and recitations after dinner, and did not get home till twelve o'clock, which is a novelty, as we usually go to bed at eight o'clock in camp.

Now, I must saddle up for a thirty-mile ride out to the front, where it is expected there will be a fight tomorrow.

Sydney Morning Herald, 12 May 1900

WITH FRENCH'S COLUMN

Bloemfontein, 2nd May 1900

It is eight days since I last wrote — eight days that for variety of incident and startling experiences would about represent eight years of one's ordinary life. Many letters come to me asking for details of a war correspondent's life. Well, in those eight days I have seen three or four fights: have captured two cities: have been in among the Boers and out again; have slept, variously in a bed, in the unburnt end of a burning house, in a Boer stable, out on the open veldt, in an ambulance, and under a cart which during the night was dragged from over me by a frightened horse. So that if this letter is rather long, and rather full of personal experiences, your readers will understand that it cannot well be otherwise under the circumstances.

At time of my writing the last letter there was a general feeling of unrest and uncertainty. The Boers had driven out of Bloemfontein, and were occupying fine, cool, and airy compartments on the hillsides in the surrounding country. East of here, and in sight of the town, is a big hill called Leuwkop, and it was known that the Boers had established themselves there. About forty miles south-east from here is a town called Dewetsdorp, and the Boers were holding this town against General Rundle, who was trying to force his way through there with a large force. And about thirty-six miles east is Thabanchu, which we had for some time, and then allowed the Boers to reoccupy. North of here is Karee Siding, where there also were Boers — plenty of them, and very venomous, mostly Johannesburg police.

It was uncertain, therefore, in which direction we should move, and as the British generals don't advertise their fights in advance, the war correspondents have to trust a lot to luck, and a little to judgment, in deciding which general they will follow. They may travel for days and days with a large force and see nothing, or they may fluke on to a series of exciting incidents, and it must be explained that the British army is so full of generals that it resembles Mark Twain's famous ship, in which you couldn't throw a stone without hitting a captain. We had General Tucker at Karee, and it was known that he might move forward at any moment. General Pole-Carew (pronounced "Poole-Carey") was organizing his troops for a march, and it was not known where he was going. Rundle was fighting at Dewetsdorp; Brabazon and Brabant were at Wepener; Hamilton and Hutton were collecting the colonial division at Bloemfontein; Dickson and Gordon, with the third and fourth cavalry brigades, were under orders to be ready to march at a moment's notice; while Kitchener, French, Macdonald, Knox, Campbell, Wood and some others were all in Bloemfontein, ready to go anywhere, and do anything that might be ordered. Troops were moving in all directions all day long.

Under these circumstances, it was purely by accident that I happened to get on the march with French's column, and saw one of the best parts of the campaign. Probably, in the doctrine of averages, I shall miss something good later on — I may be missing it now — to make up for it.

It happened in this way, Mr B.B. O'Conor, a member of the New South Wales Assembly, was at the New South Wales Lancers' camp. He was very anxious to see a shot fired in action, but the Lancers had no horses fit for service, and they were out of action for the time, and there was no hope of seeing anything with them. Antill and Knight's people were coming in to be refitted with horses and clothes, so they were not likely to show him anything. Still, we all wanted to do our best in the way of entertaining a visitor — if he got shot, that was his lookout — and one day we saw troops going out to Leuwkop, so we got him a horse, and off he and I went together in the hope of possibly seeing an afternoon's shooting. We rode out to Leuwkop, and heard guns in the distance, but could not come on a fight. We found the usual thing in the field of battle; we found a lot of African volunteers and Roberts's Horse sitting under shelter of a big stony hill holding their horses. Some were making small fires to cook their provisions. They had been there all day, and had not seen a shot fired. They said that a lot of troops had gone on about five miles round the far end of Leuwkop, and were, they believed, fighting somebody somewhere, but they didn't know where, and they didn't seem to care much.

It was too far to ride round Leuwkop in pursuit of these phantom troops, so we rode back to a farmhouse, and bought two fine fat ducks, at eighteen pence per duck, and were going dismally home, when we heard the clatter of the pom-pom gun about three miles off, round the nearer end of the big blue hill known as Leuwkop. We rode off to see what was doing, giving Leuwkop a wide berth, and as things turned out, it was just as well we did so. After a long, hot, weary ride we came on a big cluster of troops, cavalry, and guns, huddled up under the side of a rolling hill. Most of the men were asleep by their horses. There was no sign of life or movement whatever, and it looked as little like a battlefield as one could imagine. Our luck had failed us. The fight, such as it was, was evidently over, and the Boers had gone home to lunch.

Lunch, alas! It was midday, very hot, ten miles from camp, and we had nothing to eat but two raw ducks. There was no chance of getting anything from the troops, as it is the unwritten law of the army, "Thou shalt not cadge". Suddenly at the other end of the big cluster of troops we saw an ambulance drawn by horses, and knew that we were sure of something to eat, anyhow, even if we saw no fight. We knew it was an Australian ambulance because the Australian ambulances are the only ones drawn by horses. All the rest use mules. We found that Captains Perkins and Marshall,

of the New South Wales Army Medical Corps, had been lent from
Hutton's Brigade to come with the third and fourth cavalry brigades. We went down and found them hard at work patching up
wounded men. It appeared that the whole outfit — cavalry, guns,
ambulances, and all, had marched in a solid mass right up into
easy range of the row of hills in front, from which the Boers had
suddenly opened fire on them with a pom-pom. No doubt someone had blundered. It had been bad scouting to let them get so
close without detecting the presence of Boers on the hill. The
Boers evidently couldn't believe their eyes when they saw this mass
of troops come into such easy range, as they actually fired the first
instalment of shells — half-a-dozen or so — right over our troops,
and the shells burst harmlessly out in the plain beyond.

A hurried retreat at once followed, a regular general hustle to
get out of range. The only patients in the ambulance at the time
were two ducks and a fine fat sheep, who were lying there securely
fastened but the men said that our non-commissioned officer was
so anxious to expedite the retreat that he actually hove the ducks
and sheep overboard to lighten the wagon. The pom-pom again
sent her hail of iron shells, each weighing a pound, in among the
retreating troops, and this time with some effect. A trumpeter of
the 8th Hussars was killed on the spot, a sergeant of the 14th was
shot right through the body by a piece of shell, several others were
wounded; and many horses were killed. Our New South Wales
stretcher-bearers, headed by Sergeant Airey (son of Colonel
Airey) and Sergeant Dart, were at once beside the wounded men,
and brought them out of action even while shells were still falling.

As soon as the troops were out of range they halted, and our 12-
pounder guns opened fire, but the Boer gun was moved into shelter, and when we got up all firing had ceased; we saw nothing but
the great stretch of open veldt; the huddled mass of troops, and
the medical men bending over the wounded. Quickly and skilfully
each man's wounds were dressed, and really they were as well
looked after as they could have been in an ordinary hospital.

A grave was dug for the dead trumpeter by the men of his own
regiment, and there, out in the open veldt, with the Boers sitting
on the their hills watching, we formed a small funeral procession
and buried the boy, the short service being read by his captain. A

curious thing was that the troops had been singing the previous
night, and a very favourite song with them is one of Sergeant
Rose's about a bugler —

> There in the snow,
> Lieth he low,
> Gallant old bugler facing the foe,

and the first man killed next day was this trumpeter.

Orders soon came to move back along Leuwkop and as we did
so we could see the Boers fetch up their horses and take away their
guns at a gallop. They moved along the ridge parallel with us, and
at the end of the hills we opened fire with the 12-pounder guns, firing at the foot of a hill. We could see nobody, but evidently someone was there, as our other guns were shelling the same place
somewhere in front, and shell after shell streamed over into this
place for an hour or more, and all the time a crackling rifle fire
told us that the Boers were still holding their own there. Our infantry were attacking the hill from the front, but we could not see
them, as each man was lying absolutely flat on his face in the long
grass, and only firing stealthily and quickly. Our shells flew right
over a large farmhouse which was surrounded by magnificent
gum-trees. At last, just as darkness fell, we saw a few Boers hurriedly run out of the stones at the foot of the hill, jump on their
horses, and dash away at a gallop for the main chain of hills. The
clatter of a maxim, fired from in front, showed that our men had
seen the retreat, but no damage was done that we could see. The
troops bivouacked where they were for the night, and I took our
New South Wales M.L.A. off back to camp.

Next day I got my cart and went out after the army. French was
in command, and nowadays that is almost a guarantee that business will be brisk. They had marched at daylight, but on going up
to the farmhouse where the fight had been I found Lieutenant Edwards, of the New South Wales Army Medical Corps, with one
ambulance, waiting to take a wounded officer into Bloemfontein.
The officer was Protheroe, of the Welsh, and he had been shot
right through the head just above the eyes. His brains were pro-
truding from the sound, but he had lived through the night, and
the medical men had hopes of saving him. He was being attended
by Lieutenant Edwards and a consulting specialist, one of the civil

surgeons who are in attendance on the army. While the ambulance went off with him I joined company with the specialist, and went on after the troops.

They had gone, and, as usual, had left no stragglers, but we soon found tracks of their transport, and came on a couple of blazing farmhouses. There had been a fight there that day, and the Boers had fired from the farmhouses, though they were flying a white flag, and a major of Roberts's Horse had been fatally shot — in revenge our people had ignited the two houses. One of them was evidently a grain-store, and was piled full of horsefeed, so we camped there for the night, letting our horses revel in all sorts of luxuries.

There was still a chance that the owners of the houses might come back in the night, and if so they would no doubt have been in a nasty temper, so every time we heard a dog bark we used to listen intently, but no one showed up. Brother Boer doesn't travel about at night much. I forgot to say that in the farmhouse where Captain Protheroe was treated there were three Dutch girls, who had been there all through the shelling and rifle fire which had raged round the house. On the grass just outside the house were little pools of cartridge cases where the soldiers had been lying and firing; all about the place where shells as thick as pumpkins in a field; and yet these women had stayed there all through the affair, and neither side had harmed them. The boy who drives my cart picked up a man's finger just outside the garden gate.

To return to our march. We loaded the cart with horsefeed at the burning house, and pushed on after French, and soon came on the rear of his army and went along, past the guns, rolling and rumbling over the stony road, past the mounted foot, spreading out on either side of the road, and at last we saw the cavalry spread out over the plains like a fan, while just at their heels an ambulance was swinging along.

It was a lovely morning, the air was full of the scent of grass, the far-off blue hills had a delicate haze on them, and we rode along in front of the ambulance, smoking, and talking of Sydney and its people, and had forgotten all about the war, when all of a sudden there came the sickeningly familiar pom, pom, pom, pom, pom, whe-e-e-e-e-e-w, crack, crack, crack of the hated Vickers-

Maxim. The reader must understand that in nine cases out of ten you never see the men, you simply hear the shells coming, and until they burst you don't know whether they are fired at you or at troops half a mile off.

In this case we saw the 16th Lancers come scuttling in across a big cornfield, and our stretcher-bearers galloped over to see if any were hurt, but the shooting was very wild, and no one was touched.

The Boers were evidently in force on a big blue hill on our left, and our general, after slight discussion, decided to leave them there, and went on. As soon as we moved the Boers came galloping over to reach a ridge that ran quite close to our line of march, and as soon as French saw this he sent the cavalry to go up one side of the ridge, while the Boers were going up the other. It was very stirring to see them dash across about a mile of level ground and then dismount and run up the hill, while from the heights where we were we could see the Boers on the opposite side doing the same thing. The hill had a flat top, and our men reached the top at one side just as the Boers reached it at the other, and both sides commenced shooting at about two hundred yards apart, an extraordinarily close range for fighting of this sort. The Boer bullets were carrying over our men, over the intervening half a mile of ground, and up on to the hill where we had the ambulances.

On to this hill there soon galloped horses drawing two curious-looking guns, khaki-coloured, with shields for the gunner to sit behind, and fired by a man sitting astride the hinder part of the gun. Quick as lightning they wheeled into action, and then there burst out the most deafening clatter, pom, pom, pom, pom, pom! It was the first appearance of the famous pom-pom guns on the English side, and we almost felt inclined to cheer their debut. The exploded cartridge cases were flying broadcast out of the gun like husks from a corn-sheller.

All the time the rifle fire along the crest of the ridge was incessant, and Airey was dispatched over to see if there were any casualties. He returned to say that there were several, and he wanted to take the ambulances over there and then — a thing that Captain Perkins would not permit. The fighting was still in full swing, and an ambulance was just as likely to get in the road of our own guns as not. The men were quite indignant because they were not let move. "There's Dhanjibhoy's ambulances going!" they said; and sure enough the little Tonga ambulances did make a move in that direction, but soon were turned back.

We waited on the hill and watched the firing. Our pom-pom shells were bursting on the Boers' side of the ridge, and their pom-pom shells were bursting on our side. At last our Horse Artillery gunners got sight of the Boers' pom-pom, and bang! away went a 12-pound shrapnel exctly where it was wanted. The Boers limbered up their gun, and away they went as hard as they could gallop, and the riflemen on the ridge ran down the hill to their horses and galloped off, while our men stood up and fired at them, and our pom-poms barked and clattered, and shelled out cartridge cases till the air was full of them.

A few of the Boers dropped; the rest galloped for about three miles, and then pulled up, and were riding leisurely away, but we had a surprise in store for them. While the fight was going on, a couple of "Weary Willies", i.e., big naval guns, had been toiling along at the tails of thirty-two oxen, the men hoping frantically to be up in time, and the way they walloped those oxen was a caution. They got sight of the Boers from a hill, and the Jack Tars jumped to the guns, and hauled them into position, panting and sweating with excitement. "At eight thousand! Number One Gun! Fire!" And away went the shell on its 4½-mile trip, after the little knot of black figures that we could just see moving across the plain. We could hear the scream of the shell getting fainter and fainter in the distance, till at last we could not hear it at all, but we had no difficulty in telling when the Boers heard it, as they suddenly began to hustle along and open out their ranks. No doubt they wondered where on earth the shell was coming from. It burst right amongst them, and set them on the run in earnest till they disappeared behind a hill. We found three wounded men at a farmhouse behind that hill next morning, and the jolly Jack Tars are all morally certain that it was their shell which did the execution.

After the Boers ran, our ambulances went out. All along the ridge where the firing had been there were dead and wounded men, and on the Boers' side of it the same state of things prevailed. Captain Perkins found one Boer shot through the thigh lying beside a Cape cart with two ponies in it. He had evidently driven himself to war in his own turn-out, but it was the ambulance people who drove him back. Our ambulance people wanted to keep the cart, but the 7th Dragoon Guards dispossessed them of it by some sleight of hand, and they again lost it to some higher authority, and it was finally left behind for want of transport to bring it along.

The medical men, Perkins and Marshall, were soon busy with their wounded. One curious thing happened. Two soldiers had been lying among the rocks sideways on to the Boers. Like ostriches, they had hidden their heads, but had forgotten that their large feet were sticking out behind the stones, and a Boer marksman put a bullet right through their four feet.

The cavalry behaved splendidly in this affair. They fought dismounted, with the greatest determination, and drove the Boers back before the infantry, or "mounted foot" came up at all. We had no Australians in this show, except the ambulance.

After the Boers ran I went up on a high hill with General French's staff, and surveyed the country. We knew that General Rundle was down a few miles south-east of us engaged with the Boers. We started a heliograph working, and before long, away on a far hill, there flamed an answering helio — Rundle was there and was ending word that he was actively engaged with the Boers. Away on our left another helio flared a message — Pole-Carew was advancing parallel with our line of march. A brigade signaller with another helio was vainly trying to attract attention in our rear. Every hill seemed to blaze with a helio; and suddenly, from a cleft in a far hill, like an evil spirit for a moment let loose above ground, a Boer helio sprang glittering into the sunlight, worked with inconceivable rapidity for a few seconds and then subsided again. Our signallers had read the message, "Who are you?" They answered back. "French". The Boer helio again flashed out for a few seconds. It sent a coarse obscene message to the general, and then, like an evil thing, disappeared once more into the shadow of the hill.

That was all we saw or heard of the Boers that day. Ten dead were gathered, but they got their wounded away. The ponies of the dead men followed their mates, but many were crippled by fragments of the pom-pom shells, and stood patiently suffering about the field. Poor brutes, they had broken legs, broken shoulders, all sorts of wounds.

We marched on after the Boers for a few miles, and camped for the night. I dined with Gwynne, Reuter's correspondent. The Turkish attaché could only speak French and Turkish, another guest could only speak Dutch, the cook could only understand Kaffir, and so the dinner rather resembled a feast in the Tower of Babel. The unspeakable Turk was a most polished gentleman, and was full of praise of our most valiant army. I met the unspeakable Russian attaché later on, and found him a much more outspoken person; but I must hurry on, or I will never get to the end of this march.

Sydney Morning Herald, 12 June 1900

THE BATTLE OF RETIEF'S NEK

Outside Fouriesberg, 22nd July 1900

The army under command of General Hunter left Bethlehem and came down here with a view of capturing the Free Staters under De Wet. It must be explained that by occupying all the towns and roads in the Orange River Colony the Boers were gradually forced down into the mountains at the eastern corner of the Colony, and touching the Basutoland border, and at length they were hemmed inside a circle of rugged mountains, through which only a few passes existed. There are real genuine mountains in this country. The whole place is about four thousand feet above the sea, and these mountain-chains ran up another one thousand feet or fifteen hundred feet, and are as steep as the Rock of Gibraltar. Consequently, when we had them penned in a circle of mountains, with the Basutos at their back, it seemed a simple matter of tactics to block all the passes and advance on them from all sides and overwhelm them by numbers.

With this object in view, General Hunter sent Paget's force to a place called Stabbat's Nek to prevent the Boers getting out that way. Bruce Hamilton was at Naauwpoort Nek with a like object. Clements was further round on the west, and Rundle on the south at Commando Nek, just near Ficksburg. The New South Wales Rifles were with Hunter at Bethlehem, which blocked Retief's Nek, the only other passage into this circle of hills. Suddenly one morning there was heard heavy firing out towards Stabbat's Nek, and all Ridley's Brigade, which included our Mounted Rifles, were ordered out to see what had happened. News soon came in that a large commando had come out of Stabbat's Nek in the night; they had marched quite close past Paget's camp with five guns and a hundred wagons, and no one had seen them, although Paget's force comprised about three hundred of our Australian Bushmen. At daylight the Boers opened fire on Paget's people, and engaged them all day; meanwhile sending their wagons on ahead. Paget failed to stop their northward march, and Broadwood's Cavalry and Ridley's Mounted Infantry were sent to fetch the Boers to a halt. They chased them nearly to Lindley, but here the wily Boers managed to give them the slip. How it was done is a mystery, when you remember that the Boers had bullock-wagons, which can only travel about fifteen miles a day, and they were pursued by mounted men, who could do thirty miles a day.

Near Lindley the Boer forces crossed a convoy of ours coming down to Bethlehem, and the two parties camped in sight of each other for the night. I was following Ridley's Brigade up, but found that the Boers had given him the slip, so I came back to headquarters with the convoy. The after history of the Boer flying commando had reached us here by wire to the effect that they got on to the line and captured a train. Whether they have been headed off since that is not known.

It was expected that Ridley's Brigade, with the New South Wales Mounted Rifles, would rejoin Hunter, but so far they have not put in an appearance, and at date of writing they may be still following the Boer commando over trackless leagues of open veldt on a sort of "Here we go round the mulberry bush" business. One thing is certain, if our people do get sight of the Boer wagons they are just the troops to hang on to them. It is said that De Wet himself is in charge of this flying column, and that Steyn, the President, is with him; but this was only rumour, while we knew for certain that a lot of Boers, with wagons and guns, had not left the circle of hills; so, leaving Ridley and Broadwood to chase the flying lot, Hunter came on to this place to carry out the scheme of driving them into a corner and capturing them; and whatever be the result of this movement I, at any rate, am glad that I came, as I have seen the Highland Brigade in action, and this alone was worth the miseries of the march down here.

We moved out from Bethlehem and crossed the Jordan (a dry creek) and advanced on Retief's Nek. The only Australians with the forces were Colonel Williams, P.M.O., of the Division, and Captain Martin, his secretary. The colonel had the largest medical command in the army at the time, as Hunter had two infantry divisions and a lot of Yeomanry and sundries, and when Macdonald joined us with his Highlanders, it brought the strength of the troops under Hunter's command up to a very high figure.

As there were so many passes to hold it was not possible to concentrate a very large force on any one point for fear of leaving the others unguarded, so we advanced on Retief's Nek with only the Highland Brigade — three regiments, Black Watch, Seaforths, and Highland Light Infantry — supported by the Sussex Regiment, three batteries of field artillery, two "cow" guns, and a lot of irregular mounted men, namely, Lovatt's Highland Gillies and Remington's Guides.

And now a word as to the Highlanders. These are the finest troops I have ever seen. They are much more intelligent-looking men than the ordinary Tommies. They are not particularly big men, but all strong, well-proportioned, and alert-looking, very neatly turned out, and evidently in a high state of discipline. The army people say that the Highlanders have not done as well as the Irish troops in this war, the Munsters and Dublin Fusiliers and the Royal Irish being cited as cases in point. There is no doubt the Highlanders were driven off at Magersfontein, and they failed to carry the Boer trenches at Paardeberg; but no other troops have been asked to do such tasks as were put to these men at those two places. Whatever be the respective merits of the troops, no one could fail to be struck by the bearing and appearance of the Highlanders, or the "Jocks", as they are always called in the army; and in this fight at Retief's Nek they acted up to the best possible standard.

Leaving Bethlehem, we advanced to within five miles of the Nek and camped at a farmhouse. Before us there rose a chain of hills about a thousand feet high, with a narrow gap or passage cleft between two of them. This passage, about a quarter of a mile wide, was the Nek through which we were to force our way. Along to the right-hand side of it the hills stretched for miles in an unbroken chain; on the left there were hills for a few miles, and then a patch of open ground, and then more hills. At the back of all were the mountains of Basutoland — great peaks and crags and fortresses of stone towering to the sky.

It was bitterly cold and windy the night of our camp there, and, behold, when we came out in the morning all the hills by the Nek and all the mountains at the back were white with snow. It was a glorious sight — those miles of snow-covered mountains gleaming in the sun. But we had something else to think about than the scenery. About ten o'clock the tramp of feet and the challenge of the pipes told us that the Highlanders were on the march. Grim and stern, with Fighting Macdonald at their head, the Highland Light Infantry field out to march up the long valley of death that led to Retief's Nek; the Black Watch moved up parallel with them to attack the little bit of open ground that lay to the left of the hills guarding the Nek; and away on the right the Sussex Regiment advanced along the foot of the hills which converged on the attack of the Highland Light Infantry. The Seaforths were left in camp go guard the huge convoy we had with us. The two Generals, Hunter and Macdonald, took their positions on a big bare hill facing the Nek, and from that height the whole battlefield lay before us like a scene in a theatre. Down on the right hand was a long, clear, grassy valley leading up to the Nek. On the far side of this valley the Sussex Regiment could be seen making its way along the foot of the mountains. On the near side of the valley, and only a stone's throw below us, the Highland Light Infantry opened out into long lines and advanced straight up the frowning hills that guarded the pass; and on the left the Black Watch made a similar advance on the bare ground that lay to the left of the Nek.

This bare ground looked as if it might be easily taken, but it turned out that it simply led to the edge of a precipice some hundred feet deep, and down at the foot of the precipice was a huge plain something like the Hollow described by Boldrewood in

Robbery Under Arms. It was into this Happy Valley that we wished to get, and the only way was to go through the Nek or down the sides of this precipice. The Black Watch pushed their attack first. They were to go to the edge of this precipice and see if there was any way down. The wailing of the pipes died away, and the men opened out and marched in open order across the brown grass, till suddenly a hot musketry fire broke out from the edge of the precipice itself, showing that the Boers had got up it from the lower side and were holding it in force; in addition to this, a hot fire was opened from the chain of hills on either side. The men dropped in the grass and advanced, crawling along the ground, and actually seized an outlying hill, driving the Boers off it in confusion; but the price paid was too high, and, when the ambulances began to come in with wounded, and the second in command was fatally hit, the advance was stopped, and the men lay motionless in the grass under fire, while an attack was tried by the Highland Light Infantry and Sussex on the Nek itself.

This looked a hopeless task from the start. The hills rose sheer and rugged, scarcely offering foothold for a goat. All along the tops of the hills the Boers had made stone breastworks and shelters and were shooting at their leisure, undismayed by the shower of shells that the "cow" guns and the two field batteries poured forth at them. The crackle of their musketry rattled all along the mountainside, and yet not a man could be seen. From the hilltop where we were we could see down below us just a series of little dots of black — these were the kilts of the Highlanders lying flat on the ground. Inch by inch they pushed their way towards the foot of the hills. Now and again an officer would stand up for a moment or so and look through his glasses, and sink again into the long brown grass. They did not advance into the pass itself, as that was full of Boer trenches, but made for the hills from which the Boers were firing, in the hope of being able to get a foothold to go up them and drive the Boers off.

It was a gallant attempt to make, and we could scarcely believe our eyes when we saw what looked like a long string of black ants crawling up from the top. The Highlanders had got some little cover from a gully that ran out of the hill, and had sneaked in single file along this till they were at the foot of the hill. The Sussex had wormed their way along the rocks on the other side of the valley, but as soon as they got near the Nek itself a deafening discharge of rifle fire began, and our cannons were worked as fast as possible to try and keep it down. All along the line of hills there was incessant firing for about two hours, and no efforts of ours could dislodge the Boers from their rocks. Word came back from the Highland Light Infantry that they could not get up the rocks, and reluctantly General Hunter ordered a general withdrawal. Here Macdonald showed better judgment than the colonel in charge of the Sussex. The latter withdrew his men at once, and they suffered severely in the retirement. Macdonald didn't try to move his men till dark, and they came back safely enough. We had about a hundred killed and wounded in the fight, and it is doubtful if the Boers lost ten.

The night found us all very dismal; the task appeared hopeless. It was a good deal like trying to advance through Sydney Heads, supposing the water to be solid ground and the Heads to be strongly held by an enemy. During the night some of the Remington Guides and some of Lovatt's Highland Gillies crawled up in the hills to the left of the Nek. There was a heavy mist, and through its white clouds they heard a Dutch challenge, "Wie ist dar?" It must have been a weird business climbing about on those rocks in the bitter cold, not knowing at what moment death, in the shape of a rifle flash, might come from the gloom. It was too much for the Boers' nerves. They withdrew from all the outlying hills and held only the big hills at each side of the Nek, and they still kept the precipice which the Black Watch had vainly attacked.

Next morning (25th July) the Seaforths were brought away from the task of convoy guarding, and were sent to take this precipice, or rather to drive the Boers from it, in the hope of finding a way down. It was argued that where the Boers could get up the Highlanders could get down. The retirement of the Boers from the outlying hills during the night had made the task easier, as they could bring no cross-fire to bear. The general and his staff pushed on to one of the outlying hills, and here we looked right down into the valley below. Not a Boer could be seen, but from the edge of the cliff the bullets fairly whistled wherever a man showed himself.

We all lay down behind the stones and watched the Seaforths make their rush at this place.

As soon as the signal was given for them to advance, they came along in a long line of prostrate figures, while a terrific fire was poured on to the edge of the precipice to cover their advance. Slowly they crept on, one or two giving little convulsive struggles and lying still. Suddenly, at some signal that we could not hear, they leapt to their feet, and dashed at the run for the edge of the cliff. One or two bowled over like shot rabbits, but the others held grimly on, and when they got within two hundred yards of the edge we saw the Boers bolting out from beneath the rocks. They had clambered down to the valley and jumped on to their horses, and in twos and threes and half-dozens they began to come out from under the rocks a hundred feet below the Highlanders. They split into small parties and galloped off at full speed. About a hundred came out, and by the time the first of the Highlanders got to the edge of the rocks the Boers could not have been three hundred yards off, and yet they rode away almost unharmed under a regular fusillade.

That is the one great mystery one never ceases to marvel at — how so much firing can do so little harm. We saw a few fall, and they were taken away by their comrades. A nigger next day reported that "a wagon-load of dead Boers" had been removed; but a nigger isn't much of an authority to trust to. We saw them go under a storm of shot and shell, and hardly any dropped. The Highlanders clambered down the rocks after them and took possession of the valley, and ran round to the back of Retief's Nek, hoping to catch the Boers who were holding it. But those gentry had seen the flight of their mates, and were in full retreat long before our men got round to them. The dash on this precipice, the flight of the Boers from under the rocks, and their retreat across the big hollow valley were like a battle in a theatre — every movement was absolutely clear and open to the spectator. We followed them up, and got down the valley nearly to Fouriesberg, where we now are.

As we approached this town a few snipers began firing from the hills, and to our surprise far away up the valley ahead we could see a Boer convoy coming towards us. It is evidently being hunted in by Rundle from Commando Nek, and we are much disappointed that the general doesn't see fit to attack it. But we understand that there is only one way in which it can get out of the mountains, and Macdonald has been sent round to block that way; so in a day or two we will know if this great "early closing movement" is to come to a successful issue or not.

In any event, we hope to be on the road home before long now, and it is just possible I may come home through Basutoland. We don't know at all what is doing anywhere else. There may be fighting at Pretoria or Lyndenberg; our Mounted Rifles may have caught Steyn and De Wet. All we know is that we are here in a little circle of hills, and that the Boers, about three thousand, are cooped up in the same circle of hills. So if they don't get out there is likely to be an end of the Free State army in these parts.*

Sydney Morning Herald, 6 September 1900

---

* Paterson returned to Australia towards the end of 1900. The Boer War ended on 31 May 1902.

Army Poems

THERE'S ANOTHER BLESSED HORSE FELL DOWN

When you're lying in your hammock, sleeping soft and sleeping
      sound,
   Without a care or trouble on your mind,
And there's nothing to disturb you but the engines going round,
    And you're dreaming of the girl you left behind;
In the middle of your joys you'll be wakened by a noise,
    And a clatter on the deck above your crown,
And you'll hear the corporal shout as he turns the picket out,
    "There's another blessed horse fell down."

You can see 'em in the morning, when you're cleaning out the stall,
    A-leaning on the railings nearly dead,
And you reckon by the evening they'll be pretty sure to fall,
    And you curse them as you tumble into bed.
Oh, you'll hear it pretty soon, "Pass the word for Denny Moon,
    "There's a horse here throwing handsprings like a clown;
And it's "Shove the others back or he'll cripple half the pack,
    "There's another blessed horse fell down."

And when the war is over and the fighting is all done,
    And you're all at home with medals on your chest,
And you've learnt to sleep so soundly that the firing of a gun
    At your bedside wouldn't rob you of your rest;
As you lie in a slumber deep, if your wife walks in her sleep,
    And tumbles down the stairs and breaks her crown,
Oh, it won't awaken you, for you'll say, "It's nothing new,
    "It's another blessed horse fell down."

Bulletin, 19 May 1900 [RGLR]

WITH FRENCH TO KIMBERLEY

The Boers were down on Kimberley with siege and Maxim gun;
The Boers were down on Kimberley, their numbers ten to one!

Faint were the hopes the British had to make the struggle good,
Defenceless in an open plain the Diamond City stood.
They built them forts from bags of sand, they fought from roof
        and wall,
They flashed a message to the south "Help! or the town must fall!"
And down our ranks the order ran to march at dawn of day,
For French was off to Kimberley to drive the Boers away.

He made no march along the line; he made no final attack
Upon those Magersfontein heights that drove the Scotchmen
        back;
But eastward over pathless plains by open veldt and vley,
Across the front of Cronje's force his troopers held their way.
The springbuck, feeding on the flats where Modder River runs,
Were startled by his horses' hoofs, the ramble of his guns.
The Dutchman's spies that watched his march from every rocky
        wall
Rode back in haste: "He marches east! He threatens Jacobsdal!"
Then north he wheeled as wheels the hawk and showed to their
        dismay,
That French was off to Kimberley to drive the Boers away.

His column was five thousand strong — all mounted men — and
        guns:
There met, beneath the world-wide flag, the world-wide
        Empire's sons;
They came to prove to all the earth that kinship conquers space,
And those who fight the British Isles must fight the British race!
From far New Zealand's flax and fern, from cold Canadian
        snows,
From Queensland plains, where hot as fire the summer sunshine
        glows;
And in the front the Lancers rode that New South Wales had
        sent:
With easy stride across the plain their long, lean Walers went.
Unknown, untried, those squadrons were, but proudly out they
        drew
Beside the English regiments that fought at Waterloo.
From every coast, from every clime, they met in proud array,
To go with French to Kimberley to drive the Boers away.

He crossed the Reit and fought his way towards the Modder bank.
The foemen closed behind his march, and hung upon the flank.
The long, dry grass was all ablaze, and fierce the veldt fire runs;
He fought them through a wall of flame that blazed around the
        guns!
Then limbered up and drove at speed, though horses fell and
        died;
We might not halt for man nor beast on that wild, daring ride.
Black with the smoke and parched with thirst, we pressed the
        livelong day
Our headlong march to Kimberley to drive the Boers away.

We reached the drift at fall of night, and camped across the ford.
Next day from all the hills around the Dutchman's cannons
        roared.
A narrow pass between the hills, with guns on either side;
The boldest man might well turn pale before that pass he tried,
For if the first attack should fail then every hope was gone:
But French looked once, and only once, and then he said, "Push
        on!"
The gunners plied their guns amain; the hail of shrapnel flew;
With rifle fire and lancer charge their squadrons back we threw;
And through the pass between the hills we swept in furious fray,
And French was through to Kimberley to drive the Boers away.

Ay, French was through to Kimberley! And ere the day was done
We saw the Diamond City stand, lit by the evening sun:
Above the town the foemen camped — they knew not that we
        came;
But soon they saw us, rank on rank; they heard our squadrons'
        tread;
In panic fear they left their tents in hopeless rout they fled;
And French rode into Kimberley; the people cheered amain,
The women came with tear-stained eyes to touch his bridle rein,
The starving children lined the streets to raise a feeble cheer,
The bells rang out a joyous peal to say "Relief is here!"
Ay! we that saw that stirring march are proud that we can say
We went with French to Kimberley to drive the Boers away.

Sydney Morning Herald, 29 September 1900 [RGLR]

ON THE TREK

Oh, the weary, weary journey on the trek, day after day,
  With sun above and silent veldt below;
And our hearts keep turning homeward to the youngsters far
    away,
  And the homestead where the climbing roses grow.
Shall we see the flats grow golden with the ripening of the grain?
  Shall we hear the parrots calling on the bough?
Ah! the weary months of marching ere we hear them call again,
  For we're going on a long job now.

In the drowsy days on escort, riding slowly half asleep,
  With the endless line of waggons stretching back,
While the khaki soldiers travel like a mob of travelling sheep,
  Plodding silent on the never-ending track,
While the constant snap and sniping of the foe you never see
  Makes you wonder will your turn come — when and how?
As the Mauser ball hums past you like a vicious kind of bee —
  Oh! we're going on a long job now.

When the dash and the excitement and the novelty are dead,
  And you've seen a load of wounded once or twice,
Or you've watched your old mate dying — with the vultures
    overhead,
  Well, you wonder if the war is worth the price.
And down along Monaro now they're starting out to shear,
  I can picture the excitement and the row;
But they'll miss me on the Lachlan when they call the roll this
    year,
  For we're going on a long job now.

Rio Grande's Last Race, 1902

THE ARMY MULES

Oh the airman's game is a showman's game, for all of us watch
    him go
With his roaring, soaring aeroplanes, and his bombs for the
    blokes below.

Over the railways and over the dumps, over the Hun and the
    Turk;
You'll hear him mutter "What-ho she bumps!" when the
    Archies get to work.

But not of him is the song I sing, though he follow the eagle's
    flight,
And with shrapnel holes in his splintered wing come home to his
    roost at night.
He may silver his wings on the shining stars, he may look from
    his clouds on high,
He may follow the flight of the wheeling kite in the blue
    Egyptian sky.
But he's only a hero built to plan, turned out by the Service
    Schools,
And I sing of the rankless, thankless man who hustles the Army
    Mules.

Now, where he comes from and where he lives is a mystery dark
    and dim,
And it's rarely indeed that the General gives a D.S.O. to him.
The stolid Infantry digs its way, like a mole in a ruined wall:
The Cavalry lends a tone, they say, to what were else but a brawl:

The Brigadier of the Mounted Fut, like a cavalry colonel swanks
As he goeth abroad like a gilded nut to receive the General's
    thanks:
The Ordnance Man is a son-of-a-gun, and his lists are a standing
    joke;
You order "Choke arti Jerusalem one" for Jerusalem artichoke.
The Medicals shine with a Number Nine, and the men of the
    great R.E.
Their colonels are Methodist, married, or mad, and some of
    them all the three.
In all these units the road to fame is taught in the Service
    Schools,
But a man has got to be born to the game when he tackles the
    Army Mules.

For if you go where the depots are, as the dawn is breaking grey,
By the waning light of the morning star as the dustcloud clears
away
You'll see a vision among the dust like a man and a mule
combined;
It's the kind of thing you must take on trust, as its outlines aren't
defined:
A thing that wheels like a spinning top, and props like a
three-legged stool —
And you find it's a long-legged Queensland boy convincing an
Army Mule.

The rider sticks to the hybrid's hide as paper sticks to a wall,
For a "Magnoon" Waler is next to ride, with every chance of a
fall.
It's a rough-house game, and a thankless game, and it isn't the
game for a fool,
For an army's fate and a nation's fame may turn on an Army
Mule.

And if you go to the front-line camp where the sleepless outposts
lie,
At the dead of night you can hear the tramp of the Mule Train
toiling by:
The rattle and clink of a leading-chain, the creak of the lurching
load,
As the patient plodding creatures strain at their task in the
shell-torn road.

Through the dark and the dust you may watch them go till the
dawn is grey in the sky,
For only the sleepless pickets know when the "All-night corps"
goes by.
And far away as the silence falls, when the last of the train has
gone,
A weary voice through the darkness calls "Get on there, men,
get on!"
It isn't the hero built to plan, turned out by the modern schools,
It's only the Army Service man, a-driving his Army Mules.

Kia-Ora Coo-ee, March 1918 [ANF]

SWINGING THE LEAD
(Army term for malingering)

Said the soldier to the sergeant: "I've got noises in me head
And a kind of filled-up feeling after every time I'm fed;
I can sleep all night on picket, but I can't sleep in me bed."
   And the sergeant said
   "That's lead."

Said the soldier to the sergeant: "Do you think they'll send me
    back?
For I really ain't adapted to be carrying a pack,
Though I've humped a case of whisky half a mile upon me
    back."
   And the sergeant said
   "That's lead."

"And me legs have swelled up cruel, I can hardly walk at all;
But when the Taubes come over you should see me start to crawl;
When we's sprinting for the dug-out, I can easy beat 'em all."
   And the sergeant said
   "That's lead."

So they sent him to the trenches, where he landed safe and sound,
And he drew his ammunition, just about two-fifty round.
"Oh, sergeant, what's this heavy stuff I've got to hump
   around?"
   And the sergeant said
   "That's lead."

Kia-ora Coo-ee, April 1918 [ANF]

BOOTS

*"The Australian boots were the best of any issued to the Allied
forces."*

We've travelled per Joe Gardiner, a humping of our swag
   in the country of the Gidgee and Belar.
We've swum the Di'mantina with our raiment in a bag,
   And we've travelled per superior motor car,

But when we went to Germany we hadn't any choice,
　　No matter what our training or pursuits,
For they gave us no selection 'twixt a Ford or Rolls de Royce
　　So we did it in our good Australian boots.

They called us "mad Australians"; they couldn't understand
　　How officers and men could fraternise,
They said that we were "reckless", we were "wild, and out of
　　　hand",
　　With nothing great or sacred to our eyes.
But on one thing you could gamble, in the thickest of the fray,
　　Though they called us volunteers and raw recruits,
You could track us past the shell holes, and the tracks were all
　　　one way
　　Of the good Australian ammunition boots.

The Highlanders were next of kin, the Irish were a treat,
　　The Yankees knew it all and had to learn,
The Frenchmen kept it going, both in vict'ry and defeat,
　　Fighting grimly till the tide was on the turn.
And our army kept beside 'em, did its bit and took its chance,
　　And I hailed our newborn nation and its fruits,
As I listened to the clatter on the cobblestones of France
　　Of the good Australian military boots.

Smith's Weekly, 5 July 1919

CASSIDY'S EPITAPH

Here lies a bloke who's just gone West,
　　A Number One Australian;
He took his gun and did his best
　　To mitigate the alien.
So long as he could get to work
　　He needed no sagacity;
A German, Austrian, or Turk.
　　Were all the same to Cassidy.

Whenever he could raise "the stuff"
   — A liquor deleterious —
The question when he'd have enough
   Was apt to be mysterious.
'Twould worry prudent folks a lot
   Through mental incapacity;
If he could keep it down or not,
   Was all the same to Cassidy.

And when the boys would start a dance,
   In honour of Terpsichore,
'Twas just an even-money chance
   You'd find him rather shickery.
But once he struck his proper stride,
   And heard the band's vivacity,
The jazz, the tango, or the slide
   Was all the same to Cassidy.

And now he's gone to face the Light,
   With all it may reveal to him,
A life without a drink or fight
   Perhaps may not appeal to him;
But when St Peter calls the roll
   Of men of proved tenacity,
You'll find the front-rank right-hand man
   Will answer: "Here . . . Cassidy."

Smith's Weekly, 14 June 1919

5
Racehorses and Racing
— Bush and City

EDITOR'S NOTE

Horseracing was a passion with Paterson all his life and it seems appropriate that a section of this book should be devoted to his writings on the sport. Certainly his love of racing was the spur to the writing of some of his best-known equestrian ballads.

Paterson was introduced to the turf as a small boy living at Illalong when a station hand took him to the Bogolong picnic races. A Snowy River mountaineer borrowed his saddle so that his horse, Pardon, could win the main race of the day. Probably from that day, nurtured by his own love of riding (he rode his pony to school and back each day, a distance of some dozen kilometres), the excitement of watching horses racing against each other entered his veins. Certainly he never forgot Pardon's race, and it was the subject of one of his first and best-known racing ballads, ''Old Pardon the Son of Reprieve'', the first poem in this section. This was not, however, his first racing ballad: that was ''A Dream of the Melbourne Cup'', printed by the *Bulletin* in October 1886, and the second set of his verses to be signed ''The Banjo''. The ''Pardon'' ballad followed two years later.

In the 1890s as a young man Paterson achieved a reputation as one of Sydney's most competent and fearless amateur riders and as such won several races ''over the jumps'' at the Randwick racecourse. His son, Hugh, told me in later years that Paterson had often said that his happiest newspaper years were when he was editing the *Sportsman* and reporting races for the *Truth*.

When, in 1967, I was commissioned by Angus & Robertson to compile an anthology of Paterson's prose writings, one of the firm's older staff members told me of a horseracing book by Paterson that, as far as she knew, had been locked away in one of the firm's safes since the World War I years. This I discovered to be a 257-page manuscript entitled *Racehorses and Racing in Australia*, which covered in remarkable and knowledgeable detail every aspect of racing in this country and also had much well-researched information on racing overseas. Paterson had begun writing it in his leisure time while he was running his station, Coodravale, near Wee Jasper (it was completed in 1914, up to which year its statistics and records refer), as an interesting (and characteristic) letter to George Robertson[1] revealed:

> Coodra Station
> Wee Jasper, via Yass.
> 7 Jan. 1910
>
> Dear Robertson,
> I got a circular letter from your firm about a book on horse-breeding issued by a German. I am writing a small book on racing and would like to get hold of the German's book for reference. Will you lend it to me — I take great interest in the matter and would do an article for *Herald* on the book which I think they would accept as it could not offend any advertisers. Would mention your firm as supplying it. I can't afford £2.10. for a book or would buy it right out . . .
>
> The lines I am going on in my book are that of all the thousands who attend races very few have any idea of "the game". People who go to cricket and football mostly know a bit about the games and have played them themselves. But thousands on thousands go racing and bet their money cheerfully on mysterious whispers imparted to them by men without any seat to their pants. It struck me that if one wrote a book on the practical side of racing it ought to sell well. Nothing heavy, but a sort of Royal Road to Racing. People seem to me to take racing so gloomily. One could make it very funny without much effort and it would point a good moral as I could show the folly of betting. We might get it into the schools in course of time . . .

Every detail of the sport was covered: the buying of yearlings; the training and racing of young horses; the attributes of good jockeys. He analysed systems of bookmaking and betting in the minutest detail and worked out pages of arithmetical calculations to prove his points. On the denizens of the racecourse he was superb. He described the "knowledge boxes" and "whisperers", the conmen and urgers who made a living by "telling the tale" — to separate a trusting punter from his money.

Paterson completed his book with a magnificent piece of sustained fiction in three chapters where he described, in all its bustle and activity, a day at the races, illustrating most of the points and observations he had made in the previous eighteen chapters. Probably nothing of its kind has been done as well, if at all, in our literature before or since, than in his description of the main race of

---

1. In the files of Angus & Robertson Ltd (now Collins/A&R).

the day — a weight-for-age race in which he drew together an imaginary field of champions and near-champions and poured into the telling of it all his love and understanding of a sport he knew so well.

A contemporary of Paterson wrote that up to within a few weeks of the latter's death "he was a conspicuous figure on the race-courses of Sydney with his outsize in field-glasses".[2] Another recalls him at Randwick as one of the "regulars", with his tall, lean figure and lined, saturnine face — not communicative, but obviously known to most sporting pressmen, trainers and owners with whom he sometimes yarned quietly between races. "After the races were over he would put his old glasses carefully away, stand up, look around, and depart leisurely."[3] From this environment and just as unostentatiously, this modest and unassuming man gave a welcome flash of new colour to the spectrum of our popular literature.

2. G.A. King, in a letter to the *Sydney Morning Herald*, 8 February 1941.

3. Sydney May, *The Story of Waltzing Matilda* (Brisbane: Smith & Paterson, 1944).

Bush Racing

OLD PARDON THE SON OF REPRIEVE

You never heard tell of the story?
  Well, now, I can hardly believe!
Never heard of the honour and glory
  Of Pardon, the son of Reprieve?
But maybe you're only a Johnnie
  And don't know a horse from a hoe?
Well, well, don't get angry, my sonny,
  But, really, a young un should know.

They bred him out back on the 'Never,'
  His mother was Mameluke breed.
To the front — and then stay there — was ever
  The root of the Mameluke creed.
He seemed to inherit their wiry
  Strong frames — and their pluck to receive —
As hard as a flint and as fiery
  Was Pardon, the son of Reprieve.

We ran him at many a meeting
  At crossing and gully and town,
And nothing could give him a beating —
  At least when our money was down.
For weight wouldn't stop him, nor distance,
  Nor odds, though the others were fast,
He'd race with a dogged persistence,
  And wear them all down at the last.

At the Turon the Yattendon filly
  Led by lengths at the mile-and-a-half,
And we all began to look silly,
  While *her* crowd were starting to laugh;
But the old horse came faster and faster,
  His pluck told its tale, and his strength,
He gained on her, caught her, and passed her,
  And won it, hands-down, by a length.

And then we swooped down on Menindie
   To run for the President's Cup —
Oh! that's a sweet township — a shindy
   To them is board, lodging, and sup.
Eye-openers they are, and their system
   Is never to suffer defeat;
It's "win, tie, or wrangle" — to best 'em
   You must lose 'em, or else it's "dead heat."

We strolled down the township and found 'em
   At drinking and gaming and play;
If sorrows they had, why they drowned 'em,
   And betting was soon under way.
Their horses were good 'uns and fit 'uns,
   There was plenty of cash in the town;
They backed their own horses like Britons,
   And, Lord! how *we* rattled it down!

With gladness we thought of the morrow,
   We counted our wagers with glee,
A simile homely to borrow —
   "There was plenty of milk in our tea."
You see we were green; and we never
   Had even a thought of foul play,
Though we well might have known that the clever
   Division would "put us away."

Experience *"docet"*, they tell us,
   At least so I've frequently heard,
But, "dosing" or "stuffing," those fellows
   Were up to each move on the board:
They got to his stall — it is sinful
   To think what such villains would do —
And they gave him a regular skinful
   Of barley — green barley — to chew.

He munched it all night, and we found him
   Next morning as full as a hog —
The girths wouldn't nearly meet round him;
   He looked like an overfed frog.

We saw we were done like a dinner —
　　The odds were a thousand to one
Against Pardon turning up winner,
　　'Twas cruel to ask him to run.

We got to the course with our troubles,
　　A crestfallen couple were we;
And we heard the "books" calling the doubles —
　　A roar like the surf of the sea;
And over the tumult and louder
　　Ran "Any price Pardon, I lay!"
Says Jimmy, "The children of Judah
　　"Are out on the warpath to-day

Three miles in three heats: — Ah, my sonny,
　　The horses in those days were stout,
They had to run well to win money;
　　I don't see such horses about.
Your six-furlong vermint that scamper
　　Half-a-mile with their feather-weight up;
They wouldn't earn much of their damper
　　In a race like the President's Cup.

The first heat was soon set-a-going;
　　The Dancer went off to the front;
The Don on his quarters was showing,
　　With Pardon right out of the hunt.
He rolled and he weltered and wallowed —
　　You'd kick your hat faster, I'll bet;
They finished all bunched, and he followed
　　All lathered and dripping with sweat.

But troubles came thicker upon us,
　　For while we were rubbing him dry
The stewards came over to warn us:
　　"We hear you are running a bye!
If Pardon don't spiel like tarnation
　　"And win the next heat — if he can —
"He'll earn a disqualification;
　　"Just think over *that*, now, my man!"

Our money all gone and our credit,
   Our horse couldn't gallop a yard;
And then people thought that *we* did it!
   It really was terribly hard.
We were objects of mirth and derision
   To folk in the lawn and the stand,
And the yells of the clever division
   Of "Any price Pardon!" were grand.

We still had a chance for the money,
   Two heats still remained to be run;
If both fell to us — why, my sonny,
   The clever division were done.
And Pardon was better, we reckoned,
   His sickness was passing away,
So he went to the post for the second
   And principal heat of the day.

They're off and away with a rattle,
   Like dogs from the leashes let slip,
And right at the back of the battle
   He followed them under the whip.
They gained ten good lengths on him quickly
   He dropped right away from the pack;
I tell you it made me feel sickly
   To see the blue jacket fall back.

Our very last hope had departed —
   We thought the old fellow was done,
When all of a sudden he started
   To go like a shot from a gun.
His chances seemed slight to embolden
   Our hearts; but, with teeth firmly set,
We thought, "Now or never! The old 'un
   "May reckon with some of 'em yet."

Then loud rose the war-cry for Pardon;
   He swept like the wind down the dip,
And over the rise by the garden,
   The jockey was done with the whip
The field were at sixes and sevens —
   The pace at the first had been fast —

And hope seemed to drop from the heavens,
    For Pardon was coming at last.

And how he did come! It was splendid;
    He gained on them yards every bound,
Stretching out like a greyhound extended,
    His girth laid right down on the ground.
A shimmer of silk in the cedars
    As into the running they wheeled,
And out flashed the whips on the leaders,
    For Pardon had collared the field.

Then right through the ruck he came sailing —
    I knew that the battle was won —
The son of Haphazard was failing,
    The Yattendon filly was done;
He cut down the Don and the Dancer,
    He raced clean away from the mare —
He's in front! Catch him now if you can, sir!
    And up went my hat in the air!

Then loud from the lawn and the garden
    Rose offers of "Ten to one on!"
"Who'll bet on the field? I back Pardon!"
    No use; all the money was gone.
He came for the third heat light-hearted,
    A-jumping and dancing about;
The others were done ere they started
    Crestfallen, and tired, and worn out.

He won it, and ran it much faster
    Than even the first, I believe
Oh, he was the daddy, the master,
    Was Pardon, the son of Reprieve.
He showed 'em the method to travel —
    The boy sat as still as a stone —
They never could see him for gravel;
    He came in hard-held, and alone.

*   *   *   *   *

But he's old — and his eyes are grown hollow
   Like me, with my thatch of the snow;
When he dies, then I hope I may follow,
   And go where the racehorses go.
I don't want no harping nor singing —
   Such things with my style don't agree;
Where the hoofs of the horses are ringing
   There's music sufficient for me.

And surely the thoroughbred horses
   Will rise up again and begin
Fresh races on far-away courses,
   And p'raps they might let me slip in
It would look rather well the race-card on
   'Mongst Cherubs and Seraphs and things,
"Angel Harrison's black gelding Pardon,
   "Blue halo, white body and wings."

And if they have racing hereafter,
   (And who is to say they will not?)
When the cheers and the shouting and laughter
   Proclaim that the battle grows hot;
As they come down the racecourse a-steering,
   He'll rush to the front, I believe;
And you'll hear the great multitude cheering
   For Pardon, the son of Reprieve.

Bulletin, 22 December 1888 [MSR]

MULLIGAN'S MARE

Oh, Mulligan's bar was the deuce of a place
To drink, and to fight, and to gamble and race;
The height of choice spirits from near and from far
Were all concentrated on Mulligan's bar.

There was "Jerry the Swell", and the jockey-boy Ned,
"Dog-bite-me" — so called from the shape of his head —
And a man whom the boys, in their musical slang,
Designated the "Gaffer of Mulligan's Gang".

Now Mulligan's Gang had a racer to show,
A bad un to look at, a good un to go;
Whenever they backed her you safely might swear
She'd walk in a winner, would Mulligan's mare.

But Mulligan, having some radical views,
Neglected his business and got on the booze;
He took up with runners — a treacherous troop —
Who gave him away, and he "fell in the soup".

And so it turned out on a fine summer day,
A bailiff turned up with a writ of *"fi. fa."*;
He walked to the bar with a manner serene,
"I levy," said he, "in the name of the Queen."

Then Mulligan wanted, in spite of the law,
To pay out the bailiff with "*one* on the jaw";
He drew out to hit him; but ere you could wink,
He changed his intention and stood him a drink.

A great consultation there straightway befell
'Twixt jockey-boy Neddy and Jerry the Swell,
And the man with the head, who remarked "Why, you bet!
Dog-bite-me!" said he, "but we'll diddle 'em yet.

"We'll slip out the mare from her stall in a crack,
And put in her place the old broken-down hack;
The hack is so like her, I'm ready to swear
The bailiff will think he was Mulligan's mare.

"So out with the racer and in with the screw,
We'll show him what Mulligan's talent can do;
And if he gets nasty and dares to say much,
I'll knock him as stiff as my grandmother's crutch."

Then off to the town went the mare and the lad;
The bailiff came out, never dreamt he was "had";
But marched to the stall with a confident air —
"I levy," said he, "upon Mulligan's mare."

He watched her by day and he watched her by night,
She was never an instant let out of his sight,
For races were coming away in the West
And Mulligan's mare had a chance with the best.

"Here's a slant," thought the bailiff, "to serve my own ends,
I'll send off a wire to my bookmaking friends:
'Get all you can borrow, beg, snavel or snare
And lay the whole lot against Mulligan's mare.' "

The races came round, and the crowd on the course
Were laying the mare till they made themselves hoarse,
And Mulligan's party, with ardour intense,
They backed her for pounds and for shillings and pence.

But think of the grief of the bookmaking host
At the sound of the summons to go to the post —
For down to the start with her thoroughbred air
As fit as a fiddle pranced Mulligan's mare!

They started, and off went the boy to the front,
He cleared out at once, and he made it a hunt;
He steadied as rounding the corner they wheeled,
Then gave her her head — and she smothered the field.

The race put her owner right clear of his debts;
He landed a fortune in stakes and in bets,
He paid the old bailiff the whole of his pelf,
And gave him a hiding to keep for himself.

So all you bold sportsmen take warning, I pray,
Keep clear of the running, you'll find it don't pay;
For the very best rule that you'll hear in a week
Is never to bet on a thing that can speak.

And, whether you're lucky or whether you lose,
Keep clear of the cards and keep clear of the booze,
And fortune in season will answer your prayer
And send you a flyer like Mulligan's mare.

Bulletin, 23 November 1889 [CV]

AN IDYLL OF DANDALOO

On Western plains, where shade is not,
   'Neath summer skies of cloudless blue,
Where all is dry and all is hot,
   There stands the town of Dandaloo —

A township where life's total sum
Is sheep, diversified with rum.

It's grass-grown streets with dust are deep,
    'Twere vain endeavour to express
The dreamless silence of its sleep,
    Its wide, expansive drunkenness.
The yearly races mostly drew
A lively crowd to Dandaloo.

There came a sportsman from the East,
    The eastern land where sportsmen blow,
And brought with him a speedy beast —
    A speedy beast as horses go.
He came afar in hope to "do"
The little town of Dandaloo.

Now this was weak of him, I wot —
    Exceeding weak, it seemed to me —
For we in Dandaloo were not
    The Jugginses we seemed to be;
In fact, we rather thought we knew
Our book by heart in Dandaloo.

We held a meeting at the bar,
    And met the question fair and square —
"We've stumped the country near and far
    "To raise the cash for races here;
"We've got a hundred pounds or two —
"Not half so bad for Dandaloo.

"And now, it seems, we have to be
    "Cleaned out by this here Sydney bloke,
"With his imported horse; and he
    "Will scoop the pool and leave us broke
"Shall we sit still, and make no fuss
"While this chap climbs all over us?
                    *   *   *   *   *
The races came to Dandaloo,
    And all the cornstalks from the West,
On ev'ry kind of moke and screw,

Came forth in all their glory drest.
The stranger's horse, as hard as nails,
Look'd fit to run for New South Wales.

He won the race by half a length —
    Quite half a length, it seemed to me —
But Dandaloo, with all its strength,
    Roared out "Dead heat!" most fervently;
And, after hesitation meet,
The judge's verdict was "Dead heat!"

And many men there were could tell
    What gave the verdict extra force:
The stewards, and the judge as well —
    They all had backed the second horse.
For things like this they sometimes do
In large towns than Dandaloo.

They ran it off; the stranger won,
    Hands down, by near a hundred yards
He smiled to think his troubles done;
    But Dandaloo held all the cards.
They went to scale and — cruel fate! —
His jockey turned out under-weight.

Perhaps they'd tampered with the scale!
    I cannot tell. I only know
It weighed him *out* all right. I fail
    To paint that Sydney sportsman's woe.
He said the stewards were a crew
Of low-lived thieves in Dandaloo.

He lifted up his voice, irate,
    And swore till all the air was blue;
So then we rose to vindicate
    The dignity of Dandaloo.
"Look here," said we, "you must not poke
Such oaths at us poor country folk."

We rode him softly on a rail,
    We shied at him, in careless glee,

Some large tomatoes, rank and stale,
   And eggs of great antiquity —
Their wild, unholy fragrance flew
About the town of Dandaloo.

He left the town at break of day,
   He led his race-horse through the streets,
And now he tells the tale, they say,
   To every racing man he meets.
And Sydney sportsmen all eschew
The atmosphere of Dandaloo.

                  Bulletin, 21 December 1889 [MSR]

THE OPEN STEEPLECHASE

I had ridden over hurdles up the country once or twice,
By the side of Snowy River with a horse they called "The Ace."
And we brought him down to Sydney, and our rider Jimmy Rice,
Got a fall and broke his shoulder, so they nabbed me in a trice —
Me, that never wore the colours, for the Open Steeplechase.

"Make the running," said the trainer, "it's your only chance
     whatever,
"Make it hot from start to finish, for the old black horse can
     stay,
"And just think of how they'll take it, when they hear on Snowy
     River
"That the country boy was plucky, and the country horse was
     clever.
"You must ride for old Monaro and the mountain boys to-day."

"Are you ready?" said the starter, as we held the horses back,
All ablazing with impatience, with excitement all aglow;
Before us like a ribbon stretched the steeplechasing track,
And the sun-rays glistened brightly on the chestnut and the black
As the starter's words came slowly, "Are — you — ready? Go!"

Well, I scarcely knew we'd started, I was stupid like with wonder
Till the field closed up beside me and a jump appeared ahead.

And we flew it like a hurdle, not a baulk and not a blunder,
As we charged it all together, and it fairly whistled under,
And then some were pulled behind me and a few shot out and
    led.

So we ran for half the distance, and I'm making no pretences
When I tell you I was feeling very nervous-like and queer,
For those jockeys rode like demons; you would think they'd lost
    their senses
If you saw them rush their horses at those rasping five foot
    fences —
And in place of making running I was falling to the rear.

Till a chap came racing past me on a horse they called "The
    Quiver,"
And said he, "My country joker, are you going to give it best?
"Are you frightened of the fences? does their stoutness make
    you shiver?
"Have they come to breeding cowards by the side of Snowy
    River?
"Are there riders on Monaro? — "but I never heard the rest.

For I drove the Ace and sent him just as fast as he could pace it,
At the big black line of timber stretching fair across the track,
And he shot beside the Quiver. "Now," said I, "my boy, we'll
    race it.
"You can come with Snowy River if you're only game to face it,
"Let us mend the pace a little and we'll see who cries a crack."

So we raced away together, and we left the others standing,
And the people cheered and shouted as we settled down to ride,
And we clung beside the Quiver. At his taking off and landing
I could see his scarlet nostril and his mighty ribs expanding,
And the Ace stretched out in earnest and we held him stride for
    stride.

But the pace was so terrific that they soon ran out their tether —
They were rolling in their gallop, they were fairly blown and
    beat —

But they both were game as pebbles — neither one would show
    the feather.
And we rushed them at the fences, and they cleared them both
    together,
Nearly every time they clouted, but they somehow kept their feet.

Then the last jump rose before us, and they faced it game
    as ever —
We were both at spur and whipcord, fetching blood at every
    bound —
And above the people's cheering and the cries of "Ace" and
    "Quiver,"
I could hear the trainer shouting, "One more run for Snowy
    River."
Then we struck the jump together and came smashing to the
    ground.

Well, the Quiver ran to blazes, but the Ace stood still and waited,
Stood and waited like a statue while I scrambled on his back.
There was no one next or near me for the field was fairly slated,
So I cantered home a winner with my shoulder dislocated,
While the man that rode the Quiver followed limping down the
    track.

And he shook my hand and told me that in all his days he never
Met a man who rode more gamely, and our last set to was prime,
And we wired them on Monaro how we chanced to beat the
    Quiver.
And they sent us back an answer, "Good old sort from Snowy
    River:
"Send us word each race you start in and we'll back you every
    time."

Bulletin, 19 December 1891 [MSR]

TOMMY CORRIGAN
(Killed, Steeplechasing at Flemington)

You talk of riders on the flat, of nerve and pluck and pace —
Not one in fifty has the nerve to ride a steeplechase.

It's right enough, while horses pull and take their fences strong,
To rush a flier to the front and bring the field along;
But what about the last half-mile, with horses blown and beat —
When every jump means all you know to keep him on his feet.
When any slip means sudden death — with wife and child to
    keep —
It needs some nerve to draw the whip and flog him at the leap —
But Corrigan would ride them out, by danger undismayed,
He never flinched at fence or wall, he never was afraid;
With easy seat and nerve of steel, light hand and smiling face,
He held the rushing horses back, and made the sluggards race.

He gave the shirkers extra heart, he steadied down the rash,
He rode great clumsy boring brutes, and chanced a fatal smash;
He got the rushing Wymlet home that never jumped at all —
But clambered over every fence and clouted every wall.
You should have heard the cheers, my boys, that shook the
    members' stand
Whenever Tommy Corrigan weighed out to ride Lone Hand.

They were, indeed, a glorious pair — the great upstanding horse,
The gamest jockey on his back that ever faced a course.
Though weight was big and pace was hot and fences stiff and
    tall,
"You follow Tommy Corrigan" was passed to one and all.
And every man on Ballarat raised all he could command
To put on Tommy Corrigan when riding old Lone Hand.

But now we'll keep his memory green while horsemen come and
    go;
We may not see his like again where silks and satins glow.
We'll drink to him in silence, boys — he's followed down the
    track
Where many a good man went before, but never one came back.
And, let us hope, in that far land where the shades of brave men
    reign,
The gallant Tommy Corrigan will ride Lone Hand again.

Bulletin, 18 August 1894 [CV]

HOW THE FAVOURITE BEAT US

"Aye," said the boozer, "I tell you it's true, sir,
"I once was a punter with plenty of pelf,
"But gone is my glory, I'll tell you the story
"How I stiffened my horse and got stiffened myself.

"'Twas a mare called the Cracker, I came down to back her,
"But found she was favourite all of a rush,
"The folk just did pour on to lay six to four on,
"And several bookies were killed in the crush.

"It seems old Tomato was stiff, though a starter;
"They reckoned him fit for the Caulfield to keep.
"The Bloke and the Donah were scratched by their owner,
"He only was offered three-fourths of the sweep.

"We knew Salamander was slow as a gander,
"The mare could have beat him the length of the straight,
"And old Manumission was out of condition,
"And most of the others were running off weight.

"No doubt someone 'blew it', for everyone knew it,
"The bets were all gone, and I muttered in spite
"If I can't get a copper, by Jingo, I'll stop her,
"Let the public fall in, it will serve the brutes right."

I said to the jockey, "Now, listen, my cocky,
You watch as you're cantering down by the stand,
"I'll wait where that toff is and give you the office,
"You're only to win if I lift up my hand."

"I then tried to back her — 'What price is the Cracker?'
"Our books are all full, sir," each bookie did swear;
"My mind, then, I made up, my fortune I played up
"I bet every shilling against my own mare.

"I strolled to the gateway, the mare in the straightway
"Was shifting and dancing, and pawing the ground,
"The boy saw me enter and wheeled for his canter,
"When a darned great mosquito came buzzing around.

"They breed 'em at Hexham, it's risky to vex 'em,
"They suck a man dry at a sitting, no doubt,

"But just as the mare passed, he fluttered my hair past,
"I lifted my hand, and I flattened him out.

"I was stunned when they started, the mare simply darted
"Away to the front when the flag was let fall,
"For none there could match her, and none tried to catch her —
"She finished a furlong in front of them all.

"You bet that I went for the boy, whom I sent for
"The moment he weighed and came out of the stand —
"Who paid you to win it? Come, own up this minute."
"Lord love yer," said he, "why you lifted your hand."

"'Twas true, by St. Peter, that cursed 'musketeer'
"Had broke me so broke that I hadn't a brown,
"And you'll find the best course is when dealing with horses
To win when you're able, and *keep your hands down*.

Rosehill Race Book, 9 November 1894 [MSR]

RIO GRANDE'S LAST RACE

Now this was what Macpherson told
    While waiting in the stand;
A reckless rider, over-bold,
The only man with hands to hold
    The rushing Rio Grande.

He said, "This day I bid good-bye
    "To bit and bridle rein,
"To ditches deep and fences high,
"For I have dreamed a dream, and I
    "Shall never ride again.

"I dreamt last night I rode this race
    "That I to-day must ride,
"And cant'ring down to take my place
"I saw full many an old friend's face
    "Come stealing to my side.

"Dead men on horses long since dead,
    "They clustered on the track;
"The champions of the days long fled,
"They moved around with noiseless tread —
    "Bay, chestnut, brown, and black.

"And one man on a big grey steed
  "Rode up and waved his hand;
"Said he, 'We help a friend in need,
" 'And we have come to give a lead
  " 'To you and Rio Grande.

" 'For you must give the field the slip,
  " 'So never draw the rein,
" 'But keep him moving with the whip,
" 'And if he falter — set your lip
  " 'And rouse him up again.

" 'But when you reach the big stone wall,
  " 'Put down your bridle hand
" 'And let him sail — he cannot fall —
" 'But don't you interfere at all;
  " 'You trust old Rio Grande.'

"We started, and in front we showed,
  "The big horse running free:
"Right fearlessly and game he strode,
"And by my side those dead men rode
  "Whom no one else could see.

"As silently as flies a bird,
  "They rode on either hand;
"At every fence I plainly heard
"The phantom leader give the word,
  " 'Make room for Rio Grande!'

"I spurred him on to get the lead,
  "I chanced full many a fall;
"But swifter still each phantom steed
"Kept with me, and at racing speed
  "We reached the big stone wall.

"And there the phantoms on each side
  "Drew in and blocked his leap;
" 'Make room! make room!' I loudly cried,
"But right in front they seemed to ride —
  "I cursed them in my sleep.

"He never flinched, he faced it game,
  "He struck it with his chest,
"And every stone burst out in flame,
"And Rio Grande and I became
  "As phantoms with the rest.

"And then I woke, and for a space
  "All neverless did I seem;
"For I have ridden many a race,
"But never one at such a pace
  "As in that fearful dream.

"And I am sure as man can be
  "That out upon the track,
"Those phantoms that men cannot see
"Are waiting now to ride with me,
  "And I shall not come back.

"For I must ride the dead men's race,
  "And follow their command;
"'Twere worse than death, the foul disgrace
"If I should fear to take my place
  "To-day on Rio Grande."

He mounted, and a jest he threw,
  With never sign of gloom;
But all who heard the story knew
That Jack Macpherson, brave and true,
  Was going to his doom.

They started, and the big black steed
  Came flashing past the stand;
All single-handed in the lead
He strode along at racing speed,
  The mighty Rio Grande.

But on his ribs the whalebone stung,
  A madness it did seem!
And soon it rose on every tongue
That Jack Macpherson rode among
  The creatures of his dream.

He looked to left and looked to right,
  As though men rode beside;

And Rio Grande, with foam-flecks white,
Raced at his jumps in headlong flight
   And cleared them in his stride.

But when they reached the big stone wall,
   Down went the bridle-hand,
And loud we heard Macpherson call,
"Make room, or half the field will fall!
   "Make room for Rio Grande!"

             *   *   *   *   *

"He's down! he's down!" And horse and man
   Lay quiet side by side!
No need the pallid face to scan,
We knew with Rio Grande he ran
   The race the dead men ride.

Sketch, 16 December 1896 [RGLR]

THE WARGEILAH HANDICAP

Wargeilah town is very small,
   There's no cathedral nor a club,
In fact the township, all in all,
   Is just one unpretentious pub;
And there, from all the stations round,
The local sportsmen can be found.

The sportsmen of Wargeilah side
   Are very few but very fit:
There's scarcely any sport been tried
   But what they held their own at it
In fact, to search their records o'er,
They held their own and something more.

'Twas round about Wargeilah town
   An English new-chum did infest:
He used to wander up and down
   In baggy English breeches drest —
His mental aspect seemed to be
Just stolid self-sufficiency.

The local sportsmen vainly sought
   His tranquil calm to counteract,
By urging that he should be brought
   Within the Noxious Creatures Act.
"Nay, harm him not," said one more wise,
"He is a blessing in disguise!

"You see, he wants to buy a horse,
   "To ride, and hunt, and steeplechase,
"And carry ladies, too, of course,
   "And pull a cart and win a race.
"Good gracious! he must be a flat
"To think he'll get a horse like that!

"But since he has so little sense
   "And such a lot of cash to burn,
"We'll sell him some experience
   "By which alone a fool can learn.
"Suppose we let him have The Trap
"To win Wargeilah Handicap!"

And here, I must explain to you
   That, round about Wargeilah run,
There lived a very aged screw
   Whose days of brilliancy were done:
A grand old warrior in his prime —
But age will beat us all in time.

A trooper's horse in seasons past
   He did his share to keep the peace,
But took to falling, and at last
   Was cast for age from the Police.
A publican at Conroy's Gap
Then bought and christened him The Trap.

When grass was good, and horses dear,
   He changed his owner now and then
At prices ranging somewhere near
   The neighbourhood of two pound ten:
And manfully he earned his keep
By yarding cows and ration sheep.

They brought him in from off the grass
  And fed and groomed the old horse up;
His coat began to shine like glass —
  You'd think he'd win the Melbourne Cup.
Ad when they'd got him fat and flash
They asked the new-chum — fifty — cash!

And when he said the price was high,
  Their indignation knew no bounds.
They said, 'It's seldom you can buy
  "A horse like that for fifty pounds!
"We'll refund twenty if The Trap
"Should fail to win the handicap!"

The deed was done, the price was paid,
  The new-chum put the horse in train:
The local sports were much afraid
  That he would sad experience gain,
By racing with some shearer's hack,
Who'd beat him half-way round the track.

So, on this guileless English spark
  They did most fervently impress
That he must keep the matter dark,
  And not let any person guess
That he was purchasing The Trap
To win Wargeilah Handicap.

They spoke of "spielers from The Bland,"
  And "champions from the Castlereagh,"
And gave the youth to understand
  That all of these would stop away,
And spoil the race, if they should hear
That they had got The Trap to fear.

"Keep dark! They'll muster thick as flies
  "When once the news gets sent around
"We're giving such a splendid prize —
  "A Snowdon horse worth fifty pounds!
"They'll come right in from Dandaloo,
"And find — that it's a gift to you!"

* * * * *

The race came on — with no display,
  Nor any calling of the card,
But round about the pub all day
  A crowd of shearers, drinking hard,
And using language in a strain
'Twere flattery to call profane.

Our hero, dressed in silk attire —
  Blue jacket and a scarlet cap —
With boots that shone like flames of fire,
  Now did his canter on The Trap,
And walked him up and round about,
Until the other steeds came out.

He eyed them with a haughty look,
  But saw a sight that caught his breath!
It was! Ah John! The Chinee cook!
  In boots and breeches! Pale as death!
Tied with a rope, like any sack,
Upon a piebald pony's back!

The next, a colt — all mud and burrs!
  Half-broken, with a black boy up,
Who said, "You gim'me pair o' spurs,
"I win the bloomin' Melbourne Cup!"
These two were to oppose The Trap
For the Wargeilah Handicap!

They're off! The colt whipped down his head,
  And humped his back and gave a squeal,
And bucked into the drinking shed,
  Revolving like a Cath'rine wheel!
Men ran like rats! The atmosphere
Was filled with oaths and pints of beer!

But up the course the bold Ah John
  Beside the Trap raced neck and neck:
The boys had tied him firmly on,
  Which ultimately proved his wreck,
The saddle turned, and, like a clown,
He rode some distance upside down.

His legs around the horse were tied,
  His feet towards the heavens were spread,
He swung and bumped at every stride
  And ploughed the ground up with his head!
And when they rescued him, The Trap
Had won Wargeilah Handicap!

And no enquiries we could make
  Could tell by what false statements swayed
Ah John was led to undertake
  A task so foreign to his trade!
He only smiled and said, "Hoo Ki!
I stop topside, I win all 'li!"

But never, in Wargeilah Town,
  Was heard so eloquent a cheer
As when the President came down
  And toasted, in Colonial Beer,
"The finest rider on the course!
  "The winner of the Snowdon Horse!"

"You go and get your prize," he said,
  "He's with a wild mob, somewhere round
"The mountains near The Watershed;
  "He's honestly worth fifty pound,
"A noble horse, indeed, to win,
"But none of *us* can run him in!

"We've chased him poor, we've chased him fat,
  "We've run him till our horses dropped,
"But by such obstacles as that
  "A man like you will not be stopped,
"You'll go and yard him any day,
"So here's your health! Hooray! Hooray!"

* * * * *

The day wound up with booze and blow
  And fights till all were well content,
But of the new-chum, all I know
  Is shown by this advertisement —
"For Sale, the well-known racehorse Trap,
"He won Wargeilah Handicap!"

Sydney Mail, 14 December 1901 [RGLR]

City Racing

THE ORACLE AT THE RACES

No tram ever goes to Randwich races without him; he is always fat, hairy, and assertive; he is generally one of a party, and takes the centre of the stage all the time — collects and hands over the fares, adjusts the change, chaffs the conductor, crushes the thin, apologetic stranger next him into a pulp, and talks to the whole compartment as if they had asked for his opinion.

He knows all the trainers and owners, or takes care to give the impression that he does. He slowly and pompously hauls out his race-book, and one of his satellites opens the ball by saying, in a deferential way,

"What do you like for the 'urdles, Charley?"

The Oracle looks at the book and breathes heavily; no one else ventures to speak.

"Well," he says, at last, "of course there's only one in it — if he's wanted. But that's it — will they spin him? I don't think they will. They's only a lot o' cuddies, any 'ow."

No one likes to expose his own ignorance by asking which horse he refers to as the "only one in it"; and the Oracle goes on to deal out some more wisdom in a loud voice.

"Billy K — told me" (he probably hardly knows Billy K — by sight) "Billy K — told me that that bay 'orse ran the best mile-an'-a-half ever done on Randwick yesterday; but I don't give him a chance, for all that; that's the worst of these trainers. They don't know when their horses are well — half of 'em."

Then a voice comes from behind him. It is that of the thin man, who is crushed out of sight by the bulk of the Oracle.

"I think," says the thin man, "that that horse of Flannery's ought to run well in the Handicap."

The Oracle can't stand this sort of thing at all. He gives a snort, wheels half-round and looks at the speaker. Then he turns back to the compartment full of people, and says, "No 'ope."

The thin man makes a last effort. "Well, they backed him last night, anyhow."

"Who backed 'im?" says the Oracle.

"In Tattersall's," says the thin man.

"I'm sure," says the Oracle; and the thin man collapses.

On arrival at the course, the Oracle is in great form. Attended by his string of satellites, he plods from stall to stall staring at the horses. Their names are printed in big letters on the stalls, but the Oracle doesn't let that stop his display of knowledge.

"'Ere's Blue Fire," he says, stopping at that animal's stall, and swinging his race-book. "Good old Blue Fire!" he goes on loudly, as a little court collects. "Jimmy B — (mentioning a popular jockey) "told me he couldn't have lost on Saturday week if he had only been ridden different. I had a good stake on him too, that day. Lor', the races that has been chucked away on this horse. They will not ride him right."

A trainer who is standing by, civilly interposes. "this isn't Blue Fire," he says. "Blue Fire's out walking about. This is a two-year old filly that's in the stall —"

"Well, I can see that, can't I," says the Oracle, crushingly. "You don't suppose I thought Blue Fire was a mare, did you?" and he moves off hurriedly.

"Now, look here, you chaps," he says to his followers at last. "You wait here. I want to go and see a few of the talent, and it don't do to have a crowd with you. There's Jimmy M — over there now" (pointing to a leading trainer). "I'll get hold of him in a minute. He couldn't tell me anything with so many about. Just you wait here."

He crushes into a crowd that has gathered round the favourite's stall, and overhears one hard-faced racing man say to another, "What do you like?" to which the other answers, "Well, either this or Royal Scot. I think I'll put a bit on Royal Scot." This is enough for the Oracle. He doesn't know either of the men from Adam, or either of the horses from the great original pachyderm, but the information will do to go on with. He rejoins his followers, and looks very mysterious.

"Well, did you hear anything?" they say.

The Oracle talks low and confidentially.

"The crowd that have got the favourite tell me they're not

afraid of anything but Royal Scot," he says. "I think we'd better put a bit on both."

"What did the Royal Scot crowd say?" asks an admirer deferentially.

"Oh, they're going to try and win. I saw the stable commissioner, and he told me they were going to put a hundred on him. Of course, you couldn't say I told you, 'cause I promised him I wouldn't tell." And the satellites beam with admiration of the Oracle, and think what a privilege it is to go to the races with such a knowing man.

They contribute their mites to the general fund, some putting in a pound, others half a sovereign, and the Oracle takes it into the ring to invest, half on the favourite and half on Royal Scot. He finds that the favourite is two to one, and Royal Scot at threes, eight to one being offered against anything else. As he ploughs through a ring, a Whisperer (one of those broken-down followers of the turf who get their living in various mysterious ways, but partly by giving "tips" to backers) pulls his sleeve.

"What are you backing?" he says.

"Favourite and Royal Scot," says the Oracle.

"Put a pound on Bendemeer," says the tipster. "It's a certainty. Meet me here if it comes off, and I'll tell you something for the next race. Don't miss it now. Get on quick!"

The Oracle is humble enough before the hanger-on of the turf. A bookmaker roars "ten to one Bendemeer"; he suddenly fishes out a sovereign of his own — and he hasn't money to spare, for all his knowingness — and puts it on Bendemeer. His friends' money he puts on the favourite and Royal Scot as arranged. Then they all go round to watch the race.

The horses are at the post; a distant cluster of crowded animals with little dots of colour on their backs. Green, blue, yellow, purple, French grey, and old gold, they change about in a bewildering manner, and though the Oracle has a cheap pair of glasses, he can't make out where Bendemeer has got to. Royal Scot and the favourite he has lost interest in, and secretly hopes that they will be left at the post or break their necks; but he does not confide his sentiment to his companions.

They're off! The long line of colours across the track becomes a shapeless clump and then draws out into a long string. "What's that in front?" yells someone at the rails. "Oh, that thing of Hart's," says someone else. But the Oracle hears them not; he is looking in the mass of colour for a purple cap and grey jacket, with black armbands. He cannot see it anywhere, and the confused and confusing mass swings round the turn into the straight.

Then there is a babel of voices, and suddenly a shout of "Bendemeer! Bendemeer!" and the Oracle, without knowing which is Bendemeer, takes up the cry feverishly. "Bendemeer! Bendemeer!" he yells, waggling his glasses about, trying to see where the animal is.

"Where's Royal Scot, Charley? Where's Royal Scot?" screams one of his friends, in agony. "'Ow's he doin'?"

"No 'ope!" says the Oracle, with fiendish glee. "Bendemeer! Bendemeer!"

The horses are at the Leger stand now, whips are out, and three horses seem to be nearly abreast; in fact, to the Oracle there seem to be a dozen nearly abreast. Then a big chestnut sticks his head in front of the others, and a small man at the Oracle's side emits a deafening series of yells right by the Oracle's ear:

"Go on, Jimmy! Rub it into him! Belt him! It's a cake-walk! A cake-walk!" The big chestnut, in a dogged sort of way, seems to stick his body clear of his opponents, and passes the post a winner by a length. The Oracle doesn't know what has won, but fumbles with his book. The number on the saddle-cloth catches his eye — No. 7; he looks hurriedly down the page. No. 7 — Royal Scot. Second is No. 24 — Bendemeer. Favourite nowhere.

Hardly has he realized it, before his friends are cheering and clapping him on the back. "By George, Charley, it takes you to pick 'em." "Come and 'ave a wet!" "You 'ad a quid on, didn't you, Charley?" The Oracle feels very sick at having missed the winner, but he dies game. "Yes, rather; I had a quid on," he says. "And," (here he nerves himself to smile) "I had a saver on the second, too."

His comrades gasp with astonishment. "D'you hear that, eh? Charley backed first and second. That's pickin' 'em if you like." They have a wet, and pour fulsome adulation on the Oracle when he collects their money.

After the Oracle has collected the winnings for his friends he meets the Whisperer again.

"It didn't win?" he says to the Whisperer in inquiring tones.

"Didn't win," says the Whisperer, who has determined to brazen the matter out. "How could he win? Did you see the way he was ridden? That horse was stiffened just after I seen you, and he never tried a yard. Did you see the way he was pulled and hauled about at the turn? It'd make a man sick. What was the stipendiary stewards doing, I wonder?"

This fills the Oracle with a new idea. All that he remembers of the race at the turn was a jumble of colours, a kaleidoscope of horses and of riders 'hanging on to the horses' necks. But it wouldn't do to admit that he didn't see everything, and didn't know everything; so he plunges in boldly.

"O' course I saw it," he says. "And a blind man could see it. They ought to rub him out."

"Course they ought," says the Whisperer. "But, look here, put two quid on Tell-tale; you'll get it back!"

The Oracle does put on "two quid", and doesn't get it all back. Neither does he see any more of this race than he did of the last one — in fact, he cheers wildly when the wrong horse is coming in. But when the public begin to hoot he hoots as loudly as anybody — louder if anything; and all the way home in the tram he lays down the law about stiff running, and wants to know what the stipendiaries are doing.

If you go into any barber's shop, you can hear him at it, and he flourishes in suburban railway carriages; but he has a tremendous local reputation, having picked first and second in the Handicap, and it would be a bold man who would venture to question the Oracle's knowledge of racing of all matters relating to it.

Evening News, 30 January 1904

KNOWLEDGE-BOXES AND WHISPERERS

"It's not the tale that matters, it's how they tell it!"
— Unpublished Sayings of Solomon.

Backers may be roughly divided into two classes — those who bet on what they are told and those who bet on what they know. The membership of the latter class is very select. Constant study of pedigrees, and of public form; constant attendance at race meetings; good judgement of condition; a close study of each horse's peculiarities, such as his ability to begin or to finish; a quick eye to detect any incident in the course of a race; an extensive acquaintance with and popularity among other turf experts; amazing capacity for keeping his mouth shut; and above all an instinct like a Jew financier to detect movements in the betting market; all these qualities are necessary to the man who aspires to be what is known on the turf as a "knowledge-box".

Strange as it may seem, there really are such men. The ruthless test of competition and selection that has evolved the racehorse has also evolved the man to back him. Not that these men are always professional backers — many of the finest judges and most constant students of racing do not bet at all; but their opinion is always thought good enough to be heavily gambled on by the punting fraternity. Even when he bets, the real knowledge-box may not always pick the winner; but at any rate he can always give a sensible reason for his choice, and if defeated he is not discredited. William of Orange was still a great general though he was constantly defeated; and we have already seen how the element of luck in running a race will upset the best calculations, and what little margin there is between the first, second, and third in a race. The knowledge-box does not bet on every race; he may even go to two or three meetings without a bet. Then something crops up that really looks good enough, and he has a go at it. Knowledge-boxes are of all classes of the turf world.

The term comprises some trainers, some owners, some sporting writers, a fair number of breeders — your successful breeder is usually a really good judge of racing — some gentlemen who live by the game (sometimes backing horses and sometimes taking a share with a bookmaker) an occasional handicapper, and a few unattracted race-goers who seem to be born with the turf instinct. One of the best judges of racing the writer ever knew was a foreman plumber, and the worst was a jockey.

Next to the knowledge-boxes in the table of turf precedence come the hard-heads. A hard-head, as the name implies, is a combative sort of person. He is invariably a backer, and bets on every race. He, too, is a good judge of racing, but his skill consists mainly in getting information and sifting it and picking out the grains of wheat from the straw of irrelevance. He is far better posted in performances than in pedigrees. The knowledge-box is the artist of racing, the hard-head is the commercial man, shrewd, and self-reliant.

Racing seems to have developed a special class of human being. Where do they all come from, these "followers of the turf", always well dressed, always clean shaven, hard featured, alert, and mysterious? They go to every race-meeting and always seem to have money. Some are simply professional gamblers, but a great many are men with trades to turn to, and should they encounter a run of bad luck, they go back to work, and their places are taken by others. When they have got a fresh start they come at it again, for backing horses is a disease for which death is the only cure. They get the best information and the best prices and very often run themselves into quite a good lump of money when luck comes their way. They often get better information than the owner, for they are of the same social class as the jockeys and stable boys, and from these latter they hear any valuable bit of news just as soon as ever it happens. A good gallop by, or an accident to, the favourite seems to be wirelessed into town, so quickly do some of the hard-heads get hold of it. Not only do they get it quickly but they get it accurately, which the owner does not always manage to do. If there were anything in backing horses these gentry would surely reap the profit of their skill, pluck, and persistence; but inquiry as to their whereabouts often is met with the curt sentence, "Bill's 'ad to get work", which shows that even for the hard-head the turf is a slippery road to travel.

Allied to the hard-heads but somewhat different in species are the whisperers. A whisperer is a man who makes a living, often a very good living, by giving tips for races. The well-dressed stranger or country man who goes to a race-meeting, as he leans over the rails and studies the horses, will find an affable stranger alongside him and they drift into conversation. The affable stranger says, "That's a good sort of a horse", and the ice is broken and before long the country man is "told the tale". Now the tale has many versions, and it all depends on the listener which version is brought forward. The crudest plot that finds patrons is the old, old, friend-of-the-owner story. In this drama the whisperer represents himself as a great friend of the owner of a certain horse, and if necessary he produces a confederate to represent the owner. The whisperer and confederate talk in a light-hearted way of putting a hundred each on, and they agree that they will do it if the price is good enough; but if they cannot get a fair price they will wait for another day. The stranger thinks he ought not to miss such a chance at this, and timidly suggests that he would like to be allowed to put a tenner on with their money. They demur and say that they have a good deal of other money to put on for friends and if they try to put too much on, it might spoil the price. However, as being entreated to do so, they take the stranger's tenner as a great favour and that is the last he sees of it or them.

This is a simple way to get money, but it has its drawbacks. If the stranger is an absolute novice he may be persuaded to back a horse with no possible chance, and then the gang never lose sight of him and they try to get another tenner out of him for the next race. If he looks like a man that knows anything at all, they have to suggest backing a horse with some sort of a chance; and if that horse happens to win they have to leave the course hurriedly, because it is a very awkward thing to have an infuriated country man looking for you with a race-course detective when you depend on your wits for a living. So the friend-of-the-owner story is tried only on novices and as a last resource, for it can be worked only on a very raw fool, and raw fools as a rule have not enough money to be worth robbing. Also, it is a breach of the law, and the true artist in whispering can "find 'em", without that.

The higher grade class of narrative depends for its success not on the tale but on the way it is told. The artistic practitioner goes to the races and picks out by some unerring instinct the right "mark". He may select a country man or a sailor or a stuck-up — anyone that looks as if he had money and was ready for a gamble. The whisperer tells the tale suited to his more educated client. This time the tale is that he has a friend in a racing stable (which is quite true), that White Cockade is favourite but has not been backed by its stable and will not try to win, and that he knows a horse that is on the whole "an absolute cert if they spur it". He can find out all about it from his friend in the racing stable. Will the client have twenty pounds on it if he can find out that it is all right? The client, anxious to be up-to-date, says he will. Off goes the whisperer and comes back very mysterious. "Good thing! Paleface, second favourite at six to one. Better have twenty on it. The favourite is as dead as mutton!" He hypnotizes the client, who soon gets the suggestion that he must back Paleface, it would be absolutely chucking a chance away not to have a good punt on Paleface, six to one's a real gift about Paleface, don't ask anybody anything, just get in quiet and back Paleface: after they have conversed for a while the client would eat a tallow candle and swear it was milk chocolate if the whisperer offered it to him. It was once said of a really great whisperer that he could talk a punter off a battleship into a canvas dinghy in mid-ocean.

Like horse-taming it is all done with the eye and the voice. Having hooked his fish, the whisperer now pilots him up to a bookmaker and sees the money put on, and they go off to watch the race. The favourite runs wide at the turn and loses his position and never quite gets into the fighting line; but Paleface hugs the rails and comes away in the straight and wins easily. The whisperer and his client go off together to draw £120 of the best and the whisperer, if he handles his client properly, should get at least £20 for himself out of it. More than that, the client will be good for more betting, certainly until the hundred is gone, and probably a bit more on the top of that. Some of these whisperers do really well when money is plentiful and sportsmen generous, and they build up quite a connection with country punters. Some of them keep the same clients for years. No one has ever actually heard of a whisperer selling his business or floating it into a Company, but that may come later on.

They deserve all they make, too. Do you think, oh most astute reader, that you could get a living by going to the race-courses and finding out winners and then inducing perfect strangers to back them and give you a share of the proceeds! Like most other professions it tends to be overcrowded. Practically every ex-jockey or stable-hand with the necessary brains has his little circle of punters, and some of the boys in the stables learn to "whisper" winners before they can see over the half-door of a stable. It takes a really good judge of racing and of human nature to keep his clientele together for long; and sometimes even the masters of the art make mistakes, as the following absolutely true tale of the trainer and whisperer will illustrate.

It was when things were dull in Melbourne but booming in Sydney that a crowd of the Melbourne followers of racing came up to Sydney on the track of the money. One of the Melbourne visitors was an expert whisperer and he had not been long on the Sydney course before he saw a genuine bushman, bearded, cabbage-tree-hatted, sunburnt, and silent. Bearing down on the bushie he told him the old tale, and said that he had a friend in Layton's stable and that one of Layton's horses was "a certainty if they backed it". Layton, it may be mentioned, was a leading Sydney trainer. After the usual spell-binding and oratory on the part of the whisperer, the bushie agreed to put ten pounds on the horse, and went away to see some friends, arranging to meet the whisperer after the race. The horse won all right and the whisperer was at the meeting-place bright and early. He had not long to wait. Up came the bushman smiling all over, and the whisperer expected a very substantial "cut" out of the winnings. "Did you back it?" he said. "What price did you get?"

"I got fives — fifty pound to ten."

"You won fifty, eh? Well, what about a tenner for me, for putting you on to it?"

"Oh, I don't know. Why should I give you a tenner? I'd have backed the horse whether I saw you or not."

The whisperer tried persuasion and even pathetic appeal; he reduced his claim to "Two quid", but even at that the pastoral individual was adamant. At last the whisperer lost his temper.

"You'd have backed it without me tellin' you! You, you great yokel! What do you know about racehorses?"

"Well, I ought to know something. My name's Layton. I train that horse. I've just been away for a holiday in the bush. But I'll tell you what I'll do. I'll give you the two pounds if you can point me out any man in my stable that told you to back it."

As he finished speaking, as the novelist says, "He looked up and found himself alone."

The World of "Banjo" Paterson, 1967

A RACE WORTH WATCHING

Now that the selling race is disposed of, comes race No. 4, the big event of the day, a mile-and-a-half, weight-for-age race, worth two thousand pounds to the winner; and now we have the best side of racing. There are six runners, all very high-class horses, all owned by wealthy men, thorough sportsmen and incapable of any sharp practice, and trained by leading trainers who get their living by training winners and not by a combination of punting and roguery, and ridden by the best Australian and American jockeys. It seems almost a profanation to draw betting into such a race as this, and we determine to let them run unbacked so that we may enjoy a real genuine first-class race without having any financial bias whatever.

What a field for equality! Oligarch, a four-year-old, winner of last year's Derby, meets Dragoon, second horse for this year's Derby; while Flint Arrow, a horse that only came to his best as he increased in years, represents the five-year-olds. Pleasantry, a filly that might have won the Oaks only for going wrong before the race, is making a reappearance and no one knows quite how good she is. The other two are Moonlighter, an Irish four-year-old that has been clearing up everything before him in handicaps and is now having a try in first-class company, and Tornado, the last of the lot, a dark three-year-old that was not trained at two years but has run very well since and apparently is that very rare thing, a real born genuine stayer — though whether he will be fast enough for this lot is another matter. It is a sight not be forgotten when the six turn out to parade — the grand swinging walk, heads held high and confidently, manners sober and determined, their frames laced and braced with bands of muscle, coats shining like glass. No other animal in the world reaches the same level of excellence as the thoroughbred horse. And this field now going to the post has been arrived at by centuries of breeding, feeding, selection, judgment, and constant weeding out of the inferior and the unfit. Turf history rises before us as we look at them. It was to produce these horses that the Darley Arabian was brought from the desert, that the Byerley Turk was taken from his work as an officer's charger, and that the Godolphin Barb was rescued from drawing a water-cart in France to be the founder of a long line of courageous and determined horses.

As they canter past, the mind goes back to the old-time races and we almost seem to see a race-meeting of a hundred years ago, the noble owners on their hacks cantering up to watch the start and galloping back across the course to see the finish; the bookmakers congregating at the betting post; Royalty in its chariot looking on; and the common people, not so educated as now, stubbornly supporting their local champions irrespective of favour or weight or distance. Where the great grandstands now are we seem to see the little booths strictly reserved for the quality — for a gentleman was a gentleman in those pre-democratic days. In that fiery chestnut rushing down the running with his head in his chest, his great stride sweeping the ground behind him, we seem to see again the mighty Eclipse — that evil-tempered, nerve-beaten equine phenomenon — going out to battle once more to make mincemeat of the opposition. In the brown colt lazily lobbing past we see again the Flying Dutchman to whom distance and weight were as nothing; while the little wiry excited bay mare reefing at her bit and gliding along like a snake — is that Bee's-Wing come back on earth again? Not a horse starting in this race today but has its pedigree as carefully kept as that of any aristocrat in the land. At its worst racing may have many faults but at its best it has always been the one sport that gripped the mind of the English, for the grim pluck, the fiery dash of the blood horse have always appealed to something deep down in the breast of every Englishman.

And so our field goes to the post to show themselves worthy of their sires; and even as the horses are good so are the owners, for not an owner in the race is racing for money or for the excitement of betting but simply for the pleasure of seeing his colours carried by a really good horse in really good company. Though we have decided not to bet on this race, still we must try to pick it, so let us see how they have run. Oligarch is a good horse in every sense of the word. He won his Derby by sheer grit against a much faster animal; he is neither sad nor sorry, does not pull or fight in a race, hard going or soft makes no difference to him: he has raced at two, three, and four years old and has never run a bad race. He has a jockey on his back who has ridden him half a dozen times already, and he is up to the mark in the matter of condition; but he has something to beat today and, though he is favourite and the public money is going on him in bushels, the ring are prepared to bet even money till the cows come home. In these weight-for-age races the price of the favourite is always short as there is no need to ask the owners' intention — one horse usually stands out as a likely winner, but at short prices the ring will take a lot of silencing. So it is even money Oligarch, and still even money though the fivers, and the tenners, and the hundreds and the thousands pour steadily in on him.

Second favourite at three to one is Dragoon, a fine three-year-old who was not too lucky in the running of the Derby and is said to have improved since. The Derby winner having gone wrong, Dragoon may be considered the best three-year-old of his year, but he has not yet met any really first-class older horses on this distance and it is not too certain that he can see the mile and a half right out if pace is on all the way; but if the pace is slow in the early part then Dragoon's great burst of speed may just land him a winner. We should see some good riding in this race as it will be a matter for rare judgment how much pace to set and when to make the final dash. Here comes Pleasantry; a beautiful, graceful, gazelle-like creature, she hardly seems to touch the ground as she moves past. She has speed enough and is bred to stay for ever, but her fiery temperament will be all against her in a race like this; she will probably fret in the race and not be able to do herself justice at the finish.

Now comes the old one, Flint Arrow, hard as flint too, an indifferent two- and three-year-old, he suddenly showed form as a four-year-old and now at five is, so it is whispered, a far better horse than he ever was before in his life. There are families in the racehorse aristocracy whose characteristic it is to develop late in life, and these are nearly always the best-constituted and best-fibred animals in the world. But the craze for early racing — large profits and quick returns — has driven these families out of fashion and Flint Arrow represents what is an almost unfashionable family on the sire's side, while on the mother's side he has a cross of Herod blood. He looks hard enough and tough enough for any trial, but the race will need to be run at a full pace, all the way, if he is to do any good, and there is nothing in the race to make a pace for him, so the books are offering sixes about him and he too has a host of followers.

Moonlighter, the handicap champion, has never met this class of field before and the general idea is that he will find himself outclassed. With him, at outside prices, is Tornado, a tough-looking, game-headed, sleepy customer that looks like staying all day but has done nothing to warrant anyone thinking he can see out a mile and half with this lot. And so they go to the post.

A little delay and the barrier goes up. The two stayers, Tornado and Flint Arrow, move off at once, settling down to the long journey with easy strides, heads stretched out and just a nice easy pull on their bridles; the two fliers, Oligarch and Dragoon, are running behind them, each a bit inclined to pull and to resent being steadied, but the superb hands of their riders calm them down and humour them, and after a hundred yards or so they settle to it contentedly enough. The handicap king, Moonlighter, bounds along, a ball of muscle, in last place; he is so used to carrying top weight in big handicaps that he is accustomed to run all his races behind and he only wonders there are so few horses in front of him. So far nothing looks like setting an extra fast pace, though the whole lot, easily as they seem to be going, are cutting up the ground at a great rate. But suddenly the fiery little mare, Pleasantry, who has failed to get a place on the rails and is running alongside the two colts, begins to show very plain symptoms that she does not think she is going fast enough. She is fighting at the bit, and her rider, to hold her, has to pull till her mouth is wide open and her neck bent so that the free current of air to her lungs, so important in long-distance racing, is sadly interfered with. She throws her head from side to side and gets out of her stride, while her rider recognizes that it is better to let her go than to let her beat herself pulling; so all at once she flashes to the front, and away she goes with a three-lengths lead, and what looks like a slow-run race gives every promise of being a remarkably fast one.

As soon as she goes out to the lead the whole field quickens and before long it is not much trouble to hold anything. They run the first half-mile in 52 seconds, and all the time the little mare draws farther away; the two stayers are getting all the pace they want and when the mile is reached in one minute 41 and a half seconds, it looks as if the fliers may not have a run left to finish with. As they begin the last half-mile the rear division imperceptibly quicken. They are "going out after the mare", because it is time now to get within striking distance to get in position for the final rush. Flint Arrow, hugging the rails and saving every inch of ground, begins to draw up on her; but his mate, Tornado, cannot go on with him. The company is a shade too good for him and in a flash he has dropped back and the two fliers, Oligarch and Dragoon, are past him. The boy on the handicap king, Moonlighter, asks him to go on after them; but it is one thing coming with a burst of speed through a lot of inferior horses and quite another to last out a mile and a half with this lot, and he soon shows that if the field are going to improve the pace they will have to improve it without him. He and Tornado drop to the rear and are no more thought of. Three furlongs from home Flint Arrow has caught the little mare, while just at their heels the other two are thundering, the riders watching each other and waiting to make a drive on the straight. They are fairly flying now and the little mare, game as she is, has taken too much out of herself to be able to finish, and rounding the turn she drops back beaten, leaving Flint Arrow in the lead. The two colts have to come round outside the mare. She rolls a little with distress and Dragoon gets a bump — the slightest thing in the world, but a very slight thing is going to make a very big difference in this race. It throws him off his balance for an instant and when he gets into his stride again Oligarch has got a clear length from him. Dragoon, owning a high-strung nervous system, refuses to make the supreme effort necessary to get in line again and in an instant he is out of the race. This leaves Oligarch, the favourite, to chase Flint Arrow down the straight; and, running straight as a gun-barrel, he swoops down on the tiring leader. How the crowd yell! Foot by foot he draws up on him, to his quarters, to his girth, to his shoulder. Can he maintain the effort? If he had been just a little bit nearer the leader at the entrance to the straight, if he had had time to get just one long breath to fill his lungs before the final dash, then his pace would be sure to prevail. But he has been racing at his very top for the whole of the last half-mile and though he draws level with the leader he seems unable to pass him.

Out come the whips and while the crowd yell themselves hoarse Flint Arrow calls on the reserve force and determination, which all really great horses seem to carry packed in their system somewhere, and with whip and spur cutting him to pieces he draws away again from the favourite and wins a desperate race by half a neck. As he comes back to weigh blood is on his sides and weals are on his ribs, but the horse knows he has won and holds his head high; and one old-time sportsman points at him a hand shaking with excitement and says, "Look at that! You don't see many nowadays would stand a question like that put to them. He's one of the old sort!" And so they come in through cheering thousands, and before the saddles are off the news is flashed to all parts of the world that Flint Arrow, who never won a really big race in his life, has beaten the best in the land at weight-for-age. We have seen a race that will make turf history.

Of course after the race there are all the usual post-mortems and excuses. If the mare had not set up such an awful pace, if Oligarch had been kept a little bit closer to the leaders, if Dragoon had not got that bump, what a different tale there would have been to tell. It is quite likely that if the race were run over again Flint Arrow might not be in the first three. Such is the luck of racing. After a tussle like this it is almost a degradation to have to watch another selling race, this time for two-year-olds. These races are always much supported by the gamblers because it is easier to keep a two-year-old dark than an older horse, and a big stake can sometimes be made almost a matter of certainty. So it is in this race, for a little wiry precocious two-year-old filly hardly bigger than a pony is put forward by a heavy betting stable, and backed as if it were all over. The mare herself has a varminty, elderly-spinster look, and there is nothing in her appearance to justify the rush that is made on her. But the knowledge-boxes and the hard-heads all seem to agree that she is the one to back. They know that the people backing her are the shrewdest of the shrewd, and they don't ask any questions. In a flash the mare is at even money and she wins all the way; whereby we win a tenner and the people who own her win about three thousand beautiful golden sovereigns.

Oh, it is a good game when nothing goes amiss. Who would work for a few sordid pounds when one can get on to a good thing like this? But the last race of the day — a mile handicap at welter weights — lowest weight seven stone seven — gives the talent something to think about. Kingfish, a big strong horse, has won several of these welter-weight races, and he is the early favourite though he is carrying ten stone ten. Then a lot of money comes in for a flying, light-framed, weedy colt called Talkative, and half a dozen others carry the confidence and money of their stables. It is what is called a "good betting" race. No matter what wins the bookmaker cannot lose anything, while they will skin the lamb to some tune should an outsider get home. They are offering five to one on the field and everybody is having a wager on something, for this is the last race of the day and people who are in pocket are playing up their winnings hoping to win a really good stake, while those who have lost on the day are going for a recovery. Pop it down, gents, if you don't put down a brick you can't pick up a castle! Twenty of them go to the post, Kingfish favourite, but in this as in most good betting races the prices vary all over the ring. Some men who have laid their full book against Kingfish are unwilling to concede a shadow of a point in the price, while others who have not laid him to any extent are willing to stretch the odds a point or two so as to "get him in". Seastream and Condamine are at sixes in one part of the ring and at eights elsewhere.

It is a big field and the matter of post positions will make a difference. A quick beginner that draws a position near the rails has a lot the best of it, as he can shoot out when the barrier lifts and get away on the rail while the slow beginners are crushed and bumped by the mass of horses drawing in towards the rail. A jockey giving evidence at an inquiry into a racecourse smash was asked, "After the barrier went up what happend?"

"Why, the same thing that always happens! The horses on the outside came in towards the rails and my horse was lifted fair off the ground. He never hit the ground at all for three strides."

In this race the one, two, and three positions next the rails are drawn by rank outsiders and as soon as the barrier rises one of them, Solitaire, a nervous, excitable mare jumps out like a flash. While the others are scuffling with each other she hits her stride at once and is away with one, two, three, four, lengths lead of anything. Half maddened by the roar of hoofs behind her she races like a scared rabbit, and five hundred hard-heads all yell the same question at once, "Here, what price that thing in front?" The bookmakers who bet while the race is being run offer ten to one but won't lay it to much money. They don't want to spoil a real good "skinner", by laying a lot of money in running. What they will lay is snapped up like a flash. Still in front the bay mare holds her advantage well, her novice rider crouching down on her neck in a frenzy of excitement, but mercifully sitting still as a rock on her, letting the mare run her own race. The half-mile is reached and she still has her four lengths lead. Will she last it out? By this time the good horses have fought their way clear of the ruck and are being sent along after her for all they are worth. Only two furlongs to go and they have hardly made an impression on her, and the cry is raised, "She walks in."

Backers look vainly in the mass of colour behind her for something to run out and settle her in the last four strides. The whips come out, but nothing gets near enough to really ask her a question and the unthought-of mare races home with a two-lengths lead and it takes her rider another three furlongs before he can get her pulled up. The ring give one might roar of exultation, and hustle back to their positions laughing and joking with each other. "'Ere, I'll pay this winner!" they yell exultantly; but backers are like the oysters in *Alice in Wonderland* for, "answer came there none." The public stream off home — "If I'd only left that last race alone —" And we, too, join the crush through the gates, having come out pretty well square on the day; and so off home to buy an evening paper and read all about it and to speculate on what might have happened if we hadn't been stupid enough to back the wrong ones, or had been plucky enough to back the right ones a little more heavily. The bookmakers pack up their satchels and depart; the trainers hood and rug their horses and get them away home; and in half an hour's time the saddling paddock is a vast emptiness littered with torn-up tickets, paper bags, tipsters' cards, and blighted hopes. The day's racing is over.

The World of "Banjo" Paterson, 1967

6
Poems for Children

EDITOR'S NOTE

Whatever elegance of simplicity and explicitness and grace of poetic expression Paterson had developed in the writing of his verses down the years came most felicitously to fruition in his last volume of verse, *The Animals Noah Forgot*, published in 1933 by the Endeavour Press, the *Bulletin*'s first and only venture into book publishing. Written as poetry for children and gloriously illustrated by Norman Lindsay, it reaches out — like all the classic examples of this genre in our literature — to all ages. In this work, Paterson has written the most charming verses imaginable about Australian animals and birds, which sadly his poems may well outlast.

It is doubtful if better children's poetry about animals and birds has been written before or since. Somehow here best of all, Paterson's love of the bush, his poetic sense, his innate humour and his accurate observation combined to give his writing the most delicate touch. Happy the children who have numbered these poems in their literary education!

THE ANIMALS NOAH FORGOT

by A. B. PATERSON ("Banjo")

ILLUSTRATED BY NORMAN LINDSAY

PUBLISHED BY THE ENDEAVOUR PRESS
Bulletin Buildings, 252 George Street, Sydney, N.S.W.

Original title page for 1933 Endeavour Press edition.

The Animals Noah Forgot

PROLOGUE

The Mountains

A land of sombre, silent hills, where mountain cattle go
By twisted tracks, on sidelings steep, where giant gumtrees grow
And the wind replies, in the river oaks, to the song of the stream
    below.

A land where the hills keep watch and ward, silent and wide
    awake
As those who sit by a dead campfire, and wait for the dawn to
    break,
Or those who watched by the Holy Cross for the dead
    Redeemer's sake.

A land where silence lies so deep that sound itself is dead
And a gaunt grey bird, like a homeless soul, drifts, noiseless,
    overhead
And the world's great story is left untold, and the message is left
    unsaid.

The Plains

A land, as far as the eye can see, where the waving grasses grow
Or the plains are blackened and burnt and bare, where the false
    mirages go
Like shifting symbols of hope deferred — land where you never
    know.

Land of plenty or land of want, where the grey Companions
    dance,
Feast or famine, or hope or fear, and in all things land of chance,
Where Nature pampers or Nature slays, in her ruthless, red,
    romance.

And we catch a sound of a fairy's song, as the wind goes
    whipping by,
Or a scent like incense drifts along from the herbage ripe and dry
— Or the dust-storms dance on their ballroom floor, where the
    bones of the cattle lie.

FOREWORD

The big white English swan, escaped from captivity, found himself swimming in an Australian waterhole fringed with giant
gumtrees. In one of the lower forks of a gumtree sat a placid
round-eyed elderly gentleman apparently thinking of nothing
whatever — in other words, a native bear.

"Excuse me, sir," said the swan, "can you tell me where I am?"

"Why, you're here," said the bear.

"I know I'm here," said the swan, thinking that his new acquaintance was dull-witted; "but where is 'here'? You see. I'm an
English swan" —

"Excuse me," said the bear, "swans are black. I've seen thousands of 'em."

"They're black in this country," said the swan, "just the same
as the aboriginals are black; but they are white in England, just the
same as the people there are white. I don't like mentioning it, but
our family are very highly regarded in England — one of the oldest
families. We came to England from Cyprus with Richard Coeur-
de-Leon."

"I'm a bit in that line myself," said the bear. "Did you ever
hear of the Flood, when Noah took the animals in the Ark? Well,
my people wouldn't go in the Ark. They didn't see any chance of
getting fresh gumleaves every day, and they heard that this Noah
was not too reliable. A capable chap — he must have been a capable chap to organise that outfit — but inclined to drink. So our
people climbed trees and lived on gumleaves till the water went
down. They say the Flood wasn't as high here as it was in other
places, but I've never seen a flood yet but what somebody would
tell you it was higher at his place than at yours. Have you any
friends here?"

"I'm afraid not," said the swan, "but you never know. I'll give
a call."

So he put up his head and sent a call echoing through the bush like the clang of a great brazen gong. Twice he repeated it, but no answer came.

"No luck," said the bear. "Anyone within two miles would be deaf if he didn't hear that. I'm pretty good, myself, at making people hear me. We got a lot of practice in the Flood, shouting to each other from the trees, and when we saw old Noah drifting to a sandbank, we'd give him a hail. Listen to me."

And throwing his head back, he emitted the weirdest and most unmusical noise you ever heard. It sounded like an empty train running over an iron bridge.

"I could have had good money to go on the stage," he said, "but of course in my position I couldn't consider it. What would people think?"

"I suppose you have a lot of friends," said the swan.

"Well, not exactly friends," said the bear. "You see, we of the old families have to be a bit particular. We can't associate with these *nouveaux riches* and Johnny-come-lately people that you see about. Now, there's the 'possums — people that pretend to be relations of mine, but they're not. I saw one of them hanging upside down by the tail from a limb one night. Most undignified. Thank goodness, no matter what has happened to us, we have never grown tails. The Platypus family is as old as we are, but they live in the water, and I have never touched water, inside or outside, in my life; so we don't see anything of them."

"Do *they* date back to the Flood?" said the swan, who was thinking that after all Coeur-de-Leon seemed quite modern compared to these people.

"Oh, yes," said the bear. "They wouldn't go in the Ark either. Couldn't see any hope of getting their regular food, and there was a first-class chance of getting trodden on by the elephant. So they took to the water and they had the time of their lives. Plenty of food, and they drifted about on floating logs and fence-posts all day long. Didn't even have to swim. That was a gentleman's life, if you like."

"What is there up this creek?" said the swan. "Do you travel about much?"

"Me travel!" said the bear. "Do I look like it? Why should I?

They say there are better trees up the creek, but what was good enough for my fathers is good enough for me. One of our people went wandering all over the place, half a mile up the creek, and he climbed a tree with a bees' nest in it and they stung him till his nose swelled up like an elephant's trunk. That's what he got for being one of these revolutionary chaps. Served him right.''

"Well," said the swan, "I'm glad to have met you, and I think I'd better be moving on.''

"Not a bit of it," said the bear, "not a bit of it. Never move on when you're lost. If people that are lost would sit still they'd be all right; but they will keep moving about and they die before people can catch up with them. Stay where you are and someone's sure to hear of you and they'll come here to look for you.''

While they were talking, the surface of the waterhole below them was as smooth as glass. Then, without a splash or a ripple, a lithe brown creature rose to the surface and drifted there soundlessly, looking up at them with bright little eyes.

"Good-day, Mr. Platypus," said the bear. "This," he went on, indicating the swan with a wave of his hand, "is an English friend of mine. I want you to take him where he can get a good feed of waterlily roots and frogs, and then fetch him back here. We'll boil the billy and make a night of it. He can tell us about Richard Coeur-de-Leon, and we can tell him about these neighbours of ours.''

And it is from what the native bear and the platypus said that night that this book is written.

— A.B. PATERSON

OLD MAN PLATYPUS

Far from the trouble and toil of town,
Where the reed-beds sweep and shiver,
Look at a fragment of velvet brown —
Old Man Platypus drifting down,
Drifting along the river.

And he plays and dives in the river bends
In a style that is most elusive;

With few relations and fewer friends,
For Old Man Platypus descends
From a family most exclusive.

He shares his burrow beneath the bank
With his wife and his son and daughter
At the roots of the reeds and the grasses rank;
And the bubbles show where our hero sank
To its entrance under water.

Safe in their burrow below the falls
They live in a world of wonder,
Where no one visits and no one calls,
They sleep like little brown billiard balls
With their beaks tucked neatly under.

And he talks in a deep unfriendly growl
As he goes on his journey lonely;
For he's no relation to fish our fowl,
Nor to bird nor beast, nor to horned owl;
In fact, he's the one and only!

WHY THE JACKASS LAUGHS

The Boastful Crow and the Laughing Jack
Were telling tales of the outer back:
"I've just been travelling far and wide,
At the back of Bourke and the Queensland side;
There isn't a bird in the bush can go
As far as me," said the old black crow.

"There isn't a bird in the bush can fly
A course as straight or a course as high.
Higher than human eyesight goes
There's sometimes clouds — but there's always crows,
Drifting along for a scent of blood
Or a smell of smoke or a sign of flood.
For never a bird or a beast has been
With a sight as strong or a scent as keen.
At fires and floods I'm the first about,

For then the lizards and mice run out:
And I make my swoop — and that's all they know —
I'm a whale on mice," said the Boastful Crow.

The Bee-birds over the homestead flew
And told each other the long day through
"The cold has come, we must take the track."
"Now, I'll make you a bet," said the Laughing Jack,
"Of a hundred mice, that you dare not go
With the little Bee-birds, my Boastful Crow."

Said the Boastful Crow: "I could take my ease
And fly with little green birds like these.
If they went flat out and they did their best
I could have a smoke and could take a rest."
And he asked of the Bee-birds circling round:
"Now, where do you spike-tails think you're bound?"
"We leave to-night, and our present plan
Is to go straight on till we reach Japan.

"Every year, on the self-same day,
We call our children and start away,
Twittering, travelling day and night,
Over the ocean we take our flight;
And we rest a day on some lonely isles
Or we beg a ride for a hundred miles
On a steamer's deck,* and away we go;
We hope you'll come with us, Mister Crow."

But the old black crow was extremely sad.
Said he: "I reckon you're raving mad
To talk of travelling night and day,
And how in the world do you find your way?"
And the Bee-birds answered him: "If you please,
That's one of our own great mysteries."

* * * * *

Now, these things chanced in the long ago
And explain the fact, which no doubt you know,
That every jackass high and low
Will always laugh when he sees a crow.

* The writer has seen Eastern steamers green with the migrating bee-eaters.

BENJAMIN BANDICOOT

If you walk in the bush at night,
In the wonderful silence deep,
By the flickering lantern light
When the birds are all asleep
You may catch a sight of old Skinny go-root,
Otherwise Benjamin Bandicoot.

With a snout that can delve and dig,
With claws that are strong as steel,
He roots like a pigmy pig
To get his evening meal,
For creeping creatures and worms and roots
Are highly relished by bandicoots.

Under the grass and the fern
He fashions his beaten track
With many a twist and turn
That wanders and doubles back,
And dogs that think they are most astute
Are baffled by Benjamin Bandicoot.

In the depth of the darkest night,
Without a star in the sky,
He'll come to look at a light,
And scientists wonder why:
If the bush is burning it's time to scoot
Is the notion of Benjamin Bandicoot.

THE BILLY-GOAT OVERLAND

Come all ye lads of the droving days, ye gentlemen unafraid,
I'll tell you all of the greatest trip that ever a drover made,
For we rolled our swags, and we packed our bags, and taking
    our lives in hand,
We started away with a thousand goats, on the billy-goat
    overland.

There wasn't a fence that'd hold the mob, or keep 'em from
    their desires;
They skipped along the top of the posts and cake-walked on the
    wires.
And where the lanes had been stripped of grass and the
    paddocks were nice and green,
The goats they travelled outside the lanes and we rode in between.

The squatters started to drive them back, but that was no good
    at all,
Their horses ran for the lick of their lives from the scent that was
    like a wall:
And never a dog had pluck or gall in front of the mob to stand
And face the charge of a thousand goats on the billy-goat
    overland.

We found we were hundreds over strength when we counted out
    the mob;
And the put us in jail for a crowd of thieves that travelled to
    steal and rob:
For every goat between here and Bourke, when he scented our
    spicy band,
Had left his home and his work to join in the billy-goat overland.

AN EMU HUNT

West of Dubbo the West begins
The land of leisure and hope and trust,
Where the black man stalks with his dogs and gins
And Nature visits the settlers' sins
With the Bogan shower, that is mostly dust.

When the roley-poley's roots dry out
With the fierce hot winds and the want of rain.
They come uprooted and bound about
And dance in a wild fantastic rout
Like flying haystacks across the plain.

And the horses shudder and snort and shift
As the bounding mass of weed goes past,
But the emus never their heads uplift

As they look for roots in the sandy drift,
For the emus know it from first to last.

* * * * *

Now, the boss's dog that had come from town
Was strange to the wild and woolly West,
And he thought he would earn him some great renown
When he saw, on the wastes of the open down,
An emu standing beside her nest.

And he said to himself as he stalked his prey
To start on his first great emu hunt:
"I must show some speed when she runs away,
For emus kick very hard, they say;
But I can't be kicked if I keep in front."

The emu chickens made haste to flee
As he barked and he snarled and he darted round,
But the emu looked at him scornfully
And put an end to his warlike glee
With a kick that lifted him off the ground.

* * * * *

And when, with an injured rib or two,
He made for home with a chastened mind,
An old dog told him: "I thought you knew
An emu kicks like a kangaroo,
And you can't get hurt — IF YOU KEEP BEHIND."

FLYING SQUIRRELS

On the rugged water-shed
At the top of the bridle track
Where years ago, as the old men say,
The splitters went with a bullock-dray
But never a dray came back;

At the time of the gumtree bloom,
When the scent in the air is strong,
And the blossom stirs in the evening breeze,
You may see the squirrels among the trees,
Playing the whole night long.

Never a care at all
Bothers their simple brains;
You can see them glide in the moonlight dim
From tree to tree and from limb to limb,
Little grey aeroplanes.

Each like a dormouse sleeps
In the spout of a gumtree old,
A ball of fur with a silver coat;
Each with his tail around his throat
For fear of his catching cold.

These are the things he eats,
Asking his friends to dine:
Moths and beetles and new-born shoots,
Honey and snacks of the native fruits,
And a glass of dew for wine.

FROGS IN CHORUS

The chorus frogs in the big lagoon
Would sing their songs to the silvery moon.
Tenor singers were out of place,
For every frog was a double bass.
But never a human chorus yet
Could beat the accurate time they set.
The solo singer began the joke;
He sang "As long as I live I'll croak, Croak, I'll croak,"
And the chorus followed him: "Croak, croak, croak!"

The poet frog, in his plaintive tone,
Sang of a sorrow was all his own;
"How shall I win to my heart's desire?
How shall I feed my spirit's fire?"
And the solo frog in his deepest croak,
"to fire your spirit," he sang, eat coke, Coke, eat coke,"
And the chorus followed him: "Coke, coke, coke!"

The green frog sat in a swampy spot
And he sang the song of he knew not what.

"The world is rotten, oh cursed spite,
That I am the frog that must set it right.
How shall I scatter the shades that lurk?"
And the old-man bull-frog sang "Get work, Work, get work,"
And the chorus followed him: "Work, work, work!"

* * * * *

The soaring spirits that fain would fly
On wings of hope to the starry sky
Must face the snarls of the jealous dogs,
For the world is ruled by its chorus frogs.

WHITE COCKATOOS

Now the autumn maize is growing,
Now the corn-cob fills,
Where the Little River flowing
Winds among the hills.
Over mountain-peaks outlying
Clear against the blue
Comes a scout in silence flying,
One white cockatoo.

Back he goes to where the meeting
Waits among the trees.
Says "The corn is fit for eating;
Hurry, if you please."
Skirmishers, their line extending,
Shout the joyful news;
Down they drop like snow descending,
Clouds of cockatoos.

At their husking competition
Hear them screech and yell.
On a gumtree's high position
Sits a sentinel.
Soon the boss goes boundary-riding;
But the wise old bird,
Mute among the branches hiding,
Never says a word.

Then you hear his strident squalling:
"Here's the boss's son,
Through the garden bushes crawling,
Crawling with a gun.
May the spiny cactus bristles
Fill his soul with woe;
May his knees get full of thistles.
Brothers, let us go."

Old Black Harry sees them going,
Sketches Nature's plan:
"That one cocky too much knowing,
All same Chinaman.
One eye shut and one eye winkin' —
Never shut the two;
Chinaman go dead, me thinkin'.
Jump up cockatoo."

Select Bibliography

WORKS BY A.B. PATERSON

Books

The Man from Snowy River and Other Verses. Sydney: Angus & Robertson, 1895.

Rio Grande's Last Race and Other Verses. Sydney: Angus & Robertson, 1902.

Old Bush Songs (collected and edited with an Introduction). Sydney: Angus & Robertson, 1905.

An Outback Marriage. Sydney: Angus & Robertson, 1906.

Saltbush Bill J.P. and Other Verses. Sydney: Angus & Robertson, 1917.

Three Elephant Power and Other Stories. Sydney: Angus & Robertson, 1917.

Collected Verse. Sydney: Angus & Robertson, 1921.

The Animals Noah Forgot. Sydney: Endeavour Press, 1933.

Happy Dispatches. Sydney: Angus & Robertson, 1934.

The Shearer's Colt. Sydney: Angus & Robertson, 1936.

Banjo Paterson Tells His Own Story (newspaper series). *Sydney Morning Herald*, 4 February-4 March 1939.

Later Collections and Anthologies

The World of "Banjo" Paterson. Ed. Clement Semmler. Sydney: Angus & Robertson, 1967.

A.B. "Banjo" Paterson: Complete Works. Vol. 1. Singer of the Bush (18835-1900); Vol. 2 Song of the Pen (1901-1941). Eds. Rosamund Campbell & Philippa Harvie. Sydney: Lansdowne, 1983.

WORKS ABOUT A.B. PATERSON

Books and Monographs

Semmler, Clement. *The Banjo of the Bush: The Life and Times of A.B. "Banjo" Paterson*. St Lucia: University of Queensland Press, 1974 repr. 1987.

____. *A.B. (Banjo) Paterson* (Australian Writers and Their Work series). Melbourne: Oxford, 1972.

____. *A.B. Paterson* (Great Australians series). Melbourne: Oxford, 1967.

Essays and Studies

Coombes, A.J. "A. B. Paterson". In *Some Australian Poets*. Sydney: Angus & Robertson, 1938.

Elliott, Brian. "Australian Paterson". *Australian Quarterly* (June 1941).

Glasson, W.R. "Famous Australian Poet". *Queensland Geographical Journal* (1960-61).

Green, H.M. "Banjo Paterson". In *Fourteen Minutes*. Sydney: Angus & Robertson, 1961, pp. 360-70.

Hanna, Cliff. *The Penguin New Literary History of Australia*. Melbourne: Penguin, 198?.

Heseltine, H.P. "Banjo Paterson — A Poet Nearly Anonymous". *Meanjin* 4 (1964).

Hooper, Florence Earle. "A. B. Paterson, Some Adjustments". *Southerly* (October 1949)

Howard, Donald. "So the Man from Snowy River Is a Myth". *Riverlander* (September 1956).

Jose, A.W. "Paterson and Lawson". In *The Romantic Nineties*. Sydney: Angus & Robertson, 1933.

Long, Gavin. "Young Paterson and Lawson". *Meanjin* 4 (1964).

Macartney, F.T. Introduction to *The Collected Verse of Banjo Paterson*. Sydney: Angus & Robertson, 1965.

Magoffin, Richard. *Fair Dinkum Matilda*. Charters Towers: Mimosa Press, 1973.

Manifold, John. "The Banjo". *Overland* (Spring/Summer 1954-55).

____. "The Australian Literary Balladists". In *Who Wrote the Ballads?*. Sydney: Australasian Book Society, 1964.

May, Sydney. *The Story of Waltzing Matilda*. Brisbane: Smith & Paterson, 1944.

Mendelsohn, O. *A Waltz with Matilda*. Melbourne: Lansdowne, 1966.

Palmer, Vance. "Literature Emerges". In *The Legend of the Nineties*. Melbourne: Melbourne University Press, 1954.

Semmler, Clement. "Banjo Paterson and the Nineties". *Southerly* (Spring 1964).

____. Introduction to *A Tribute to the Man from Snowy River*, Sydney: Angus & Robertson, 1982.

Sheridan, R.C. "Banjo Paterson — A Biographical Note". *Biblionews* (May 1951)

Stewart, Douglas. "Banjo, the Minstrel". *Bulletin:* Red page, n.d.

Stone, W.W. "Materials Towards a Checklist of *Bulletin* Contributions by A.B. Paterson to 1902". *Biblionews* (December 1957).

Thomas, Elizabeth S. "Banjo and his Grandmother". Playreading in three scenes, unpublished.

Ward, Russell. "Waltzing Matilda". In *Australian Signpost*. Melbourne: Cheshire, 1956.

Waters, Edgar. "Ballads and Popular Verse". In *The Literature of Australia*. Ed. Geoffrey Dutton. Melbourne: Penguin, 1976.

Unsigned. "The Banjo of the Bush". *Salt* (April 1945).

_____. "Whose Matilda?" *Nation*, 27 November 1965.

GENERAL REFERENCE BOOKS

Turner, Graeme. *National Fictions: Literature, Film and the Construction of Australian Narrative*. Sydney: Allen & Unwin, 1986.

White, Richard. *Inventing Australia: Images and Identity, 1688-1980*. Sydney: Allen & Unwin, 1980.

UQP AUSTRALIAN AUTHORS

The Australian Short Story
edited by Laurie Hergenhan
Outstanding contemporary short stories alongside some of the best from the past. This volume encompasses the short story in Australia from its *Bulletin* beginnings in the 1890s to its vigorous revival in the 1970s and 1980s.

Writings of the 1890s
edited by Leon Cantrell
A retrospective collection, bringing together the work of 32 Australian poets, storytellers and essayists. The anthology challenges previous assumptions about this romantic period of galloping ballads and bush yarns, bohemianism and creative giants.

Catherine Helen Spence
edited by Helen Thomson
An important early feminist writer, Catherine Helen Spence was one of the first women in Australia to break through the constraints of gender and class and enter public life. This selection contains her most highly regarded novel, *Clara Morison*, her triumphant autobiography, and much of her political and social reformist writing.

Henry Lawson
edited by Brian Kiernan
A complete profile of Henry Lawson, the finest and most original writer in the bush yarn tradition. This selection includes sketches, letters, autobiography and verse, with outspoken journalism and the best of his comic and tragic stories.

Christopher Brennan
edited by Terry Sturm
Christopher Brennan was a legend in his own time, and his art was an unusual amalgam of Victorian, symbolist and modernist tendencies. This selection draws on the whole range of Brennan's work: poetry, literary criticism and theory, autobiographical writing, and letters.

Robert D. FitzGerald
edited by Julian Croft

FitzGerald's long and distinguished literary career is reflected in this selection of his poetry and prose. There is poetry from the 1920s to the 1980s, samples from his lectures on poetics and essays on family origins and philosophical preoccupations, a short story, and his views on Australian poetry.

Australian Science Fiction
edited by Van Ikin

An exotic blend of exciting recent works with a selection from Australia's long science fiction tradition. Classics by Erle Cox, M. Barnard Eldershaw and others are followed by stories from major contemporary writers Damien Broderick, Frank Bryning, Peter Carey, A. Bertram Chandler, Lee Harding, David J. Lake, Philippa C. Maddern, Dal Stivens, George Turner, Wynne N. Whiteford, Michael Wilding and Jack Wodhams.

Barbara Baynton
edited by Sally Krimmer and Alan Lawson

Bush writing of the 1890s, but very different from Henry Lawson. Baynton's stories are often macabre and horrific, and her bush women express a sense of outrage. The revised text of the brilliant *Bush Studies*, the novel *Human Toll*, poems, articles and an interview, all reveal Baynton's disconcertingly independent viewpoint.

Joseph Furphy
edited by John Barnes

Such is Life is an Australian classic. Written by an ex-bullock driver, half-bushman and half-bookworm, it is an extraordinary achievement. The accompanying selection of novel extracts, stories, verse, *Bulletin* articles and letters illustrates the astounding range of Furphy's talent, and John Barnes's notes reveal the intellectual and linguistic richness of his prose.

James McAuley
edited by Leonie Kramer

James McAuley was a poet, intellectual, and leading critic of his time. This volume represents the whole range of his poetry and prose, including the Ern Malley hoax that caused such a sensation in the 1940s, and some new prose pieces published for the first time. Leonie Kramer's introduction offers new critical perspectives on his work.

Rolf Boldrewood
edited by Alan Brissenden

Australia's most famous bushranging novel, *Robbery Under Arms*, together with extracts from the original serial version. The best of Boldrewood's essays and short stories are also included; some are autobiographical, most deal with life in the bush.

Marcus Clarke
edited by Michael Wilding
The convict classic *For the Term of His Natural Life*, and a varied selection of short stories, critical essays and journalism. Autobiographical stories provide vivid insights into the life of this prolific and provocative man of letters.

Nettie Palmer
edited by Vivian Smith
Nettie Palmer was a distinguished poet, biographer, literary critic, diarist, letter-writer, editor and translator, who played a vital role in the development and appreciation of Australian literature. Her warm and informative diary, *Fourteen Years*, is reproduced as a facsimile of the original illustrated edition, along with a rich selection of her poems, reviews and literary journalism.

Colonial Voices
edited by Elizabeth Webby
The first anthology to draw on the fascinating variety of letters, diaries, journalism and other prose accounts of nineteenth-century Australia. These colonial voices belong to adults and children, some famous or infamous, others unknown, whose accounts reveal unusual aspects of Australia's colourful past.

Eight Voices of the Eighties
edited by Gillian Whitlock
These eight voices represent the crest of the wave of women's writing that has characterised the 1980s. Short fiction by Kate Grenville, Barbara Hanrahan, Beverley Farmer, Thea Astley, Elizabeth Jolley, Jessica Anderson, Olga Masters, and Helen Garner is supported by a selection of their criticism, reviews, interviews and commentary, to give an unusual perspective on the phenomenon of women's writing in Australia today.

Randolph Stow
edited by Anthony J. Hassall
Stow's most powerful novel, *Visitants*, is reproduced in full, together with episodes from *To the Islands*, *Tourmaline*, the semi-autobiographical *The Merry-go-Round in the Sea*, the satiric comedy *Midnite* and *The Girl Green as Elderflower*, as well as a generous selection of his poems, many not previously collected.

David Malouf
edited by James Tulip
A well-balanced, compact selection of David Malouf's intricately connected work. Short stories, poems, essays, interviews and the classic novel *Johnno*, reproduced in full, show the range of his remarkable achievement.

John Shaw Neilson
edited by Cliff Hanna
John Shaw Neilson was the most original poet of his time, able to imbue the Australian landscape with a universal significance. This volume gathers together Neilson's poetry, arranged chronologically from his earliest work to the confidence and maturity of his last poems, his autobiography, and correspondence. It also includes an interview with members of his family.

Kenneth Slessor
edited by Dennis Haskell
This collection of Kenneth Slessor's writing — poetry, essays, journalism, war despatches and diaries, personal notes and letters — allows a fuller, more rounded view of his work than has previously been possible. Slessor emerges as a sensitive, complex and sophisticated person and writer — in any medium.